The Trilogy:

Redstripe and other Dachshund Tales

Another Redstripe, Please!

Redstripe's Inn

by Jack Magestro

Copyright © 2008 by Jack Magestro

All rights reserved under Title 17, U.S. Code, International and Pan-American Copyright Conventions. No part of this work, whether in printed or digital form, may be reproduced or transmitted in any form or by any means, electronic or mechanical, including (but not limited to) photocopying, scanning, recording, live performance or broadcast, or duplication by any information storage or retrieval system without prior written permission from the author(s) and publisher(s).

Unlimited Publishing LLC ("UP") works with professional authors and publishers, serving as distributing publisher. Sole responsibility for the content of each work rests with the author(s) and/or co-publisher(s). Information or opinions expressed herein may not be interpreted as originating from, or endorsed by UP, nor any of its officers, members, contractors, agents or assigns.

This is a work of fiction. All characters, products, corporations, institutions, and/or entities of any kind in this book are either the product of the author's imagination or, if real, used fictitiously without any intent to describe their actual characteristics.

CASTAWAYS TRAVEL™ is used with permission.

OMNIBUS TRILOGY EDITION
First Edition
ISBN-13: 9781588329943

Contributing Publisher:
Jack Magestro

Distributing Publisher:

Unlimited Publishing LLC
http://www.unlimitedpublishing.com

Dedication

*For my grandmother,
Rose Svanda-McCall, 1906-1983,
who taught me tolerance, to cook, and was too polite to tell me
she suspected I would never grow up.*

Foreword:
About the REDSTRIPE books and their author, Jack Magestro

AS JACK MAGESTRO'S PUBLISHER, I've been one lucky dog. His three *Redstripe* books have certainly been warmly received by the public over the years. But much more importantly, as a result of the popularity of his books, Jack and I started working together. And then he became my friend, as well as a co-worker.

Jack and I are both animal lovers, so I could relate to his stories personally. Granted, my dog Hap is a big dumb mutt, not nearly as clever as Belle and her companions — but just the same Hap "owns" me and my amazing wife Jenny the same way Redstripe, Belle and Lampshake control Jack and his aptly-named human counterpart Jill.

As co-workers, Jack and I have published dozens of books by other writers together. Many of these writers, like Jack and I, started small with a dream of finding larger audiences. I'm pleased to say that several of them have succeeded.

Jack has worked hard, and sometimes with considerable frustration, to make good old books, and promising new ones, widely available to readers across the nation and around the world. But now back to his own books...

We're both old dewds now, Jack and I, but I hope that our books will reach untold numbers of readers in the 21st century and possibly even beyond.

Personally, I'm pretty confident that readers like you will be enjoying the *Redstripe* books decades from now, after Jack and I are gone.

For now, it's enough for me to thank Jack for lending his talents and skills to both readers and writers.

It's probably not worth more than a small footnote in literary history, but I want to thank Jack, Jill, Belle, Lampshake and Redstripe for making my life a little better — and yours.

Sincerely,

Danny O. Snow
Publisher
Unlimited Publishing LLC
http://www.unlimitedpublishing.com
December, 2007

Redstripe
and Other Dachshund Tales

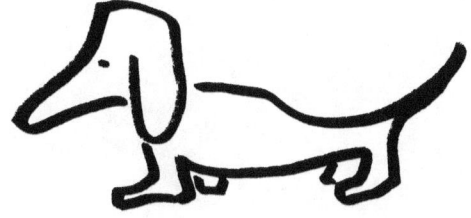

Redstripe
and Other Dachshund Tales

By Jack Magestro

Redstripe
Bernard
Bernard's Visit
The Mouse That Was Saved
The Real Christmas Story

Unlimited Publishing
Bloomington, Indiana

Copyright © 2003 by Jack Magestro

Distributing Publisher:
Unlimited Publishing LLC
Bloomington, Indiana

http://www.unlimitedpublishing.com

Contributing Publisher:
Jack Magestro

Cover and book design by Charles King. Copyright © 2003 by Unlimited Publishing LLC. This book was typeset with Adobe® InDesign®, using Myriad® and Adobe Jensen® typefaces. This book makes use of one or more typefaces specifically licensed by and customized for the exclusive use of Unlimited Publishing LLC.

All rights reserved under Title 17, U.S. Code, International and Pan-American Copyright Conventions. No part of this work may be reproduced or transmitted in any form or by any means, electronic or mechanical, including photocopying, scanning, recording or duplication by any information storage or retrieval system without prior written permission from the author(s) and publisher(s), except for the inclusion of brief quotations with attribution in a review or report. Requests for reproductions or related information should be addressed to the author(s) c/o Unlimited Publishing LLC. See www.unlimitedpublishing.com for mailing address.

Unlimited Publishing LLC provides worldwide book design, printing, marketing and distribution services for professional writers and small to mid-size presses, serving as distributing publisher. Sole responsibility for the content of each work rests with the author(s) and/or contributing publisher(s). The opinions expressed herein may not be interpreted in any way as representing those of Unlimited Publishing, nor any of its affiliates.

This is largely a work of fiction. All characters, products, corporations, institutions, and/or entities of any kind in this book are either the product of the author's imagination or, if real, used fictitiously without any intent to describe their actual characteristics.

First Edition

Copies of this book and others
are available to order online at:

http://www.unlimitedpublishing.com/authors

ISBN 1-58832-078-2

Unlimited Publishing
Bloomington, Indiana

Contents

Prologue to "Redstripe" • 1

Redstripe: A Tale of a New York Dachshund • 3

Bernard • 47

Bernard Visits Belle • 57
A story in which the families of the two dogs gather after the rescue of Bernard.

The Mouse That Was Saved • 77
The Story of the Puppies of Belle and Bernard, the Adventures of a Field Mouse, the Intervention of Luck and the Application of Things That Are Good and Kind.

The Real Christmas Story • 91
(or, What Happened to the Gold, Frankincense and Myrrh)

Prologue to "Redstripe"

Many of the people we have met during our many travels may remember us; Jack and Jill and Belle. Our names really *are* Jack and Jill so most folks don't have a tough time remembering us. We introduce ourselves as "Jack and Jill—really". Jill and I met a while back after we had both experienced our own failures with the institution of marriage. Belle is our dachshund. She is a ten pound smooth miniature female. She is a little lamb with an attitude usually held in check.

Long ago (at least in the realm of cyberspace it seems long ago) we started to write back and forth over the internet with others we met during our travels to Mexico and the Caribbean. In this day and age, everyone has an e-mail address and shares it. Lots of information was exchanged between our discovered friends and us over time over the net. Many stories were traded and many life experiences, good and bad, unfolded on our computer monitor. We learned of career changes, planned trips and met friends. We were updated about families and woes and concerns. We were informed of the births of babies and grandbabies, and read about dark hours and joyful days.

We shared our own trials and tribulations with these friends. Often, over the internet, we shared the adventures and misadventures of our own travels.

This group of friends, whose homes are located from Canada to Australia, has remained in touch with each other over a very long period. We have never met face-to-face all at one time. But our contacts have remained in place due to the efforts of some very special people.

For some reason or another, there seems to have grown an incredible bond between all of us. Joined through the internet only because we had met while vacationing in one Caribbean spot or another, we have come to rely upon each other via e-mail during grim days and have rejoiced with one another the same way during sunny times.

It is for this group that the "Redstripe" story was put into actual words. It is for them; our friends.

We must thank Carol and Sue, two members of the group who helped organize things for us for this story and made sure we had all of the little parts together.

And we must thank Sam. He has continued to orchestrate our group connections over the net. Look for him in Texas. He is a gray haired guy who sometimes rides a big motorcycle. Should you want to find him, just approach every biker in Texas who has gray hair and ask if the guy has dachshunds. If he squints at you and appears annoyed, run. When one says yes, you will have found Sam.

This is a story about Jamaica that involves a dachshund. Or it may be a story about a dachshund that involves Jamaica. It's hard to say. You decide. In any event, this is a treasured family story that has taken some time to discover during our many trips from the United States to Jamaica and back. You are free to believe the story or not. We make no claim that the story is fact. The first section is about to begin, and please be warned—you may have trouble concentrating on other important matters until you read the end. So, get a glass of rum, grab this little tale and put your feet up.

Redstripe

A Tale of a New York Dachshund

On one of our trips to Jamaica, we ran into a rastamafarian named Cirtron. Now, if you don't know what a rastamafarian is, well, it is easy to explain. Sort of. Rastamafarians believe in "GA." GA is god. And one of the main beliefs of the rastamafarians is that it is just fine to consume an awful lot of "ganja." Ganga is marijuana. "GA" is said to acknowledge this consumption and it seems to be accepted in Jamaica that the "rasta" men smoke a great deal of marijuana. Our Cirtron is no exception.

Cirtron is black. He is night-black. He has a short wiry frame usually covered only by a pair of khaki pants—no shirt. One does not see him much in the light of day and he is usually stoned at night. He makes his living weaving baskets and bracelets that he sells to the tourists he finds as he wanders the beaches of Negril. His black hair cascades down and around his shoulders in dreadlocks.

He also functions as an "escort" to a certain class of lonely or adventurous gals looking for something new. And yes that escort service is exactly what it implies. In fact, the literature from the Jamaican tourism board warns about people like Cirtron. But Cirtron is a happy and carefree man, would not harm a flea (or the dachshund on which it lived) and we have found him to be reasonably trustworthy and a good friend. Of course, he is not someone who understands a clock.

When we first met Cirtron, he told us of a trip he took to New York to visit a "girlfriend" he had met (escorted) while the lady was

· Redstripe ·

visiting Jamaica. It is Cirtron's trip to New York that marks the beginning of the story,

It seems that a young woman named Sheila had taken a liking to Cirtron during her vacation to the island. She was so taken with him that she wrote him when she returned home and eventually paid for a plane ticket so that Cirtron could travel to see her in New York. Sheila was a bit wild and she knew what she wanted. She wanted Cirtron, dreadlocks and all; in part to show him off to her friends.

Sheila worked in an insurance agency assembling various quotes and documents for the people responsible to underwrite various contracts. She lived in a six-story brownstone apartment building with no elevator. Her apartment was on the fourth floor and she had two bedrooms with windows that faced the street. The apartment had a small bath, walk-in kitchen and a living room with cheap prints of the work of Georgia O'Keefe in expensive frames on the walls. Sheila was gorgeous. She was blonde, slim, had hair that cascaded down her back like a waterfall and was prone to wearing tight clothing and stiletto heels. She could turn a lot of heads.

When Sheila picked Cirtron up at the airport and then drove him to her home, he was amazed. Cirtron's home was in the hills of Jamaica with his family and the various aunts, uncles, lots of pigs, goats, chickens and children. A visitor would have no exact idea of who the parents of the children are; it doesn't matter. They are all loved in Cirtron's extended family. Cirtron was not prepared for the trip and the plane. But he knew what a house was and he was stunned by Sheila's apartment. Running water? HOT water?! Oh, mon!

Sheila had a dachshund. A female dachshund that had just delivered three puppers eight weeks before Cirtron arrived.

• Redstripe •

New York and Cirtron

Cirtron spent a month and a bit more in New York with Sheila. He became a great friend and buddy of Paris, Sheila's mom dachshund. Sheila astounded Cirtron by taking him to all the right places in New York and making the rounds of the parties so many of her friends threw because, well, that's what they did. Cirtron was just as great a hit with Sheila's friends as he was with Paris. Paris was a bit of a greater hit with Cirtron than Sheila's friends.

Cirtron astounded Sheila with his ability to deal with cab drivers. He was good at this because back home, in Jamaica, his uncle drove a rundown old heap as a cab to help with the finances of Cirtron's extended family up in the hills. Cirtron had learned well from his uncle and the rules for cabbies in New York are no different than in Jamaica.

Rule one: get a fare. Rule two: keep him. Rule three: get a tip. Cirtron could deal with cab drivers and shamelessly negotiated the fare regardless of what the meter read. He explained to us how he had saved so many nickels and quarters left over from change after he had tipped the drivers. In spite of Cirtron's knack with cabs, we never have known if he really understood American money. A Jamaican dollar is only about one thirtieth of a U.S. dollar and yet he was adept (too much so) at trading "j's" for U.S. Changing from U.S. to U.S. was another matter for him, but somehow the cab driver always ended up short. Cirtron's uncle would have been proud. You'll learn more about him later.

Because Cirtron had taken such a liking to Paris and her puppies and because Sheila had such a soft spot and affinity for Cirtron, Sheila gave him one of the pups.

Now before we explain how the pup left the country with Cirtron, breaking through all kinds of rules and red tape, we need to explain the puppy's name. In Jamaica, the most predominant local beer is called "Red Stripe." It bears a red stripe on white on the label. It is rather a heavy beer. As an import in the United States it is expensive but in Jamaica it is cheap, common and plentiful. It's sort of like the local equivalent of an Old Style or an Old Milwaukee beer.

Cirtron and Sheila, in fond memory of their time in Jamaica, agreed the puppy's name would be Redstripe. Then they began to plan how to get the little dog out of the country and back to Jamaica with Cirtron.

The Airport

As part of their plan to get Redstripe to Jamaica with Cirtron while avoiding all kinds of red tape and quarantines, Sheila bought a ventilated gym bag for Cirtron to use as carryon luggage for his trip back to the island. You see, Redstripe is a mini-red dachshund. When she finally "grew up" she did not even tip the scales at eight pounds. As a little twelve-week-old puppy, she was not much more than two handfuls. She was probably only one handful for Cirtron. He had big hands. It's a Jamaican thing, we think. The ventilated gym bag had a specific purpose in the plan.

Sheila, of course, being Sheila, purchased a good amount of clothing for Cirtron during his visit. She always had her own view of how things should be. She equipped him with new jeans, an embroidered sweatshirt and docksiders; all for the trip home. She tried convincing him to take some silk boxers as well. They

· Redstripe ·

were not well received. Certain barriers exist between cultures. When Cirtron explained his reluctance to take the silk boxers, we understood. Somehow, skinny, black Cirtron, in paisley print silk boxers, wandering the beaches of the Caribbean, did not seem to fit our image of the rastamafarian.

You need to picture this, please, as Cirtron walks through the airport clutching boarding pass and plane ticket in an envelope from the airline.

Cirtron is ready to go. He is dressed in the sweatshirt with some catchy New York phrase embroidered on the front. He has new jeans. They are stiff. He has no jacket because he will not need it and his feet are without socks, encased only in the new smooth docksiders that fall and flip up against his heels as he walks. This American tourist look is in complete contrast to Cirtron the person and his color and hair and beard. Rastamafarians do not cut their hair, or beard, for that matter. And their locks tangle in long cascades of twisted dreadlocks. Part of this is due to their African ancestry. Part is due to the length of hair that is not combed out over years of time. The dreadlocks look like little tight fuzzy braids. Cirtron's reach to the middle of his back. It is almost a human mane.

Only his beard diminishes the dreadlocks. It is formidable, to say the least. We have joked that small children could hide in its largess.

The plan, of course, as you may have guessed, was to hide Redstripe in the ventilated gym bag taken as a carry on. So the little pupper was sedated and placed in the bag with the rest of Cirtron's things for the trip. We do not mean to imply that this is the way to treat dachshunds, but that is what we were told happened. We don't know what the sedative was and didn't ask.

· Redstripe ·

Sheila accompanied Cirtron through the airport. Redstripe was in the bag, blissfully unaware, asleep and tunneled amongst Cirtron's clothes in the gym bag. Cirtron craned his neck about, trying to take in all of the sights of the busy airport. They had a major hurdle to deal with. They reached the mezzanine and it was time to check Cirtron's carry on through the x-ray machine and metal detector before proceeding to the gate for the plane.

Cirtron placed the bag; Redstripe snuggled inside, on the conveyor belt. Sheila watched with baited breath. Cirtron stepped through the portal of the metal detector and the bag moved forward through the hanging straps and disappeared into the depths of the machine.

The security man did not even blink an eye at Cirtron. There was a flight leaving soon for Jamaica, after all, and he was used to seeing the rasta men. Cirtron was not even wearing one of the red, green, black and yellow knit hats so common in Jamaica. Cirtron was invisible to the security man.

The belt brought the bag out the far end of the machine.

No one had noticed the skeleton shadow of the little dog on the screen. They were all too bored to pay attention. Cirtron snatched the bag and turned back to wave at Sheila. She smiled and waved back with a teary smile.

Cirtron and Redstripe were headed home. Next stop: Montego Bay.

• Redstripe •

Flying Dachshund

Most of Cirtron's and Redstripe's air trip back to Jamaica was uneventful. Cirtron had his lunch balanced precariously on the little fold down tray and managed to keep most of the food out of his beard. Redstripe slept on.

The East Coast of the United States drifted by beneath the right side of the airplane. Nothing but ocean showed to the left. Soon, the airplane headed off from the Florida coast and continued on over the waters around Cuba. Cuba looked green and peaceful from thirty thousand feet. The view belied the political strife that was so much a part of the history of the green and brown island.

Somewhere, just past the waters around Cuba, Redstripe began to wake.

At first Cirtron heard only a murmur from beneath his seat. Then he heard a snort and then a squeak. The bag began to jostle around and Cirtron became alarmed. "Ah, mon," he thought to himself, "dis be naht good." But before he could collect his thoughts and decide what to do, his seat partner, Andrea Sue, suddenly perked up and looked down over Cirtron's knee at the bag beneath his seat.

She said, "Mister? What's in your bag? It's *moving!*"

Andrea Sue was nine years old and her parents dozed in the two seats behind Cirtron. For many adults, Cirtron's appearance would have put them off. But children are not infected by the foibles of adults and Andrea Sue did not care who or what Cirtron was. She was interested only in that jostling gym bag. "Mister, what's in there?" she begged.

Cirtron said to Andrea Sue, "No problem, mon. Eezz jus mah dog. Be still little miss. Irie?"

"Can I see? Please, can I see?"

"Ahhh," said Cirtron. "I dunno. De dog, she be sleepy. Keen?"

Andrea Sue looked back to where her parents were sleeping in the next back seats and turned back to Cirtron. She was not about to be dismissed. She was nine.

"Please? Can I please see your dog, Mister?"

"Ahhh, little miss. Oh, kay. Irie. But not to tell, Ah?"

Cirtron leaned over and reached down to pull the bag from under his seat. He unzipped the lengthwise zipper. Andrea Sue peered into the bag and she saw two bright little black eyes gazing up. Those little eyes were a bit dazed, but ready to go and happy to see the little girl.

"Shsss, little miss," said Cirtron. "Not to tell. She be Redstripe and needs her sleep. Oh kay, mon?"

"Okay, man. I won't tell." Andrea Sue grinned hugely and scratched the little Redstripe on the top of the head. She allowed Cirtron to zip the bag and place it back under his seat and she settled back, aglow with her secret.

Montego Bay was just ahead. Andrea Sue's parents began to stir, as did the rest of the passengers, as the island of Jamaica came into view.

The plane, with Cirtron and Redstripe and Andrea Sue and her parents and the rest of the passengers, came down out of the sky toward the airstrip at Montego Bay. All could see the emerald ocean glisten in the Caribbean sun. Cirtron felt the pulse of the engines change and Redstripe started, alarmed, at the sound of the wheels chucking down for the landing. The plane bumped down and the roar of the engines, as the baffles came to play to reverse them, was nearly more felt than heard.

• Redstripe •

Andrea Sue leaned over to speak to Cirtron. "Where do you live? Is Redstripe going there too? Do you have other dogs for her to play with? Do you have children? Isn't it too hot here for little dachshunds? My mom told me it's hot here."

"Ahhh, chile. Ya' mon. All of dese tings. Redstripe, she be ta go wid me to de mountains. But, no. Naht to be too hot. Ga takes, he takes de care to look at all tings under de sun. Redstripe, she be happy, mon. And welcome to Jamaica, girl. Wanna say de good bye to da Redstripe?"

Andrea Sue certainly was not going to pass up that offer. So Cirtron unzipped the bag once again and Andrea Sue reached in to pet the little dog. She grinned back at Cirtron and then frowned. "She must be hungry!"

"Ya' mon! But de ladies, make her de goat 'soon as we get dere. She be eating well and me too. No problem, mon."

Cirtron rezipped Redstripe's temporary home as the passengers on the plane all got up to stretch and gather their bags from under the seats and from the overhead compartments. Andrea Sue's father gathered up his daughter with a jaundiced look at Cirtron.

Cirtron shrugged and said "Welcome to Jamaica, mon!"

Cirtron and Redstripe faced one more barrier. They had to pass the security at the Mo-Bay airport. Cirtron was hopeful, however. The security guards were more concerned with what left the country than with what came in.

Cirtron felt hopeful. He just needed for Redstripe to be still.

• Redstripe •

Security Check—Jamaican Style

After the plane landed and everyone had gotten up to gather their belongings and then stood in the aisle of the airplane to await their chance to depart, Cirtron joined the queue, Redstripe in the bag over his shoulder, to leave the plane too. There is no "tunnel" at the Mo-Bay airport leading from the plane to the terminal. An old fashioned set of steps is rolled up to the plane and everyone just clambers down right onto the tarmac. Cirtron stepped out of the plane and onto the first step as the heat hit like a warm moist mist.

It was quite a trek from the plane to the terminal and customs. Redstripe began to fidget.

She fidgeted a lot. Cirtron tried to calm the little creature without drawing attention. He opened the bag just enough to reach in and give Redstripe some air. "Ahhh, little dog, be still, mon, 'need to be quiet, keen?" And he rubbed Redstripe's neck and head.

Across the tarmac they trudged, down the corridors of the terminal, and then on to the security check. There were four lines with impatient and sweating Jamaican officials whom checked visas and passports and stamped this and that. Cirtron got his passport stamped, handed in the forms he had filled out on the plane about what and why and who he was, and then submitted his bag to the checkers. Sometimes these people opened things and sometimes they did not. It all depended on luck.

Luck was not in store for Cirtron and Redstripe this day.

Redstripe was just too excited and restless after being confined for so long in the gym bag to stay still. She wriggled and squirmed as the bag lay on the counter. And the checker saw the bag move.

· Redstripe ·

"Ai! What you be carrying? Open it please, mon. What have you inside there?"

Now please, you need to understand about the Jamaican people. After all else, respect is most important. Trouble is just not part of the Jamaican view of the world and no one wants to offend. The checker was embarrassed to have to confront a fellow countryman. One people, one blood, means a lot. But duty called. And Cirtron would have to answer. He did. He answered in a silly and simple style that would simply not work in the United States. But in Jamaica, there is "no problem, mon!"

"Ya, mon, no problem, mon," said Cirtron and he slid the zipper open to the show the head of Redstripe. Her eyes shown out from the dim recesses of the bag expectantly, all but her head covered by Cirtron's clothes.

The checker was surprised, to say the least. "Wat is dese, mon? Ya may not move de dog to de country widout de quarantine and papers, mon. Ai!"

Please withhold your disbelief and judgment. Remember that this is in Jamaica.

Cirtron leaned over the counter and whispered in a conciliatory fashion. "No dog, mon. My sister's chile, mon. She de comeback wid me to home, mon."

What the checker said was not translatable. He issued a long stream of patois that no one not born on the island could understand.

Cirtron admonished the checker, "Dese is a chile of god, mon. I tell you, eez my sister's chile. Ya know, mon, sometime, de ladies smoke de ganga up in de hill, mon. Dese affect de chiles. Not always well. But she still be a chile of god, mon. My sister, she be de wait for her chile, mon."

Cirtron flashed his smile, yellow teeth in a black face, the most Sunday best he could muster.

The checker looked Cirtron in the eye and said, 'Hey, mon, what d'you tink, keeping de baby in de bag likkel dat? Have you no respect, mon?'

Cirtron just smiled as best he could.

Cirtron and Redstripe were passed through. And Redstripe was now officially, sort of anyway, in Jamaica. They went out the front of the terminal to look for Cirtron's uncle in the lane with all of the cabs and vans that took tourists to the resorts.

The checker remained and shook his head of black curls in amusement. He went on to check out the real problems—the American and European tourists.

Into the Mountains with Goats and Girls

Uncle Basi was there, out side of the Mo-Bay terminal. He had driven his 1969 Chevrolet Impala down from the cockpit country. This was Cirtron's transportation home. There were a few extra passengers on the trip, all installed on the broken and sun-split back seats, and one or two on the hood. As the tourists crowded into the busses and vans that would take them to the resorts and villas and other vacation destinations, a small plane took off from the main runway. It had as passengers those that had a few extra dollars to spend in order to avoid the road trip to the resorts in Ochos Rios, Runaway Bay and Negril. Basi hugged his nephew, and the nieces and others from the car piled out with their hellos on their lips for Cirtron.

• *Redstripe* •

Redstripe was still confined to the gym bag slung over Cirtron's shoulder.

Uncle Basi squandered quite a bit of money buying Ting and beers from the hawkers who all reached through the fence at the edge of the parking lot to sell to those just arriving. The hawkers were not allowed on the airport grounds, but did a brisk business through the fence. Basi haggled a bit for two beers, one for himself and one for Cirtron. The little girls got their sodas. He paid four hundred "j" for the two beers and around seventy five "j" for each of the little girl's sodas. He had haggled a bit and got a decent deal considering it was the airport.

The tan Chevy Impala had been in the family for more than three generations. Basi was proud of the red license plate that the government of Jamaica had awarded him after his application was approved to allow him to be an "official" cab driver. Americans, of course, upon seeing the car, were a little apprehensive about riding with Basi because of the car's vintage. But, nonetheless, Basi earned a sort of living from being a cabby and was the only member of the family from the hills that did so. Cirtron was more than happy to see Basi and all of those in and on the car and was lucky to have the transportation.

Uncle Basi hugged Cirtron again as a greeting and as recognition of Cirtron's return.

Cirtron exclaimed, "Basi, my aunt! How be my aunt? Are you still be de treating her so?"

"Ya, mon. I be treating her so! Same as before. Ai! Ha! Where you b'en doing?"

"None so much. De car. She still to be alrigh' to be de go back home?"

"Irie! She be sound an' fit, mon.'

In the back of the car, with its sun-damaged plastic seats and dash, the little girls grasped their sodas, (a rare treat) and listened to the exchange between the two men. They were sure that Cirtron would have something for them. And of course, we knew that he did.

"Ahhh, little ladies. You be waiting de s'prise? Yes, mon?"

The response was not negative. The little girls all giggled and strained to lean out of the car's windows at once.

Cirtron unzipped the gym bag. His black hand, pink palm and long extended fingers produced Redstripe from the bag. Cirtron is not a big man, not in stature. But his hand was large enough to cradle Redstripe with his fingertips under her chest and the heel of his hand supporting her tummy. Redstripe's legs gripped nothing but air and paddled as if to swim to a more secure spot. Her little black eyes rolled back to show the whites for just a moment.

The little girls squealed with delight. Cirtron handed Redstripe through the back window (it had not had glass in it anyway for eight years) and into the collective laps of the little girls.

Basi said that they should go. "K' de bottles, mon. We t'in later, mon."

Once in the car, Redstripe busied herself with her newfound freedom, jumping from willing lap to willing lap, to shoulder and then arms and to the back seat ledge and everywhere. As Uncle Basi started the Chevy and drove off, the little girls began to pester Cirtron asking just what sort of creature Redstripe was.

Uncle Basi headed the old car away from the airport toward the mountains.

The way Uncle Basi took home was long, twisted and arduous. The old set of wheels bumped and wheezed down the dirt lanes.

Redstripe

Basi drove, in spite of the roads, like a driver doing the Indy 500. Most Jamaicans drive like this.

Norman Manley Boulevard, a road right near the airport, was paved. It was paved between the potholes in any event. But after all, the Jamaican concept of "road" is just a wide spot of mud or dirt (depending on the weather) dividing two groups of huts or trees. Actually, the goats of Jamaica are the real legitimate denizens of the roads, not cars. Once Basi left the boulevard, things got interesting.

Goats in Jamaica are indeed a hazard on the roads on the island. The first time the car bearing Cirtron and Basi and the little girls came across these bleating and hairy creatures, they got, well, Redstripe's "goat." There, it is said.

Goats do not understand that they should cooperate in any way with human beings. The first time a group of them blocked the progress of the old Chevy, Basi leaned out to shout while he leaned on his horn. Cirtron assisted with great animation and shouts as well. "Leave by de road, mon!" "Away, mon! Go, Gaahhh!"

Redstripe entered the fray with complete dachshund abandonment. The first time she "saw goat," there were three. They were big. Still, Redstripe was sure she could help clear the road of the goats. After all, the humans were shouting and gesticulating. Certainly she could help.

"Raaarrrrfff!" said Redstripe and then "RAAARRRFFF!" again. She jumped to the front seat and onto the dashboard. "Raaarrrfff!" In the language of dachshunds this means "goat! I see GOAT!"

In her excitement, one of her small paws hit the blinker control in the car. Then again, another of her paws hit the radio control as she scrambled to see the goats out of the front window. With Redstripe "raarrrfffing" and Cirtron and Basi shouting, the blinkers blinking and the radio hissing, the goats moved off. They presumably wanted calmer pastures.

Redstripe could barely wait for the next goat. She remained on the dashboard, shivering and shaking.

"Ahhh, little dog. Be still!" said Cirtron. "You no to be de mess wid de goat, mon. She have de teeth, keen?"

Redstripe did not "keen" at all. All she knew was that she needed to get just as close as possible to these hairy creatures. She was bound and determined to do just that. She vibrated with tension and her hackles roses up into a strip down her back. Basi saw this as he drove on and said, "Well, mon. De Redstripe, she has de red stripe! Ya, mon!"

The journey to Cirtron's home in the hills continued while Redstripe kept a look out for goats.

Redstripe did not starve as she rode along in the old Chevy as it bumped, bumbled and bustled down the back roads of the Jamaican hills. She didn't have a chance to starve. The little girls had plenty of food they all wanted to feed Redstripe in the back seat. The food was all wrapped in cloth by the aunts and mothers back home. Cirtron and Basi were oblivious to all of this feeding going on right behind them. But the aunts and mothers would not have been pleased to see that all of the food was going to the little dog and not the little girls. Eyebrows would be raised and brooms would swing. Redstripe, though, was happy to feed on bits of yam, carrot and greasy chicken.

Cirtron, of course, had saved a bread roll from the plane and that went to Redstripe too. Eventually, Redstripe, bloated and hot, settled down and snoozed off in the laps of the little girls. The little girls had worn themselves out as well and the whole pile of girls and puppy slept in the back seat of the Chevy; the sight of which would become quite common.

They approached Cirtron's home.

Redstripe's Dubious Arrival

From the air, one would see lush foliage and a few narrow paths following the ridges of the gently rounded mountains. A few steel roofs marred the sight, rusting in the moist air and baking in the relentless sun. From above, the oppressive humidity could not be felt there in the interior of the island. Nor could one hear the constant buzzing of insects nor smell the fecundity of the tropical jungle.

On the ground, a visitor would see the smaller huts, roofed with woven thatch that made up the sleeping quarters of the children. These were wooden-floored and were raised off of the jungle floor. The resulting space created an abode underneath for various chickens and pigs that dwelled in the relatively cool and shaded soil.

Several goats wandered about, and the chickens owned the place.

The old Chevy wheezed into the small group of huts and dwellings that Basi, Cirtron and the girls called home. Their approach had been heard from a long way off and all of the relatives were at hand and waiting anxiously. Not a whole lot happened there, up in the Jamaican Mountains. Cirtron was the prodigal son and his returns from his travels always held the promise of tales of mischief.

Amongst shouts and waves and cheers and squawking chickens and squealing pigs, the old Chevy let loose a hissing cloud of steam

· Redstripe ·

from its old and devastated radiator. The car rolled to a dusty stop. An inquisitive pig snuffled around the side of the car. Cirtron had arrived back home.

Redstripe woke up.

The crowd that had rushed the car stopped upon seeing Redstripe in the back seat. They were stone still. They had never seen a dachshund and had no idea what they were looking at there in the laps of the yawning little girls.

Someone pointed and asked, "Waht be dis?" and peered into the back seat with a worried look. Someone else, alarmed, said "de baby rat? Cirtron! Waht be you de bring ta here, mon?"

Another, "Ahh, y'find de pig, de baby pig!"

"No, mon! Never see de pig like so, mon! Too much hair!"

"Cirtron, mon. Ayie! *Wahd be dis?*"

Cirtron, cool as always, said, "No problem, mon. She be Redstripe, she be a dach—"

But it was too late. Redstripe smelled *pig*! And she leaped from the laps of the little girls, clambered out the open window and tumbled to the ground, feet scrambling for purchase in the dust as soon as she landed. The little girls burst from the doors, the snuffling pig, now alarmed, took off and the chase was on.

It was Redstripe in the lead, second only to the pig, paws a blur and ears flapping. Her tongue blew back out of the side of her jaws from the wind caused by her speed. Next was Cirtron. Then came the little girls who were followed by the shouting crowd. The men ran and waved and the women held up their long skirts as they chased after the dog and girls and Cirtron. Basi stayed and leaned on the car. He was way too smart for this nonsense. Not so for the pig.

The pig had never seen anything like this!

• Redstripe •

And it didn't like it. Not one bit.
Redstripe had arrived.

Interlude at Maddie's Bar, Negril

It may now be time to take a moment to describe just how we met Cirtron. After all, it is Cirtron who first told us this story. We met him late at night as we leaned up against the rail of one of the many bars that sit back from the edge of the beaches in Negril. There are countless numbers of these. And none are fancy. They are all "open air" and quite rough. Almost anything anyone wants can often be had. We have declined many offers over time.

Some of the bars do not even have refrigerators for beer. The operators rely on coolers and ice to keep things chilled. After the sun goes down, many travelers would not even go near the smaller places. But we pride ourselves in experiencing places avoided by the faint of heart. Drinking a tepid beer in the dark with strangers in another country may not be everyone's idea of a good time. We live for it. That's Jamaica. Those travelers who stay within the walls of their all-inclusive resorts are missing the whole point of the island. Cirtron's story is only one of many we have collected by the light of the Jamaican moon.

We stopped one night, during one of our walks, at a palm frond roofed hut called "Maddie's." The slow night waves washing on the beach and the stars glinting silently in the sky had lost their charm for a bit. Unbelievable, but one gets immune to the Jamaican beauty after a while. This can happen after a week or so. We turned away from the beach to approach Maddie's. You would not know it was Maddie's—there was no sign—you had to ask. But not right away, please. This is not polite. This would not demonstrate respect. All that was in the bar was a bartender, two rastamafarians, a cooler and a Coleman lantern that hung from a wire. The lantern hissed quietly and cast a pale yellow glow onto the scarred surface of the plywood bar.

"Ya, mon." said the woman behind the bar. She was huge. But she was well dressed for the situation; colorful dress and gold necklaces.

"Irie," we said back.

And we asked for two Redstripes, sixty "j."

Cirtron and Asha, brothers, we discovered later, were perched on rickety stools at the bar. They each bummed a smoke from us; a practice we came to understand was part of the price of the beer in many places. Cirtron was dutifully weaving a bracelet from green, yellow and black threads he held in a tangled pile on his lap. He sold bracelets like the one he was making on the beach. To watch him was wondrous. His long black fingers, with their contrasting pink nails flew as he manipulated the rolls of thread in his lap to the work at hand. How he did what he did in the dim light is still a mystery to us.

"Ahh, lady, be you de want de bracelet? I make you one, mon. I make you one."

"Well, I don't know," Jill said cautiously.

I glanced at another man, not seen at first, on the side of the little hut. He was holding a baseball bat and stood as though he meant to use it. Cirtron caught my eye.

"Ahh, mon. Not to worry, mon. He dere to watch for you! See, we love all de people day come by. See? Keen, mon. We want no one de bother you."

"I see."

"No, mon. Be it de truth, mon. You see. Go wid Ga, respect."

We began a long talk with Cirtron and Asha. And we agreed to pay Cirtron to weave bracelets for our kids with their names on them. The bracelets were woven in black, green, yellow and red over armatures cut from plastic milk bottles. The colors have certain meanings. The yellow and green are the sun and the earth. The red is the blood of the people. The black represents the joining of all cultures and people. From this comes the phrase that is so commonly used in Jamaica, "one people, one blood."

It took a while, but finally Cirtron made us feel at ease. So it was there in the shadows under the lantern in Maddie's bar, bat-equipped guard on hand, the ocean sighing in the distance, unseen, that Cirtron told us his story about Redstripe and Sheila. It was two years later, during a chance meeting with Cirtron at the same place that we heard the end of the story and it was completed.

Redstripe Settles In and Tastes Jamaican Cooking

Once Redstripe and Cirtron were settled into the village in the hills, the days came and went, one day pretty much like the one before it. The women spent most of their days tending the gardens. They grew yams, heavenly tomatoes, and carrots as the main crops. The men of the conclave spent most of their days being lazy. So it was with the men that Redstripe spent most of her time during the days.

The chickens and goats and pigs eventually came to an understanding with Redstripe. Redstripe would not chase them and in exchange the goats and pigs would not bite her. The chickens and Redstripe lost interest in each other and the chickens kept to

Redstripe

themselves. Redstripe did end up with some scars that did heal on her head. If one would part the coat on her hindquarters, a small scar would be seen that had been caused by the teeth of a goat who had not been interested in being herded about by the likes of the little red dog. The goat made that clear.

At night, when it was time to really rest, Redstripe slept with the little girls in one of the raised wooden huts. The girls and Redstripe lay in heaps on the cots like piles of so many puppies snoozing during the cool nights in the mountains. Redstripe always found a way to insert herself warmly between two or more little bodies The mothers and aunts were not thrilled with this arrangement but finally gave up and let it go. Redstripe was then safe from the "brooms of discipline."

No one can visit Jamaica and not become acquainted with jerk sauce. This is the Jamaican equivalent of barbecue sauce but it can be unbelievably hot. Tomatoes (the heavenly ones), peppers onions and spices make up the sauce but the main bite comes from a small little pepper, a Chile-like fruit, called a Scotch Bonnet. Scotch Bonnet, Scottish Basket and Habenero are all names for this little wicked pepper.

These little peppers (they look like miniature yellow pumpkins) grow on a tall, bush-like plant. They are so hot, they cannot be handled safely with bare hands. Gloves of some kind must be worn when preparing them and only the cooking and cutting utensils can touch the raw ones. Rub one of their seeds between your fingers and just run your finger against your nose and you won't see a thing for half an hour. And that half an hour will be pure misery. Believe this. Been there and done that!

Yet, no one can resist the mouth-watering smell of this sauce when used while cooking pork or chicken or goat. When used as a

Redstripe

sauce, the dish in which it is used becomes jerked chicken or jerked pork or jerked goat. Redstripe couldn't resist the smell either. She discovered the power of the Scotch Bonnets the hard way.

A pot of this jerk sauce, not fully cooked, but warm from the fire, was placed for a moment on a low bench. Redstripe, being a dachshund, just *had* to investigate.

It took only one lick and a noseful of the stuff. Redstripe rocketed off, shaking her head furiously, trying to rid herself of the sting. She ran this way and that, rubbed her head on the ground nearly hard enough to lose her hide and then pawed at her snout all the while making loud wooking noises. She dashed right. And then reversed and dashed left. She whirled. It was all to no avail.

She sneezed in reverse; a loud hoarse and painful sound. She sneezed again with such force she was knocked back unto her haunches. She was a mess. It *hurt*!

But one of the Jamaicans, being a Jamaican, knew what to do to rescue the little dog and end her discomfiture. Gently smiling and in good humor, he grabbed the little dog and held a bowl of goat's milk up to the poor little dog's nose.

But Redstripe wanted no part of that. She bucked away. She wanted nothing to do with goat and besides she could not think straight from the pain and did not understand that someone was only trying to help.

"Ahh, well, den, little dog. So, mon." said her helper. The Jamaican carried Redstripe over to a larger metal bucket of goat's milk. There was just enough to submerge a struggling and wriggling dachshund's little head. She was dunked once and came up snorting and flapping her ears like mad. Another dunk and she came up but sneezed a bit less violently. Three dunks and her benefactor could tell that the goat's milk was neutralizing the sting of the jerk sauce. Redstripe looked ridiculous with her white-soaked head in contrast with her red body. But she felt lots better.

"Ahhh, little dog," said her savior, "Not to be de drink de sauce, mon. Eeez too hot, mon. Too hot for de little dog."

Redstripe never, ever, went near anything "jerked" after that. But she'd walk a mile for some goat's milk.

Easter Monday

Anyone who visits Jamaica would notice that the Christian religion of the western world is held in high regard on the island. This may come as a surprise to visitors. After all, Jamaica has a very different culture than the culture of the North American or the European Continent. The existence of Christian worship on the island has, we think, something to do with the various peoples who, at one time or another during the last few centuries, have visited the island and left their marks, blood and influence. There have been French, British and African contributions that have all blended together with the original local culture. Of course, when it comes to religion on Jamaica, the women show a much greater interest in the theological teachings of Western Europe and North America than do the men.

This western Christian influence shows itself in at least two holidays. One is a "Mardi Gras" type celebration called "Carnival." The other is "Easter Monday." Easter Monday is named for the calendar date that it implies. It is always the Monday of the week just after Easter Sunday. Cirtron, Basi, the little girls and the rest of the family headed out of the mountains and into Negril for the holiday of Easter Monday. Redstripe was included, of course. The goats, chickens and pigs stayed behind. So did an uncle or two that never woke up early enough to make the trip.

Basi was really the only one of the group who had any reliable income at all. Cirtron made some money selling his bracelets and services, but, more often than not, very little of what Cirtron made came back to the village. Basi's money came from the fares he transported in the old tan Chevy around the resorts and hotels in Negril. He also made a bit of money from repairing small gasoline engines in a little hut he built for himself in the hills. Most often, the repairs he made were only completed when he managed to order parts. Sometimes it took a year before those parts he ordered came by mail so that he could fix the pumps and chain saws and other little engines that were brought to him.

Basi had enough mechanical knack to keep that old tan '69 Chevy going. The Chevy that had brought Cirtron and Redstripe home was the same transportation used by the group to get to Negril for Easter Monday. The food was packed. The little girls were stuffed into the back seat with Redstripe. The blankets and tents and relatives all were piled into and onto the car. Negril was the destination, then, for the Easter Monday holiday.

Once at Negril, after the trip down from cockpit country in the mountains, the group first piled off and out at Bloody Bay. The bay was named centuries ago for the slaughtering of whales that were brought up into its shallow waters. Booby Cay, a small island, lies just off shore. It is not really within swimming distance and is guarded by jellyfish. But it is just a small haul for the fish vendors that hunt the reefs nearby with their carved canoes and then hawk their catches on the beach. There, at Bloody Bay, at the public park, the adults set down their food bags and tents just north of the main area.

· Redstripe ·

Everyone crammed back into and onto Uncle Basi's old Chevy and Uncle Basi pulled out of the park and aimed the car toward the more populated stretches of the seven miles of Negril Beach.

Redstripe would soon learn all about crabs

Basi's car lumbered down the narrow strip of asphalt road that ran parallel to the seven miles of beach in Negril. Various resorts and other establishments separated the road from the beach. Grand Lido, Hedonism II, Sandals, Yellow Bird and the Tree House all passed by on the right side of the road as the group continued. They stopped at about mid-beach and pulled into the parking lot at Alfred's, the very-Jamaican beachfront restaurant and bar that would be their passage to the beach. Cirtron was well known at Alfred's.

Everyone piled out. Redstripe was carried in the arms of one of the little girls and the little dog sniffed and snorted at the smell of grilling lobsters in the shell. She could also smell conch being grilled over open coals. The smell of jerk sauce was in the air as well, but Redstripe knew better than to become interested in that aroma. The women and little girls, with Redstripe, headed for the beach. The men headed for the bar "Ya, mon. De rum, mon!"

Alfred's is just about in the middle of the beach that starts in Negril Village and ends seven miles later to the north at the high priced resorts near Booby Cay. On Easter Monday, the entire stretch is filled with people. The water is nearly obliterated by bodies in the ocean, frolicking and just having a good old time in the warm waters and sun of the Caribbean. Hawkers roam the beach selling bracelets, fresh fish and lobster, juice and fruit. Jamaican entrepreneurs entreat the crowd to parasail or to rent jet-skis. The place is pure pandemonium. And everyone has a great time on Easter Monday.

· Redstripe ·

Redstripe could not get enough of the excitement. She ran back and forth on the beach and then toward the water, challenging the waves, getting an occasional unplanned dousing of salt water after a miscalculated lunge. She trotted after those walking along and hawking their goods and did a great job of being a general nuisance to everyone in sight.

Sand coated her. She was a mess of wet fur, beach sand and smelly dead things she had found to play with. Now and again, one of the little girls would carry her into the ocean and dunk her clean. The girls would shriek and shout as Redstripe was encouraged to paddle about in the water, her eyes pulled back and showing their whites. The girls would pluck her from the water and then deposit the little dog back on the sand where she would proceed to get just as filthy as possible all over again, scampering and rolling until every last inch of her reddish fur was covered with sand and slop.

The beaches of Negril, if one would take a close look on a day when there are not a lot of people around, are dotted here and there with little dime sized-holes; the homes of small crabs that are about the same size as the holes. To Redstripe, the smell in those holes was absolutely irresistible. Sniff, *sniff*! Snort, *snort*! Dig and dig and *dig*! Redstripe just had to get to one of those little crabs and was digging like crazy. In our house, we like the phrase, "Don't wish too hard for something, you might get it."

Redstripe got her wish.

Excavating like mad, Redstripe's long body was halfway down into the sand when she found a crab. It made a good try to scuttle away up the hole that the dog had dug but it was just too slow for the determined little dachshund. Little jaws snapped, nearly closing on the hapless crustacean. It backed away sideways just as quickly as it could manage and then lifted up one small claw

· Redstripe ·

toward the menacing little hound and clamped onto a soft, velvety ear.

Yipe! Shake! Yipe! This had not been in the plans. Redstripe whirled about and headed for the water, plunging, paws forward, in a panic. The crab still clung to her ear. Once in the water, the crab let go; meandering off to do whatever it is that crabs do in crab land. And no one really knows what that might be.

Redstripe clambered out of the water and back onto the sand. She shook off the saltwater, ears flapping, and plunked down. She looked up as if to say, "Crab? What crab? I didn't see a crab."

But she dug no more holes that day.

The Easter Monday holiday for all of the aunts and uncles and children passed by in Negril. The men spent the days trying to sell this and that on the beach. They sold bracelets they had woven (not as good as Cirtron's) and packs of cigarettes they hauled about in netted bags. The women and the children spent their time splashing about in the warm ocean waters and sitting on the sand in the sun. Redstripe eventually just tired herself out and deposited herself down in the shade of an aloe bush. These aloe bushes grow to be more than six feet tall and the lush leaves are broken off by hand. The thick leaves are then split to release a jell that can be rubbed onto the sun bruised skins of the tourists who chose not to heed the warnings about he Caribbean sun and its power.

By Tuesday, the seven miles of the white sands of the beaches of Negril were deserted. The Jamaicans all headed back home and the tourists boarded the chartered busses to travel back over the goat strewn roads to Montego Bay and the airport there. Uncle Basi, Redstripe and the family gathered at the camp at Bloody Bay and prepared for the trip back to their home in the mountains.

Cirtron had made other plans.

"Basi," said Cirtron. "I made de call to ma friend back, she be, in New York. I not to be de go back t' home jus' now, mon. You go ahead wid de family."

Basi said, "Ya not to be no good, mon. We be ready to leave, mon. Up witch you!"

Cirtron continued, "Well, ah, y'see, mon. I make de call to de lady and she be wanting de visit, once more, mon. I used de collect, d'y see, mon?"

Basi sighed. There was no reasoning with Cirtron. There never had been. Cirtron had snuck off during the holiday to make a collect call to Sheila in New York. She had promised him another airline ticket and wanted to see him once again. Redstripe, of course, was invited. Sheila had been happy to take Cirtron's collect call. She wanted dearly to see the little Redstripe once again. Cirtron was part of the deal.

Basi and the family headed for the hills in the old Chevy. Redstripe was deposited in her now-normal means of conveyance, the gym bag. The Chevy rumbled off in one direction and Cirtron, Redstripe in the bag over his shoulder, held his thumb out for a ride in the other. Montego Bay Airport was the destination for the Rasta Man and the little red dog. This time, things would not go as smooth at the airport.

Return to Mo-Bay

Cirtron and Redstripe made their way from Negril to Montego Bay by thumb, foot and paw. The rest of the family made their way back to their home in the hills. It took a few days for the man and little dog to bum rides to the airport in Mo-Bay. Cirtron shamelessly used Redstripe to get people to stop. It was hard to turn Cirtron down with Redstripe panting in his arms in the Caribbean sun.

They walked at times. They rode at times. Once in a while, Redstripe would faithfully trot along on her own four feet beside Cirtron, watching out for goats. Usually, she spent the trip riding in the gym bag, head out, sphinx-like, and sniffing the smells of Jamaican countryside. For the most part, Redstripe held the day. Cirtron stopped frequently where his credit was still somewhat accepted and Redstripe was always assured of some scraps from the back of somewhere. The little dog did not go hungry and Cirtron did not go thirsty. The proprietors were quick with food and water for the little dog. Cirtron got scraps and beer as an afterthought. He told stories not so much as payment, but rather as a distraction to the settling of the tabs.

It rained once each of the days of the three-day trek. Twice, they were lucky enough to be inside a bar or car. But once they were caught in the warm and windy rains of the afternoon Jamaican Caribbean climate. Cirtron was soaked but he dried later in the sun. Redstripe was not so lucky to get dry. The gym bag filled with water and they had to stop for a while to empty Redstripe's little traveling bag and let it dry. Redstripe and Cirtron slept under a tree during this. Passers by just ignored the rasta man and the snoozing little dog. The two of them didn't really smell all that pleasant, anyway.

The two continued, begging, riding and walking along the coast road; Norman Manley Boulevard. Redstripe was happy to ride in the old cars that picked them up and just as happy to ride along in the gym bag, swinging against Cirtron's hip as he made his unhurried way to Montego Bay. From the neck down, Cirtron appearance was that of any black man in an urban area of the states. He had on the new jeans from Sheila and a somewhat fresh shirt. From the neck up, his beard and dreadlocks stated his origins.

Finally, after three days and some adventures to be told in a later story, the black man and the little red dog arrived at the Mo-Bay airport. They were both a bit scruffy so Cirtron hauled the gym bag into the men's restroom. Redstripe got sort of a bath in the sink. It was not a happy process at all. Others visiting the restroom cast strange glances at the man holding the strange little animal under the faucet. But this was Jamaica and no one created a fuss. Cirtron did what he could for himself.

A ticket, again paid for by Sheila, awaited them at the Trans Am desk. Cirtron proudly showed his passport and received his boarding pass and seat assignment. Redstripe was in the black gym bag, zipped in securely and asleep after the indignity and rigors of bathing in a restroom sink.

Cirtron, Redstripe a sling, left the confines of the terminal when the flight was called and made his was out over the tarmac to the huge jet. He clambered the metal and somewhat rickety stairs to board the plane.

New York lay ahead. And things would be a bit dicey on the return trip.

Flight to New York

Cirtron boarded the plane with Redstripe ensconced in the gym bag from Sheila. There were no questions about Cirtron's carry-on. They were lucky at that point, anyway. Once on the plane, Redstripe's bag was deposited safely under Cirtron's seat. Cirtron took a nap and he snored. Loudly. After all, he had been traveling for three days and both the Jamaican and the little dachshund were dog dead tired.

Redstripe, asleep (mostly) in the gym bag beneath Cirtron's seat, heard the snorts and fluttering sounds from Cirtron as he slept. She had heard enough of these in the mountains and on the trip to Montego Bay to know what those sounds meant and she was not alarmed. She settled down in the confines of the black gym bag, secure and warm in the spot beneath Cirtron's seat.

After about an hour and a half into the flight, Cirtron woke up. He needed to make a trip to the washroom. He hesitated. He did not want to leave Redstripe in the bag beneath the seat while he took care of business. So he gently wrested the gym bag out from under his seat and slung the bag and little dog over his shoulder once more. He headed for the front of the plane. No one really took notice. It was not unusual for anyone to take carry-on luggage into the washrooms on the planes so that they could use the contents to freshen up or change clothes. All was calm. No one remarked on the rasta man's passage.

Cirtron made his way into the washroom, locked the door after some effort, and deposited the black gym bag on the small counter. It took a while, but Cirtron finally puzzled out the instructions for the toilet. He found the "flush" button and watched in amazement as the blue water swirled around noisily to clean and hiss its way out of the bottom of the "head."

It was loud. Very loud. And Redstripe barked out in concern from her bag that was settled on the counter in the small washroom.

"Rarrf?" (What was THAT?!) "Rarrf!"

Cirtron tried to calm the little hound. "Shsssss, little dog. No to be de get us in de trouble, mon! Jus' be de water, mon. Eezz alrigh', mon. Be still, Irie."

Just outside the washroom, in the galley, two flight attendants were straightening things. They heard Redstripe bark. They looked at each other in surprise and went to listen outside of the washroom door.

Cirtron opened the door to the washroom to see two very pretty and yet sternfaced young ladies, their arms crossed . One asked, " Sir? What is going on here? We heard a dog bark. What is this?"

"Ahhh, ladies. Ahhh, eeezz jus a …" Cirtron paused. He sensed that 'A chile of god' would not work here.

"Dog? Haa, Haa! No, mon! Dog? No. Not you be to find de dog here. Eez me, mon, d'you see? I have de cough. Carrphg! Carrphg! Have de little cough, mon. No dog, mon. Haa, Haa! D'y'see? Carrphg!"

The flight attendants were not convinced, but they let Cirtron return to his seat with his bag and hidden dog unmolested for a time.

Of the two attendants, the senior flight attendant was not convinced. Not to be outdone, she entered the flight deck to speak with the captain. She asked for his support. It seemed one of those *Jamaicans* had a small animal in a bag. They needed to get to the bottom of it, and right now! The captain wearily followed the two flight attendants and headed back to the passenger cabin to confront Cirtron. The youngest lady was in the lead, followed by the senior attendant. The captain brought up the rear.

The aisles, even on big jets, are narrow, of course and it is only possible to pass single file. When the group of investigators reached Cirtron's assigned seat, only the first person, the least senior flight attendant, could actually get right abreast of Cirtron. He was in the window seat and she had to lean over to get his attention.

"Sir? Excuse me, sir?" said the captain from two seats ahead of Cirtron. "We have to ask you to open that bag you have under your seat, sir. There seems to be a problem."

Cirtron froze. Nothing creative came to his mind. This was real bad.

As his hands trembled slightly and a gleam of sweat popped out on his forehead, he pulled Redstripe's traveling bag from under his seat. He slowly unzipped the bag, his eyes closed and expecting the worst. The captain and the older attendant could not see from where they stood. The younger attendant peered down into the gym bag.

Up gazed the little red dog, ready and waiting to meet another new friend. She had just woken up, really, and her little black eyes focused on the pretty girl. "Another friend?" she thought. "Oh, good! Maybe she has *food!*" Redstripe waited in gleeful anticipation. Her front paws pedaled up and down in excitement.

The flight attendant was stunned. "Uh!" she said. "Oh my! Well, um, gee!"

"Well, what is it?" said the captain, impatience clear in his voice.

Redstripe looked up at the attendant and then to Cirtron. Cirtron opened his eyes and gave his best baleful look to the attendant. The girl looked at Cirtron and then back down at Redstripe. She did not know what to do. But her heart did.

She looked Cirtron in the eye and said, "Sorry, sir. We've made a mistake. We apologize. You know, we have to be very careful for the safety of all the passengers on our flights. Sometimes we need to check things for everyone's benefit."

"Ya, mon. Irie!" (whew!)

"Captain? There is nothing here to be concerned about. Sorry."

• Redstripe •

"Honestly," said the captain. "Sir," he addressed Cirtron, "Please accept my apology on behalf of Trans Caribbean. Enjoy the rest of your flight, please. If there is anything you require, please let the attendants know." He turned on his heel, and harrumphed back to the flight deck, shaking his head.

The younger attendant turned to her senior and said, "Do you think the captain is mad?"

"Guess the guy really has a cough. Go figure!"

Cirtron closed the zip on the gym bag in a blink and no one bothered him the rest of the flight. But, funny, there was an extra tuna sandwich on Cirtron's tray when it was time for lunch.

Drug Sniffing Dogs

Now that the crisis of a possible discovery of the smuggled little red dog was over, Redstripe and Cirtron settled down for the rest of the flight back from Jamaica. Both of them were full of tuna sandwich. The man next to them, on the aisle seat, had chosen a meal of Salisbury steak for himself. It had interested the all-knowing nose of Redstripe for a bit, but the tuna had sufficed.

Well, mostly it had sufficed.

Cirtron's seat partner had spilled some of the gravy from the Salisbury Steak onto the lower leg of his pants. Redstripe stuck her head out of the bag from under the seat to take a preliminary and desultory sniff. Cirtron admonished the little dog to be still and behave. The seat partner was just a little irritated. But for some reason he did not want to cause attention to himself and let the incident go. Cirtron and Redstripe were still safe.

• *Redstripe* •

The plane, bearing Cirtron, Redstripe and the Salisbury Steak guy, dropped down and out of the upper regions of the sky over the eastern coast of the United States and it banked to make a final approach to the airport. Cirtron, bag and dog in lap (which was against the airline rules… all carryons need to be beneath your seat or in the overhead compartments), waited for the landing. The wheels chucked down and the pilot made his final flare. The big jet touched down. First one wheel hit and screeched and then the others. Thump, thump..whirrr. They were down and safely back in New York.

Customs lay ahead. And in the United States, things are different and less "tolerant" for incoming visitors than in Jamaica.

Cirtron, dog in bag on shoulder, found himself in a long line. There were people there with all kinds of luggage. They had bags and cardboard cartons tied with twine. They had duffel bags and they had suitcases that bulged from poor packing. Long items suggested golf clubs, narrower ones suggested skis. Who knew what was in all of this stuff?

Cirtron waited and shuffled forward as the officials checked and asked questions. Cirtron waited some more. Redstripe was getting restless in the confines of the gym bag.

The Drug Enforcement Agency men were there among the lined-up passengers. The men and women of the agency all had dogs. The dogs were there as they had been trained to sniff about for things that should not be allowed to come into the United States. One particular dog, a seventy five-pound golden retriever named Shadow, was there with his trainer-agent.

Shadow was not, as his golden retriever ancestry might suggest, the calmest of dogs. But he loved to smell things. He had been trained to smell for things that were not appropriate to bring into

· Redstripe ·

the United States. His trainer-agent had no clue that Shadow just liked to smell things and wanted to smell everything. Shadow did not just want to smell the scents he had been trained to find during his time in the DEA facilities in Vermont. He just wanted to smell everything.

As Cirtron stood in line, he took a chance. He opened the gym bag's zipper a bit to let Redstripe have some fresh air. Cirtron noticed that the man from the aisle seat, the one with the spilled gravy on his lower pant leg, was just in front in line.

Shadow was sniffing around the arriving passengers just a few yards away. Redstripe looked up and out of the open bag, craning her neck to see the sights. Without warning she took a leap up and out her little cradle and hit the floor running. She streaked over the tiles to head for the big golden retriever. "Another new friend to meet!" thought Redstripe.

"Ahh! No! y'little dog. AIE, mon! Get y'back ya little dog!"

It was too late. The people waiting in lines began to stir and notice the dachshund galloping toward Shadow.

She sprinted right up to the big dog as fast as she could pump her little legs. Shadow's agent looked down at the dachshund and held tight to Shadow's leash. But he could not prevent the big dog from lowering his shoulders and sniffing the little red creature that seemed to have appeared from nowhere. Shadow sniffed and snorted and gave a loud "*Wuff!*"

It sent Redstripe backpedaling as fast as she could. She wheeled around and scampered back to the line where she had been in the bag with the waiting Cirtron. Shadow had a new smell to pursue; Redstripe. And his paws scrabbled on the tile in pursuit of the little hound; the adult in charge of him in tow.

Well.

· Redstripe ·

Redstripe got back to Cirtron's line. Shadow was following but Redstripe had already forgotten about the golden. She did smell Salisbury Steak. And she quickly found the source of that smell on the cuff of the passenger that had been on the plane next to Cirtron. The man with the smelly cuff was standing in line for the customs check.

Her jaws clamped down on the savory cuff.

Shadow skidded up to the encounter.

The rest of the DEA agents in the airport, heretofore undercover, descended on the area to see what was going on. Their guns were not drawn, but lots of hands hovered over holstered weapons. It became absolute bedlam. Shadow jumped into the fray and knocked over the Salisbury Steak guy. Redstripe hung on to the guy's cuff, growling and readjusting her jaws, hanging on for dear life. Agents came from everywhere. They were rudely jostling through the travelers and pushing over luggage to get to the two dogs. Some cases fell over and fell open, spilling their contents among some of the people who were already down on the floor. Cirtron was among them.

He scrambled on his hands and knees to try to reach Redstripe. There were people and bags and clothes and dogs and everything in a tangle. Cirtron could not quite get to Redstripe. People were yelling, the dogs were barking and growling, the agents were shouting and all the non-involved people nearby seemingly descended on the mess.

Redstripe, Shadow and Cirtron looked up and paused. "Who? Us? We were just having fun." Cirtron smiled one of his smiles. But the DEA agents looked down on the floor to see something that had fallen out of the pocket of the Salisbury Steak man. It was something he should not have been carrying. Not at all.

· Redstripe ·

After all were untangled, Cirtron was arrested. Redstripe was impounded at the airport. The man with the gravy stained cuff was arrested as well and taken away. The evidence from his pocket was in the hands of the men from DEA.

But there was some real confusion.

The men from DEA had no inkling that Shadow wouldn't smell out contraband if his life depended on it. The training had not taken. What the DEA men did think, however, was that Redstripe somehow was able to do what Shadow had not. They didn't have a clue that Redstripe had "cuffed" the passenger because of the Salisbury Steak gravy and not because she smelled what had been in the little bag the passenger was carrying. Cirtron took advantage of this confusion.

When the DEA men questioned Cirtron he said, "Ahh, she eez a good dog, mon. Was raised by ma good friend, Sheila. Here she be in New Yark, mon. Sheila!"

"Who is this Sheila?" the men asked. "Where can we find her? Is she a dog trainer? Does she work for the government?"

"Ahh, no mon! Not for me to be de say, mon. But I know, see, de Redstripe has de mother, mon. She be Paris. Sheila, she be de tell you, mon."

Somehow, by some dark method available to the American government, Sheila was found by the men from DEA. Sheila was called to the airport and Cirtron was released to her. But Redstripe was transported to a facility in Vermont run by the DEA to be studied by scientists employed by the government. They worked on improving airport security. The little red dog would fascinate them.

Redstripe would make them earn their money while she was there.

• Redstripe •

Back at Maddie's

On an undermined date, sometime in April of 1995, we were back in Maddie's Bar. The only ones there were us, Cirtron and Maddie. Maddie had made some improvements. The Coleman lantern was gone and had been replaced by a single electric light bulb hanging on wires from the roof of the place. Progress goes on relentlessly, even in Jamaica.

"And then, Cirtron? I asked.

"Cirtron, what happened to Redstripe?" asked Jill. "How did you get away from the DEA guys ?"

Cirtron had paused. His black eyes with their yellowish whites gleamed in the darkness and reflected twin bright spots from the electric bulb. "Ahh, well. She came to be de oh kay. Irie." He grinned. "All de talk, mon. I have de tirst, mon!"

I motioned to Maddie for another Redstripe. Bottle in hand, Cirtron continued while I paid for the beer.

"Well, mon, see, de govmint men, day keep de Redstripe a while in dere mountains. I stay wid Sheila. De phone, mon. De phone she be de ringing all de time, mon. Sheila, she say day be studying de little dog. I dunno what day be want wid de little dog but Sheila, she say day be doing de tests. Day be tests for de smell, mon."

"When day speak wid me at de airport, mon, day ask me de questions. Ahh, like where de little dog be come from and how she come to be in de bag. Day had many of de questions, mon. I dunno how to be de answer for them and day had not patience, mon. They had no respect."

Redstripe

"Respect!" I said and brushed the knuckles of my closed fist with Cirtron's. Anyone, one, with any sense, learns this gesture when in Jamaica. It paves the way out of a lot of misunderstandings. This time, it was used just to get Cirtron to go on with his tale.

Cirtron took a long swallow of beer. The liquid's passage showed down Cirtron's skinny neck; a passing bulge like a snake swallowing a little rat. "Irie!" said Cirtron. "Couple days, day be de bring back de little dog to Sheila. De mother? Paris? She be de know de little dog once more and day be happy back together. De mother, she be Paris, mon."

"We remember," I said. "But what did the men from the government say, Cirtron?"

"I don't know so. Day be talk to Sheila. She say day be ass—, uh, day be people wid no respect."

Indeed, by phone, Sheila had many conversations with the men from DEA. They were insistent that Redstripe must have some innate ability to smell things not wanted in airports. But they were frustrated and felt that Sheila had some clue why Redstripe would not perform at the facility in Vermont. Redstripe was gleefully uncooperative, as only dachshunds can be, and was wearing the scientists to a frazzle.

They gave up.

If only they had asked Redstripe to find Salisbury Steak. Or maybe jerk sauce would have brought a reaction. But being men of little vision, they were unsuccessful in turning the little dachshund into a drug-sniffer. So, after two days, Redstripe was returned to Sheila in the little apartment. The notes and files of observations of the little red dog were kept in a place with other seemingly-important secrets.

· Redstripe ·

The men came in long black cars. When they got out onto the street in front of Sheila's apartment, their coats all bulged slightly over unseen things. They climbed the flights of stairs and handed Redstripe over to Cirtron at Sheila's apartment door.

"Sorry to have troubled you," one of them said in a tone that was insincere. "This has been a matter of international security. You understand this as an American, ma'am. Here is your dog."

Cirtron responded. "No problem, mon. She be de good, little dog, mon. You see?" Redstripe stretched up from where she lay cradled in Cirtron's arm and licked his neck through his beard. "You see, mon? Keen? She be a fine chile of ga!"

The men were not amused. One said, "We will be in touch when the dog has puppies. We will want to see them, of course."

"Not on your life, buddy," said Sheila over Cirtron's shoulder. "You guys have no respect!"

"Ahh, Sheila, Irie. I tink day be go now, be it oh kay." He looked at the men and raised an eyebrow. "Irie?"

"Yeah, sure. See you. We'll be in touch," they said. Then they all turned, stomped down the stairs and piled back into the black cars to leave.

All was then right with the world. Sheila was glad to have Cirtron visit once again and Cirtron was exited to see and take in the complicated sights and sounds of a city in the United States. Redstripe spent most of the time tussling and teasing with her mom. The two of the dogs, Paris and her little daughter, Redstripe, threatened major damage to the little apartment while Sheila and Cirtron would look on, laughing at the doggy antics.

In the back of her mind, Sheila remembered what the men from the DEA had said. They were interested in pups should Redstripe

· Redstripe ·

ever have any. Well, she would certainly see about *that*! But, for now, Redstripe was back in New York and Sheila and Cirtron agreed that she should stay there. After all, a busy rastamafarian's style might be a bit cramped trying to eek out a living *and* care for a dachshund back in Jamaica.

Cirtron returned to Jamaica.

When he left, the apartment held just Paris, Sheila and Redstripe. The only problem left was fitting the three of them comfortably under the same bedcovers at night. Generally, it was Sheila who ended up cold.

Bernard

We had been suspicious for a week or so. When we'd returned from a Friday night fish fry, the cushions on the living room couch had been in disarray. It hadn't been a big deal, but we noticed it. We went out other evenings. One night, all of the dog toys were strewn about the "office" in the basement. This was not something that Belle (our dachshund) would do. But we let that go. Then we noticed that throw rugs near the doors had been pushed about and were not there for our wet feet.

Later, when we returned home from some shopping trip or other, we noticed that Belle did not jump up to greet us. She was tired. Very tired. But we did not get overly concerned about that. We just felt she was just snoozing away and waiting for us to return. To wake up, it seemed to us, was just too much effort for the little dog. Generally, after we had been gone during the evening, we sent Belle out to "take care of things" and then brought her in, gave her the obligatory cookie and allowed her to wrap her self down among the covers in our bed to be warm and sleep for the rest of the night.

We were wrong about all of it. Little did we know.

The mussed cushions and rugs and Belle's energy level had an explanation. But it was not until Christmas Day that we understood.

Early on Christmas Eve, son Jeremy appeared, snaking and sliding his car up the drive. We had to get the shovel out to scrape out a semi-dry section of driveway for his wheels to grab. He made it up and then offered to help shovel the rest of the drive. While we were both out there, a dachshund appeared. It was snowing. It was cold. So we were surprised at the sight of this standard-sized

· Bernard ·

dachs we had never seen before. The little dog bristled and barked at us when we tried to approach. His teeth were bared and he looked as though he would take a piece out of anyone who tried to get close.

We kept our distance and he wheeled and disappeared into the snowy night. Belle was inside making howling sounds and barking and snorting like a rabid animal.

"What was *that* all about?"

"Dad, forget it, it's a stray."

"It can't be. It's a dachshund for Pete's sake. He just must have got loose. I hope he is all right. I'm going to look for him."

"Yeah, right, Dad. Like you're going to find him at night," said Jeremy. "I'm going in. You have anything to eat inside?"

Jeremy was right. I could find no tracks in the frozen street beyond the driveway. I returned to the house, stomped off my feet, and joined everyone in the warmth of Christmas Eve. The kids were busy grazing on the cheese and crackers, herring, pizza, chips and dips that I had set out on the kitchen table. Belle had her own little platter of neat treats on the floor. She hadn't touched it.

"What was all that about?" Jill asked. "Belle has been going nuts! She has been barking like a banshee and can't settle down."

I explained, "Well, there was this dachshund out at the end of the drive that showed up while we were shoveling. He was acting really aggressive and then he ran off. I looked for him, but, well, I dunno. Belle must have heard him."

"Do you know where he went?" asked Jill.

"No, I have no clue, we'll have to watch for him. I expect he may be from a new family that just moved into the neighborhood. I've never seen him before. I hope he's okay, but I don't know what else I can do."

· Bernard ·

Jeremy called to me from the kitchen, "Hey, Dad, do we have any more soda?"

"Uh, yeah, it isn't cold, but you can get a twelve pack out of the basement. It should be down near the laundry."

Jeremy pounded down the stairs and then called, "Dad?! Come down here, you gotta look at something."

Down in the basement, near the laundry, a window was open. It was not open very much, it was open just a crack. And from that window was a trail of wet dirt and melting snow. It started on the sill of the window, went down to a shelf, onto the dryer and then onto the clothes table and then to a trunk near the table and onto the floor.

"Dad, some animal has been in here. I can see where it went! Take a look."

Several other trails had dried there. Something had been coming and going for some time. I thought a dachshund could have made that trip from sill to shelf to dryer to table to trunk and floor, but I didn't say anything.

Instead, "Jeremy, go on upstairs, I need to fix this window, it must not be locking right."

I reached up to lock the basement window. The latch would not engage and I bruised my knuckles trying to force the window latch into its receiver. I just couldn't do it. The window frame was a bit sprung and would not close all the way.

"Hell and damnation, I don't need this on Christmas Eve!" I shouted to no one in the basement.

I tried one more time to close the window and I was shocked.

A set of claws suddenly attacked the basement window from the outside. A set of teeth appeared outside the window in the darkness. They really looked nasty. I stumbled back and fell away from the window and onto the concrete floor.

· Bernard ·

"Whoa !!! Hey, geez. What *was that!*"

Later, we would come to know that those claws and teeth belonged to Bernard.

I went back upstairs and joined everyone. "Jeremy, that dog was here again! He was right at the basement window. I thought he was going to have my head for a snack. He was wild! I think it must have been him that came in the basement window. And I couldn't get it closed completely, the latch is broken."

Jill said, "You mean the dachshund you saw when you were shoveling? Is he okay? Where'd he go? God, I hate to think of him outside like that."

"He's a stray, Dad, like I said. Don't sweat it, hey?" Jeremy said.

Jill turned to Jeremy, "Don't you care? That dog must be lost or loose. He could freeze out there. It's Christmas; have some heart, would you?"

Jeremy shrugged and slugged his soda. Belle began to bark. I went to bandage my knuckles.

None of us really could think of anything to do about the mysterious dog. I silently decided to make regular checks out the windows and particularly the basement window throughout the evening. But things settled down into the traditions of Christmas.

We ate food and opened presents, and the phone took and sent calls from and to relatives in far-away places. Tree lights and the company of family created the peace we all needed during the season. Daughter Kaylie retired upstairs with her stepsister to do what ever it is that teenage girls do behind closed doors. Jill curled up to watch television with Belle and Jeremy and I went down to computer games in the office. Belle never did eat her treats.

Around 11 o'clock on Christmas Eve, most of us were ready for bed. Except for Jeremy, of course. He was glued to the

Bernard

computer. The rest of us went to bed. But the peace that is supposed to come with Christmas Eve was just not going to be available.

Most of us had been in bed for around an hour. Midnight had passed and Jeremy was the only one up. The computer was bleeping and running cool graphics and doing what computers do when running computer games. But Jeremy heard something else. It was coming from the back of the basement, back in the laundry. Over the sound from the computer speakers, he heard thumping and scratching from the back room.

"What?"

Jeremy rose from his chair at the computer desk and went to look. He opened the door to the laundry. It was dark and he reached for a light switch and when the light came on a cacophony of barking and snarling began instantaneously. Jeremy slammed the door and ran upstairs to wake me.

"Dad! Dad! Hey, Dad! It's *back*!"

"Uh.. what ..? Oh, I hear it, what *is* that?" I was not in my most alert state.

"Dad, it's the dog again, it's in the basement. It was about to attack me, for cripes sake! You gotta come downstairs!"

That seemed reasonable to me., "All right already, I'm coming."

Jill woke, "What is going on?"

Jeremy and I raced down the stairs. Well, Jeremy raced. I stumbled. And we came to the laundry room door. By that time, all was quiet. Jill had made her way slowly down and no one noticed that Belle was in tow as well. I put my hand on the doorknob and turned it.

With Jeremy peering over my shoulder, I pulled open the door. And the barking and snarling began again. It was the dachshund.

He was right there with something brown with a little green at his feet.

He barked and backed and snarled dangerously.

I thought for just a second, "Jeremy, see if you can't grab one of those dirty towels in the pile near the washer, I'll try to get to him, but I'll need the towel to grab him so I don't get bitten."

Jeremy looked at me like I was crazy, but then he began to inch toward the dirty laundry. The dog kept barking and snarling and I still could not concentrate on what he had there on the floor long enough to make it out. No one noticed that Belle had entered the room. She padded straight to the strange dog and stopped. So did he.

"Belle, *no!*" It was a chorus.

The two dachshunds licked noses and sniffed ears, as we all stood there, stunned. In the back of my mind, I now knew what had been messing up things in the house recently. Mystery explained. This ol' dachshund had been sneaking in to see our Belle and they had been having a good ol' time while we were gone!

We stood there, still frozen, and Kaylie wandered in. "Hey, what is… oh, how *cute*! And he brought Belle a present! Cool!"

As the two dogs continued to sniff and lick, I asked Kaylie, "Present? What present?"

"Well look, silly, the dog even wrapped it for Belle. 'Course you don't have your glasses on."

Okay, I looked. And I finally got a good look at the brown and green thing on the floor. It was what was left of a pork chop with a piece of green Christmas ribbon sort of stuck to it.

The dog, turned, picked it up in his jaws and then dropped it at Belle's feet. I said, "Kaylie, that's some trash that was probably mixed in with Christmas wrappings and he dragged it in here to eat."

· Bernard ·

"Dad, it's a present for Belle." Kaylie was emphatic.

Belle certainly thought so. She lay down on the concrete, grabbed the thing in her two front paws and began to chew on the decimated chop as the mystery dog looked on. None of us quite knew what to do, but I approached the unnamed hound and bent down with a hand out. He didn't flinch and he allowed me to scratch his neck while Belle continued to chew on the chop.

While scratching him, I said, "Boy, is this guy thin. He must have been out there for a while. Where in the world did he come from? *Some*one must be missing him."

The group descended on the dog while Belle continued to gnaw.

"Hey, little guy, where do you belong?"

"Are you cold? Are you hungry?"

"Hey, we've got leftovers, you want some?"

"Oh, you poor guy, your ribs are showing!"

The dog had dropped his aggressive demeanor and welcomed the attention. We dried him off, got him water and some food and a blanket. We planned to let him sleep down in the basement for the night but when we closed the door, Belle let us know that this was not going to be. He was not to be alone unless we wanted the laundry room door scratched into splinters by Belle. They ended up in the same blanket that night. That was after I put a nail through the casement of the basement window to secure it.

Two o'clock in the morning found us around the kitchen table. It was too early for coffee and too late for any libations for the two adults. We settled on hot cider for everyone. The question was what to do.

"Dad," said Kaylie, "he has to be around from somewhere here. Let's go knock on doors, we can split up the streets."

Jill said, "Uh, I don't think so. First, no one wants to be wakened on Christmas morning at this early an hour and, well, what if someone thinks we're Santa Claus and is disappointed?"

"Santa Claus comes down chimneys, Jill," said Jeremy. "Last time I heard, he doesn't knock. But how about if I go and hit the all night grocery stores and see if there is a lost dog notice on the bulletin boards?"

"Can I go with you?" Kaylie begged.

"I suppose. I'll drive, you look."

The kids took off into the night and I sat at the table with Jill, drumming my fingers. "I have an idea, but it's a long shot. I suspect that dog downstairs has been out and around for a week or so. That's why there are multiple tracks from the basement window that didn't close and why things have been out of place around here. Belle and this guy have been, well, who knows what they have been up to."

"Jack!"

"Hey, he brought her a present. Chill out. Anyway, do you think there is a chance he has one of those chips implanted? That a vet could read it? I mean, I know our vet has that stuff and we would have to get to him later this morning, but I don't know where else to start."

The cider wasn't doing it, so we made a pot of coffee and settled down to wait to see if the kids came up with anything. An hour and a half later they came back empty-handed. I explained our plan, and we all went down to check out the hounds, who didn't seem to even notice we were there, and we went to bed. No one slept. No one admitted it either.

By five thirty in the morning, I couldn't lie in bed any longer. I got up and started pancakes and coffee and eggs and bacon. It didn't take

Bernard

long for everyone to wander down to the kitchen and it didn't take long for Kaylie to let the dogs up for their share. It was Christmas after all. Healthy stuff doesn't count. Not even for dogs.

We discussed the vet plan and it seemed to be the consensus that it was too early to call him; he might not be available, and so we should do something else. It was Jeremy who said, "Hey, what happens when all the vets are closed and the police catch a stray? Don't tell me they keep it in a jail cell, and not all of them have access to shelters. Do you think the local cops have a chip scanner?"

Brilliant. And the cop shop is always open. We left right then.

After some theatrics from the dog about getting in the car and out and into the police station, he was scanned. He was Bernard from Ohio and belonged to John Tailor. We got the name and address and called as soon as we got back.

…RRRRRinnnng…….RRRRRR.nnnnnnnnng

"Hello? John? John Tailor?"

"Yes, what is it."

John was not thrilled to hear from a stranger so early on Christmas day.

"I'm sorry to bother you, but we think we have your dachshund, we had him scanned and"

"WHAT?!"

"Your dog, he's Bernard, right? A standard short hair?"

"*My God*, wait….uh. Are you sure? I mean, we thought he was gone! He disappeared while he was with us while we were visiting my folks and, well, are you *sure*?"

"Yeah, I think so. I had the cops scan his chip. Your name came up. Seems he's been living in my basement and I didn't know it."

"I… I… hold on a second, Marge!! Marge!! Come here! They found Bernard!"

Bernard

Well, now, the rest is history and you can imagine. The Tailors left straight off from home on Christmas morning, drove through the night and arrived at our place on the twenty-sixth of December.

The reunion was something. I never asked, but I think the Tailor Christmas presents remained wrapped under their tree until they got back with Bernard.

For now, Belle looks out the front window even more diligently than ever and continues to sniff around the laundry room. So far, I have not had the heart to get her a pork chop.

Maybe next Christmas morning.

Bernard Visits Belle

A story in which the families of the two dogs gather after the rescue of Bernard.

JOHN AND MARGE TAILOR had been in touch with us by phone and letters and e-mail over the months since we had discovered their dachshund, Bernard, in our basement. The Tailors had lost Bernard while visiting relatives. We found him late on Christmas Eve and gave them the news on Christmas Day. Fortunately, the computer chip implanted between Bernard's shoulders had given us the information we needed to find his owners.

Then Christmas time was upon us once again and the memory of the rescue of Bernard the dachshund came to the forefront of our minds and an invitation was made by phone to the Tailors.

Rrrrrrinnng Rrrrrrrrring "Hello?"

"John, it's Jack, how are you doing?"

"Oh, yeah, Hi! Fine. What's up?"

I made our offer. Jill and I had thought about it for a long time. Sometimes, the relationships developed in high-stress times fade. But we thought that this one with the Tailors would hold. After all, this was over *dachshunds* for Pete's sake! We wanted to see the Tailor's again because we thought this was, well, a thing we should continue. And besides, we knew that Belle wanted to see Bernard. Well.

"Jill and I were just thinking and we wondered if you might like to make the trip up to see us here. You could bring Bernard and the two dachs could have a reunion of sorts."

Bernard Visits Belle

John replied, "Gee, that's a great idea. But after you rescued Bernard, the deal should really be on us, not you. That is really generous of you, we would love to. But…"

"Oh, I don't mean now, the holiday season is a mess, I was thinking of after Christmas. We could spend a day or two, do dinner and all of that while the dogs did their thing."

John said, "Boy, that sounds good, I have some time off from work after the New Year and we could drive up again, that is, if Marge agrees."

I said, "tell Marge it's a done deal, you guys pick the date, ok?"

"Great… it sounds great," replied John. "But let me wait until I talk to Marge and I need to fix us up with a motel room."

"Wrong answer, John, you guys stay with us, all right?"

"Okay. I'll talk to Marge. You sure we can bring Bernard?"

"That's the whole point!"

A couple of phone calls later, all of the arrangements had been made. Bernard was on his way to see our Belle.

Little did we know what would transpire.

Ahem.

Bernard, Marge and John showed up on our doorstep in mid January at about six in the evening. The doorbell rang, Belle started her customary barking and growling and we answered the door. Bernard was in Marge's arms and he immediately went airborne, leaped down to the floor and the two dogs began to bark, bare teeth, raise hackles, wag tails and sniff at each other. Privately I thought, *boy, I couldn't do all that at one time… these dogs must have a different set of nerve endings than me!* And they were FAST!

Marge said, "Oh goodness!"

I said, "Don't give a worry, the dogs will be fine, come in here already!" God, I thought, *what did I just say? "give a worry?"* My

Bernard Visits Belle

Jamaican accent must be loose. Or was that Australian? Oh well. Not to mind, bother, no problem, whatever.

The two dogs, Belle and Bernard, proceeded to race around the living room, up and down the stairs to the family room and bedrooms and continued to bark, snarl and wag tails before we even had a chance to greet the Tailor's. *Shoot, and darn it anyway,* I thought, *let the dogs go, it's THEIR reunion after all.*

Stepping into the house John said, "Hey, thanks for having us, great to see you guys again." Marge, who looked at the dogs (who had now made the circuit of the house and returned to living room) followed him in and then she said, "Oh, yes, thank you. My goodness!"

Jill took their suitcases to the guestroom and I took their coats. Marge wore a cloth coat with a fake fur collar and John had on a quilted vest. At that point, as I was hanging the coats, Jill came down after putting the suitcases away (they were just overnight bags). Marge was still clutching a black vinyl purse, the kind that you hang over the arm. The kind you see ladies carry to church on Sunday. She wore a pair of those black pumps with the squarish heels. She was *not* going to let go of that purse.

As the dog's scruffled around in the background, I looked at Marge. Under the coat, she had on a sort of "old lady's" dress: printed rayon, princess collar and a belted waist. I was tempted to look around to see if her hose had lines up the back. John was wearing a shirt and pair of pants that looked like something straight out of LL Bean.

Hmm.

We felt under-dressed. I had on a sweatshirt and my favorite jeans with the holes in all the goofy places and Jill had on her special bib overalls with a rag sweater underneath. I thought Jill looked great and the overalls had lots of pockets for dog treats and stuff. But I sensed that Marge thought we looked like a couple of Jack Pine savages not fit for company in a civilized society.

Oh boy.

Jill gave me a look that said that maybe we should have been better dressed for our guests. I had a giggly thought in my head that, well, the dogs were naked anyway, so let's not set a higher standard. Even so, I was thinking and Jill told me later that she agreed with me that Marge was dressed a little schoolmarmish. Actually, she looked a little weird. And she was a real contrast to John. I guess in all of the excitement when they had traveled up to collect their lost dachs last winter, we had not really looked at them in detail. Now we did.

Hmmm.

Ahem. (I've always kept telling myself to buy a pipe. This would have been an excellent time to pause and light one.)

I did not have a lot of time to "hmmm" to myself. The dogs were back at it.

They raced all over. They stopped in the living room, went nose to nose in full snarly mode, and pawed at each other with a vengeance. Then they took off again like the two little carpet rockets they were designed to be.

"Go to it, guys!" I said. "Enjoy yourselves!" The dogs could be heard in the other rooms. They were having a good old time. You could hear them scrabbling over the carpet and woofing and barking and snorting.

"My goodness!" said Marge.

Yes, indeed.

I had no idea how to break the ice. I should have bought that pipe!

Bernard Visits Belle

"John, Marge," I said, "Come on in the kitchen and we can pour a drink or two. Then we can plan the evening. What can I get you? Wine, beer? I've got stuff to make some mixes, the usually brown and white bottles and…"

John replied quickly, "uh, Marge doesn't drink, but I'd be glad for a beer to…"

Marge interrupted, "My Goodness, John, don't you think it is a little early? I'll take a white soda, by the way if you have one."

Oh, boy. This could be trouble. And I looked out the window. Early? It was already dark out for heaven's sake. What was going on here?

On the other hand, Marge had finally managed to string more than four words together in one breath. That was a hopeful sign.

I locked eyes with Jill, who was giving me no help at all and the dachshunds continued to wreak havoc with the carpet in the next room. I ploughed ahead as I tend to do, "Ok, a beer, a soda, Jill? White wine?" (She nodded silently, eyebrows up.)

"Coming straight away." I made the drinks and poured myself two fingers of scotch. I figured I would need it over time if I sipped it. The dogs could be heard still doing reconstructive surgery on the carpet in the next room. As I tended to things over the sink, I didn't hear even a whisper of conversation from the three adults behind me. All I could hear was the dogs.

Not good.

But we did our best for our guests.

Steaks went on the grill, potatoes went in the oven and the veggies went into the microwave. Salads were put together after much chopping and dinner was served.

Marge sort of stared at her plate.

· *Bernard Visits Belle* ·

"Marge," I asked. "Is your steak too rare or too well done? I can put it back on if it's too rare. Or I could nuke it…"

John replied for Marge. "Marge doesn't eat meat"

Oh. I wish I had known. "I guess the dogs will be having a treat, then, hey?"

No response from Marge. But she nibbled at potatoes, salad and veggies.

The rest of the evening didn't go much better. Getting a response out of Marge was a real challenge and John tried his best to sort of look past her attitude as though he was embarrassed. He told a few jokes. I told a few back. But Marge just never seemed to warm up to the situation. Jill tapped her foot a lot and put a good dent in the wine supply.

Finally, we decided to retire to bed and agreed to make plans for the next day in the morning. Belle and Bernard were taken out to the back yard and after much encouragement did their thing. Jill and I rewarded the two dogs with cookies from Belle's supply. Bed was in order. Jill and I retired to our room and the Tailors went to our guestroom with Bernard.

All seemed quiet, if not a little tense. I really thought once again about a pipe. I could have stoked it up by the fireplace and just sort of sat and thought about everything in a dignified manner. But I just turned in.

It must have been about two in the morning of the next day when there was a knock on our bedroom door. It was Marge.

I opened the door, bleary eyed and a little headachy from the scotch, to see Marge standing in the hall in a flannel set of pajamas covered by a flannel robe with our Belle under one arm. I could not help but stare, blurred vision and all, at the robe Marge was wearing. It was printed all over with little phrases. Some said "Warm

· *Bernard Visits Belle* ·

Toes—Warm Heart!" Others said "Home Is Where the Heart Is!" They were printed all over at odd angles.

"Excuse me," she said to me, "but *your* dog has snuck into our room and has been getting our Bernard way too excited. I *hope* I don't have to be specific. Would you please take her back?"

I did, of course. And then I conjured up the best sheepish grin I could give. It did not seem to have an effect. Oh, well. I was not thinking that I was being all that effectual lately anyway.

Pipe, I thought, *if I just had a pipe!*

I inserted Belle back under the covers of our bed and thought, Marge *does* talk. Hmm. I seemed to be hmming a lot. Jill rolled over, propped up on one arm and said, "grmph?"

I said, "Never mind, it isn't worth it. Go back to sleep."

"Okramph," she said.

I did go right back to sleep but I dreamed of dachshunds carrying miniature black vinyl purses in their little jaws.

In the morning, once every one was up and getting the sleep out of their eyes, we planned for Jill and Marge to do some shopping. John and I would tour some of my computer network installations. The men would find lunch separate from the women somewhere. Then we would have dinner back at the house. With some discreet inquiry, we discovered Marge would eat fish or chicken. Boiled or broiled, please, nothing rich.

We got through breakfast fine with one exception.

A chunk of butter-and-syrup-soaked pancake from one of our plates hit the floor. Bernard came racing into the room at the sound of the wet plop and stopped and stood over the messy fragment. He began to growl and snarl, his lips were drawn way back from his teeth and his ears were flat against the side of his head.

"Bernard! Stop it," exclaimed John.

• *Bernard Visits Belle* •

"My goodness!" (You *know* who said that, right?)

I reached down to Bernard with one hand to perhaps calm him only to have him snap at me. I then knew what writers talk about in horror stories about the click of the monster's teeth on air. It was a *loud* click and it startled me.

"*Hey!*" I said in surprise. (I am not eloquent when startled) Bernard continued to bristle and snarl over the piece of pancake. I was thinking that maybe I should get a paper towel. And maybe some heavy leather gloves.

As the humans sat stunned at the table and as Bernard continued to play up a miniature version of a tyrannosaurus Rex, Belle sort of wandered in. Her movement through the kitchen was slow and she paid little attention to anyone. She ambled over to the pancake particle and Bernard. We all sat transfixed for a moment.

"Belle! *No!*" (We all contributed to that one—it was sort of a chorus.)

An old song popped into my head. I think it had been recorded by the Eagles.

Somebody's gonna hurt someone, before the night is through!
Somebody's gonna come undone, there's nothing we can do!

Yet nothing happened, really. Bernard backed off, and Belle nosed down to the pancake and removed the syrup and butter off of the floor in about five licks as Bernard supervised.

Ok, I got it.

My daughter, Kaylie, during Bernard's last "visit", had tried to explain something to me when Bernard brought a pork chop scrap to Belle when he had been lost and then found in our

Bernard Visits Belle

basement the previous Christmas. She'd insisted that Bernard had brought Belle a present. I scoffed at that offering, but Kaylie insisted that Bernard had brought that scrap of pork as a present for Belle. Kaylie had been right. Bernard had a special spot in his little heart for our Belle. The pancake event must have been just a different manifestation of the behavior Kaylie had observed at Christmas.

Amazing.

Sort of cute, too.

I looked across the table and caught Jill's eye. Without looking away from Jill, I said, "Well, now. Bernard seems to continue to be the real gentleman. First it has been gifts of pork and now pancakes. He is quite the little guy, hey?"

Belle snorted and Bernard gave out a soft "wuff."

"Pork chops?" asked John. "What are you talking about?"

"My goodness," stated Marge.

Marge was *really* beginning to wear on me. But…

I explained about the pork chop. When we had finally found the lost Bernard in our basement last Christmas, he had a scrap of pork chop with a bit of green ribbon stuck to it with him. He let Belle eat the thing. Daughter Kaylie had said that Bernard had brought it as a present for Belle and I had said he just had dug it out of the garbage for himself and someone's trashed Christmas wrap had stuck to it. I was wrong, clearly. So I was told.

"So," I finished, "the pancake is the same sort of thing. You see? It's another present!"

Marge and John did not see at all. In fact, they looked at me as though I had a toad growing out of the middle of my forehead. Jill rescued me, "Jack, come help me clean up the dishes while John and Marge go up stairs and get ready. We are going out, still?"

Bernard Visits Belle

Yeah, dishes, I thought to myself. *That would be good.* The toad and I went to help clean up. Of course the dachshunds had to help, licking and slurping the remains of breakfast off of the plates. Hey, you wouldn't believe what we save in dishwasher soap at our house.

As we two men were about to leave the house in my Blazer and the two women were about to leave in Jill's car, I took Jill aside. "Are you going to be all right with Marge? I mean, she seems a little…"

Jill blew me off. "Forget it, I have plans. You'll see. Just you and John go and have a good time. Play with your 'puters and show John around some of the places around the lake. I have it under control. Okay?"

"Uh, yeah. Okay." I had doubts. But I also knew Jill. Actually, that's what scared me a little. What did she have in mind?

"See you?" I said cautiously.

"Ok, see you guys! Jill said, "Have fun. We will! C'mon, Marge. Let these two fools to themselves. You and I are going shopping." And then having said that, Jill bustled Marge out of the house, into Jill's car, and they were down the driveway before I could say another thing at all.

John looked at me with his eyebrows up and his head lowered, pressing his chin down against his chest.

I shrugged. "Let's make sure the dogs are set before we go, John. I don't know exactly when we'll be back and who knows when the ladies will be back. You fill the water dishes and I'll put some chow out. We'll have to get the two of them out for their business. You take Bernard out front and I'll take Belle in the back. They won't waste time dinking around with each other that way."

John and I climbed into my Blazer after we tended to the dogs and we were on our way. I had a thought, as we drove off, that the ladies could, well, get into some kind of trouble. But I really couldn't get that thought to coalesce. Something ticked and ticked in the back of my head that something or other was about to transpire.

"Say, Jack? Where are we going?"

"Huh? I mumbled.

John had been talking while I was ruminating. He repeated himself, "Where are we going?"

"John, I am going to show you some of my network installations in some of the buildings that I have been working in if you are interested. After that, we're going to stop at a place I know. You will like it. It's the *Golden Wolf* over on the end of Pensive Lake. We'll get a good sandwich and beer or two there. Ok with you?"

"Great, that sounds great. But I have to ask you a question."

"Sure, I said. "Shoot."

"You know, I love my wife." John sounded guilty.

"Uh, yeah? Hey, guy, how about Bernard" I thought where was *this* going?

John struggled with the next, "Sometimes she…"

John must've missed my point of humor about Bernard.

"Stop it John, not a problem. Do you think we should skip the computer tour and hit the *Golden Wolf*?"

John adjusted his frame, sat visibly straighter in his seat and said, "You know? If that's okay with you it sounds great to me. I really don't know much about computers anyway. They gave me one at work, but I don't really know much about them anyway. Let's just go."

"Great! They've got great burgers at the *Golden Wolf* and we can have a couple of beers while the wives are out spending our money."

John said ruefully, "Ain't that the truth! 'Course you know, Marge doesn't really spend that much. Not on clothes or stuff like that."

· Bernard Visits Belle ·

I bit my tongue.

John had one more thing, "Do you think the dogs will be all right?

"Yeah, sure. Don't worry. We won't stay long."

The *Golden Wolf* was full of the usual Saturday crowd; lake people that couldn't sail or get their power boats out during the winter and were looking for something to do. It was a polite group. Two or three people were at the bar sipping whatever and a half dozen pairs were at tables in the atrium overlooking Pensive Lake. I motioned John to a table and we sat. A waitress, Shannon, one that I knew, approached.

"Hi, Jack!" she said. "Who's this?" The waitress cast one of those sunrise smiles at John. (I thought, maybe I should just tell her he was married right off and be on with things, but I didn't'—I guess I thought that was John's call, not mine.)

"Hello, yourself," I posted back, "this is John. He has a dachshund, just like me."

"John, hello. Nice to meet you! Did Jack here ever tell you about the story about Bernard? It is so *cute*! I could just *die*!"

Shannon smiled again. And I thought that maybe I should be wearing my sunglasses. That, or maybe with all of those teeth in view from that smile, I might maybe call a dentist. Or maybe an orthodontist.

I told her. "This is *the* John, Shannon. He's the one who owns Bernard. He and his wife Marge are the ones in the story. They're visiting and we are here to grab a sandwich."

"*No!* You're kidding! John!? Are you the one with the, the dachshund dog who took a pork chop present to Jack's Belle? We all know Belle. She's a sweetheart, really. She's been in here! And we sneak her little treats and stuff. Oh, I shouldn't have said that.

· *Bernard Visits Belle* ·

We don't allow dogs in here, but Belle is different and she always is *so* good and, *gosh* I don't believe it!"

I laughed. "Yeah, this is John, famous owner of Bernard, right here on this very stage. And by the way, Belle and Bernard are back at the house so we need to get going here. Can you get us two mushroom and Swiss burgers, fries and a couple of light beers? Mugs?"

"You bet. That'll be right up. Bernard! I can't *believe* it!"

I looked over the table at John. He was sitting straight up, his hands were down in his lap and his eyes were casting back and forth between the view of the frozen surface of Pensive Lake and the inside of the *Golden Wolf*. For just a second, just a micro second, I thought that I was seeing Marge, not John.

No, I said to myself. *This can't be.* I was confused.

"John!"

"Hmmph?"

I told him to relax. I told him that Marge and Jill were off having a great time and that Shannon was an innocent dear and that the burgers that were coming were going to be the very best he ever had.

We inhaled the burgers. We chewed and swallowed the French fries that we had slopped with ketchup. I wrapped a piece of burger in a napkin for Belle. John did the same for Bernard. We slurped down two beers each and then headed home to the dogs.

I wondered if the women had returned before the two of us guys. Somehow, I doubted that.

After arriving back at the house, we put the dogs out, watered them and then put out the scraps of hamburger we had brought back. Staying in style, Bernard stood over his scrap of hamburger until Belle finished hers. Belle snapped up Bernard's treat as he

· Bernard Visits Belle ·

watched. (I put the extra hamburger that Shannon had snuck into my coat pocket, encased in one of those Styrofoam things, in the fridge. I figured it would make a great late night snack for me and the dogs.)

I told John to have a seat in the living room. I grabbed the remote and thumbed on a sports channel. As we watched men in expensive clothing catch fish neither of us had ever even dreamed of, Belle clambered into my lap and Bernard crawled into John's.

Perfect day.

So far.

Somewhere around fifteen fish later, the doorbell rang. Of course the two dachshunds went into doozle diddy fits. They jumped from our lazy laps, hit the floor running and attacked the front door. I had a thought that, gee, I would never match the paint needed to repair the claw marks.

Oh, well.

The two of them were barking, snarling and jumping. The two of them looked like two elongated brown popcorn kernels bouncing up from the bottom of a stove top pan.

I got up and opened the front door. Two women were standing there. One was Jill. I didn't recognize the other one.

The dachshunds were still snarling and barking and bouncing around like two unstriped matching Tiggers from *Winnie the Pooh*. John joined me at the door and was immediately foot tangled with the two dogs.

Jill said, "Hey, grab the dogs, are you going to let us in or not?"

Us?

As Jill and the other gal came into the house, stepping around the dogs, I took a good long look at the person who was not my wife.

· *Bernard Visits Belle* ·

She was a knockout. Drop dead beautiful. She wore white, skintight stretch pants and a blue semi-transparent blouse that showed off a body that could cause accidents. Her hair and makeup looked like something out of a fashion magazine; *Cosmo*, maybe.

Whew!

"What do you think?" Jill said. "We gave Marge a change. We picked out some new clothes and did one of those makeover places at the mall." Jill stood grinning.

Ok, this second lady was Marge. I was dumbfounded. I *knew* Jill would have been up to something, but boy…

"What do you think, John?" Jill asked. "Isn't she great?!"

Marge did a slow turn for John. I was glad I didn't miss it. John was darn near speechless, but he said:

"Oh my goodness!"

Jill really had done a number on Marge. The clothes. The makeup. It was unbelievable. John could not take his eyes off of her. Jill couldn't stop grinning. Bernard was barking a holy fit. He did not recognize this stranger at all. I didn't see Belle, then. I suspected she had gone upstairs to hide in her favorite closet.

I thought about joining her.

Marge, amazingly, had a little smile on her face. I guess Jill really had made a change. Inside and out.

I felt I had to say something to break the moment. "Ok, Guys. Boy, Marge. You look great! Um, let me go start dinner. I was thinking of marinated grilled chicken?

Marge was the one who answered. "That sounds scrumptious. Don't you think, John?"

John didn't answer, he just kept staring. He was completely nonplussed.

• *Bernard Visits Belle* •

Marge? I thought. I couldn't quite accept the change. She *talked!* I wanted to look over my shoulder to see if Rod Serling was around somewhere. Bernard continued to fit and bark and carry on.

I thought, hey, I'm with you, Bernard. Pretty Cool.

Jill kicked me, gently, in the ankle. She moved her lips, wordlessly, saying "Easy, Jack, remember me?"

Right. Bernard continued to bark and shuffle and I went to start dinner.

Marge had made an amazing transformation. Not only did she look like she would stop traffic; she actually participated in our conversations. She didn't say a lot, but she was not as silent and as reserved, as she had been when she first arrived.

At one point she said, "Tell me, Jack, did that story you told about the pork chop really happen? It's so hard to believe. But after seeing Bernard and the pancake this morning, I can't help but want to think it's true."

I answered her, talking around a mouthful of chicken. "Yup, it happened. Just like I said this morning. But it wasn't me who figured the whole thing out; it was my daughter, Kaylie who saw the truth of things. Your Bernard must really have a soft spot in his little heart for our Belle."

During this exchange, we all could hear the dogs whining and scruffling and snorting in the next room. None of the four of us gave it a thought. The dogs had been running around the household for two days now and the sounds they had been making had become "white noise." So, we paid no attention.

John saw fit to compliment my marinated chicken.

Jill sipped her wine.

The dogs continued to wuff and snort in the next room.

Bernard Visits Belle

As I sat at the table, my back was to the living room. Marge sat across from me so that if she chose to look, she would be able to see the room behind me in which the dogs were playing.

Suddenly, Marge turned bone white. "*Oh my God!*" Her eyes were riveted on a spot over my shoulder in the next room where the dogs were... playing.

"*Oh my God!*" Marge said again. I figured I should turn around and look at what was getting her so excited. I did.

It was Belle and Bernard that had captured Marge's attention. They had been making those snuffling and whining noises while we humans were eating dinner. Belle and Bernard, were, well...

Doing it.

Oh boy.

John jumped from his seat, knocking his chair backward in his rush to get to his dog. "Bernard! *No!*"

Too late. The two hounds separated. Belle took off for the upstairs rooms; a blurry, furry brown rocket streaking over up the carpeted stairs. Bernard stood a moment and then slumped over on his side. He appeared a little breathless.

I couldn't help it. I never can. I blurted out, "Hey, someone get Bernard a cigarette!"

No one was amused. Oh well.

John started to apologize. Marge was visibly shaken. Jill and I looked at each other....what was there to say?

Marge said in a shaken voice, "Jill, do you still have some of that white wine?"

The rest of that evening, considering what had gone on, went well. Marge's new image plus a couple of glasses of Chablis went a long way to make her feel comfortable and to open up and laugh at this or that. I caught her blinking her lashes at John on a couple

Bernard Visits Belle

of occasions. Eventually, Belle came trucking down the stairs from where she had secreted herself after the Bernard event. She put her front paws on Marge's leg and Marge pulled her up off the floor into her lap.

"What a sweetheart!" said Marge.

"That's what Shannon said," said John. I think he immediately regretted it.

"Shannon?" asked Marge.

John blustered, "Oh, Shannon, she's a waitress at the *Golden Wolf* and Jack introduced us and she knows Belle and…"

"Oh, John. Shut up, you silly." Marge didn't seem to have a care other than to hold Belle and pet her. Then she surprised us all.

"John, let's go to bed early. Jack and Jill, do you mind?"

We didn't. Both dogs snoozed in our bed that night.

Marge and John slept in the next morning. I can only guess why. I took care of feeding and watering and getting the dogs outside. Once up and awake, Marge surprised me one more time by coming to breakfast in a duplicate outfit of Jill's. She had purchased a set of bib overalls and a rag sweater, just like Jill's. She wore the outfit proudly.

I snuck a chunk of scrambled eggs to Bernard, knowing he would deliver it to Belle.

John spent a lot of time grinning that morning.

Marge and John packed, collected Bernard and prepared to leave for their trip back. Lots had changed, thanks to Jill and, maybe, the dogs. John was still grinning. Marge gave me a kiss on the cheek that lasted a split second longer than I thought it should. Maybe I just imagined it. But John looked on proudly and Jill had a smile on her face that was surely stolen from an elf.

· Bernard Visits Belle ·

Cradled in Marge's arms, Bernard looked sadly over her shoulder as his owners headed down the drive to their car. *Belle?* He seemed to say. *When can I see you again?*

Ahem, sorry, maybe that was a bit of a reach. But you get the idea.

As the Tailors backed their car down the drive and headed off, disappearing at the end of the street, Jill and I waved from the front door. Belle barked.

There was one thought left in my head after all of this; just one word, actually, and the word was not "pipe" it was—

Puppies.

The Mouse That Was Saved

The Story of the Puppies of Belle and Bernard, the Adventures of a Field Mouse, the Intervention of Luck and the Application of Things That Are Good and Kind.

I BROKE MY ARM ONCE. It was bad. My bones were sticking out of my skin and I could see them. Once, I had stitches sewn in my mouth after I fell on my face and pushed my top teeth all the way through my lower lip. I witnessed, and aided, hands-on, the birth of both of my children. I never faltered during any of these events.

But when Belle was delivering her first puppy, I fainted. I really did. And I smacked my forehead on the floor after going down and then faded away on the ceramic floor tiles in the kitchen. I fell just inches away from the birthing box we had set there for our pregnant dachshund. Jill got the vet on the on the phone, listened to Dr. Aspin's advice and took care of things while I was passed out.

After the visit of the dachshund, Bernard and our friends Marge and John, Belle had become "with puppies." And while we looked forward to the birth of these palm-sized little critters, I missed most of it. By the time I woke up (Jill just left me there on the floor, threw a blanket over me and figured I would wake up on my own), it was

The Mouse That Was Saved

time to call the Tailors and tell them about the arrival of the four puppies—three boys and a girl. They were thrilled when I called and told them that the mating between our Belle and their Bernard had finally resulted in the birth of the little pups.

Over the phone, one on each extension, both of them said, "My goodness!" It was a duet, nothing new. These folks, owners of our Belle's sire, were not always that eloquent. They were uncomplicated people. That is a different story. Read the last one. We promised to arrange a visit in the future to have the Tailors see the pups.

Belle and the puppers thrived. Belle nursed them, nosed them around as a dachshund mom should in terms of discipline and eventually, as they grew a little older and bolder and bigger, she nosed them out of the dog bed and into the real world.

The world of the kitchen, that is.

Jill and I could not help but giggle and chuckle at the pups' antics. They had nearly no control of their legs, and their little noses looked nothing like the noses of their adult peers. Their noses were so short! And it was all they could do to even get upright on the kitchen tiles. Eventually they did manage it. And then they became horrors. They were *everywhere*.

Once they found their voices, it was auditory bedlam.

An example: one afternoon I came home from work and I was looking forward to doing a little more work in my office on the lower floor of our home.

Not.

Jill greeted me at the door. Actually, greeted is the wrong word. She pounced on me. "Jack, *do* something with these *puppies!*"

I could hear them; "*Whine*", slobber, "*Whine! Rife, Rife, Riife, Riffe, RIIFFE!*" The sounds sort of really did hurt one's ears.

The Mouse That Was Saved

The four of them produced such a cacophony of puppy dog noises that I could not hear Jill's "greeting." The little dogs were galloping and darting around the enclosed kitchen like mad lizards.

"Huh?"

"Jack!"

"What was that? I can't hear you, Jill, the pups are too loud."

I was in immediate trouble. I could tell this. I'd had lots of experience.

This is what I sort of heard. I am interpreting but it's pretty close.

"I've been with these *bark* dogs all day *woof, snarl* and *yipe* you don't do a thing, and I have *yipe yipe yipe* just about had it *yip yipe* and you come home *yipe yipe* and just don't do anything and these dogs are driving me nuts and… and *woof* if you think you are going to…"

It was hard to tell which came from Jill and which came from the dogs, but, I was grateful when she ran out of breath. Jill that is. I thought so, anyway. Had I actually heard her bark? Never mind, I wasn't going there.

The pups did not, however, become breathless and their mom, Belle, joined into the fray.

Communication was out of the question. So I did what all good dog owners do in times of crises. I got food. I went to the cupboard, grabbed some dog cookies, really little ones, and threw them on the kitchen floor.

Save for the sounds of scrambling claws and paws on tiles and the crunching of sharp little teeth, miniature carnivores breaking the bones of their prey, all was quiet for a moment or two.

"Now, Jill, you were saying?"

· *The Mouse That Was Saved* ·

Too late. Jill whirled and left the room. I can't say I blamed her. I was the one, now, surrounded by pups looking for their next whatever. Belle looked up at me (I never have understood how those little dachshunds can bend their necks up so far to look at you from the floor) as if to say:

"Well, big guy? Now what?"

What indeed? And the pups, having finished their wolf bait, began to howl and yip and bark once more.

Life went on like that for a while.

Things *did* settle down. The little pups' noses grew and Belle was a good mom; nursing till it was time to stop and cooperating with the weaning. Suddenly, out of the blue, we noticed that we had five real dachshunds in the house. How did that happen? I spent more time scooping poop than I did writing or working at anything else. As cute as the little things were, it was becoming a real chore to take care of all of the feeding and cleaning and cuddling and such.

One night, Belle came up to our bedroom to take her usual place at the bottom of the bed, to be ensconced under the covers, breathing down there with a method known only to dachshunds… we have certainly never figured it out. How do they breathe like that? This time all four pups were in tow.

And up they came. Belle insisted, and we lifted each one up and each in turn found a place to burrow. Actually, there was lots of room. But the leftover space was good for only one adult human. Jill and I began each taking turns sleeping on one of the downstairs couches.

Things progressed in reasonable fashion with the puppies. We made some adjustments. The major one was that we bought a bigger bed.

The Mouse That Was Saved

The little dogs' noses elongated and they became actual dachshunds, recognizable by most anyone. This did not always include those that would see us on the street walking with five dogs. These folks would ask what kind of dogs the puppies were. We always responded that they were baby Dobermans. That usually quelled any further irritating questions. It was amazing. People would reach down to pet our crowd of pups and then snatch their hands back, (after we told them the dogs' heritage) smiling and saying, "Oh, really?" Our household has always been haunted with a strange sense of humor. It could be from the paint on the walls or something. Don't really know.

Fall came to our part of the world. Leaves colored themselves, then browned, fell and made a mess in the yard. These are pretty at first, but a real problem. And when a household has five dachshunds, the residents can become crazed trying to keep track of the dogs in the leaves. It seems the color of most dachshunds blends in just perfectly with fallen leaves. Fall has its problems.

And there are mice in fall.

Anyone who has ever lived in a four-season climate knows that the local little rodents want to invade and establish residence inside warm human habitations for the winter as fall begins. In our case, we had been through this migration for so many seasons that we were (we thought) veterans of prevention. We had always taken the usual precautions.

Belle did not think so. She began to edge.

The word "Edge" has a special definition at our house. It is a verb, actually, used in common speech as "edging." As in, "there goes Belle, she's edging!" The little dachshund began to spend lots of time covering all of the corners of the basement office and laundry room. She would stick her nose into the joints formed by the wall and

· The Mouse That Was Saved ·

floor and then travel all along the perimeter of the rooms, snuffling and snorting and (we presumed) looking for rodents.

There weren't any. We were sure of this. All of the mouse egresses had been filled, caulked, wired over and stopped up. We were mouse professionals.

But Belle continued to edge. And soon the pups joined in. This was driving us crazy. Every morning, every afternoon, every *hour* the dogs begged to go downstairs and sniff for mice. If the door wasn't open, they would sit and whine at the top of the stairs. If we were sleeping, they would bark and yip until we let them down there in the lower office and basement laundry room.

"Hey, guys! *There are no mice!*"

Yeah, right, like they would all listen to me. Good luck.

By now, in the season of the mouse hunt, the pups had names; Roller, Prancer, Snort and Lampshake. The names speak for themselves and need no explanation. That is except for Lampshake. This one was named because this pup spent most of his time running around the house like a wildcat in pursuit of dinner. In most cases, he would ram into table legs and topple the lamps on those tables. Hence; Lampshake.

I did relent on the mouse thing. I finally gave in and told the dogs that while I *really* did not think there was a mouse down below, I would set one of the live traps, just in case. I didn't think it necessary, mind you, but maybe this might keep some peace. I would show the dogs that there were no mouses once and for all.

Mice, I meant, Mice. My god! I was beginning to talk like the dogs! Did I just say that? Was I thinking that the dogs could talk? I was not in good shape. Too many dogs and too few mice, I guess.

Ahem.

· *The Mouse That Was Saved* ·

The next morning a mouse was in the live trap, feasting on the peanut butter I'd placed there as bait.

Roller was the first to find it. He had rumble bumped down the stairs to the trap and began to howl at about five thirty in the a.m. This howling woke up Snort. Snort heard Roller howling from his place under the bedcovers and began to, well, snort. Never moving from under the bedcovers, he was making all kinds of wet, messy, nose-based noises. Prancer joined in with grunts and woofs.

Down in the back of the basement, Roller held guard by the trap until I rose from my bed to see what the matter was. Belle followed me down to see Roller next to the trap, on his back, feet in air and teeth bared. The mouse cowered in the trap; peanut butter forgotten.

Well I'll be, I thought. *The dogs win, I lose. We have mice!*

And now it was time for an immediate disposal. I grabbed a piece of newspaper and placed the trap on it so as to catch the droppings out of the bottom of the wire mesh of the trap. I was a mouse expert, after all. Climbing up the stairs, dogs in tow, I carried the trap to the patio doors and then headed out to the woods behind the house with the trapped rodent. I had to shake the trap with doors opened to get the little thing loose. It fell out, adjusted its whiskers and scampered off under the fallen leaves. The score then, sat at Dogs—1, Mouse—1 and Jack—0.

Returning to the house I was greeted by all six; Belle, Prancer, Lampshake, Roller, Snort and Jill. It seemed like a homecoming save for the live trap I was holding under my arm. I had five dogs pawing at my legs and my wife pawing at my arm. The snorting, rolling, shaking and prancing told me I should allow the dogs to sniff the trap to make sure they knew the mouse was gone. The pawing at my arm; that was another problem. I had to explain to Jill that a mouse had breached our defenses. Oh boy.

I re-baited and reset the trap and placed it back in the basement. I had to put an upside-down orange crate over the top of it so the curious hounds would not trip the trap with their inquisitive noses.

The next morning, again at five, Roller took off out of the bed, scrambled to the basement and began to howl while lying on his back next to the orange crate. Snort leaped from the bed, trucked down the stairs and joined in with nose noises. Belle ambled down and sat nearby watching the festivities. There was another mouse in the live trap.

I took that little critter, again, out to the woods behind the house, cleaned, re-baited the trap and set it up under the orange crate once more. Now the score was Mice—2, Dogs—2 and Jack—0. The score changed, not in my favor, once more the next morning.

Roller woke us all up at five in the morning to make sure we knew we had caught the third mouse. This time Jill joined me down in the back room.

Rubbing the night's sleep from her eyes, Jill leaned down to peer into the mouse trap. "Ooo, look at him! He's so cute, I want to pet him."

I rolled my eyes. "You can't pet it; it's a mouse. It'll bite you."

"I want to pet him!" When an idea arrives in Jill's head, it is very, very difficult to knock loose.

Prancer and Lampshake arrived. All five dogs began to bristle and growl, ears back, heads thrust forward and ready to pounce. "Alright, fine," I said to my wife, "I'll see if I can get it out of the trap and you can pet the darn thing while I hold it. But then I have to take it outside, OK?" I reached for a work glove on the nearby bench,

The Mouse That Was Saved

lifted the trap off of the concrete floor and placed it on the bench. I wriggled the glove onto my right hand and then, securing the trap with my left, I fingered open the door and reached in.

Of all of the mistakes I have made in my life, I will not forget that one. The mouse escaped.

The racing rodent hit the top of the workbench, stumbled on its side, righted it self and leaped to the floor. It landed right in the middle of the dachshund herd. The canine reaction was electric. I don't know how this is possible, but all five of the little hounds froze in place and began to shake at the same time.

The mouse lost no time investigating. It took off across the floor and headed for the stairs in the next room.

Did you ever see one of those runaway stage coaches on some old television western being pulled by panicked horses with the wooden wheels of the coach just blurs? That was what the little mouse legs and feet looked like: blurred stage coach wheels. Up the stairs went the mouse. The dogs broke out of their suspended state, took off after the mouse and erupted into full throttle and throat.

You would have thought a pack of wolves was after an elk in our house. It was either that or a fox hunt. I thought for a second that I would hear a hunting trumpet start to blare. In any event, the chase was on and I joined in. As I scrambled up the stairs at the tail of the scrambling herd of hounds, I thought two quick thoughts. I was going to need the carpet cleaners to remove the carnage I was sure to see and I was going to need vet Aspin to check on the hounds after mouse ingestion.

The mouse reached the first floor with the dogs right behind. The howling and growling and baying were deafening. I don't think even a hunting trumpet could have been heard above the din. Carpet fibers flew. The mouse darted one way and then, in full panic, another and the hounds tried to twist and reel and keep up. At one point, the mouse completely reversed, ran right through Snort's front legs, streaked underneath his belly and out between his back legs. Snort lowered his head and tried to look down and back between his legs as the mouse exited under his tail. The mouse headed for a corner of the room and then dead-ended, cowering against the baseboards. The dogs, still barking and howling, surrounded it. But for some reason known only to them, they did not pounce.

Rigid, with lips drawn back, the dogs stood shoulder to shoulder, forming a barrier, keeping the mouse at bay in the corner. They looked like a bunch of big furry sardines crammed in a can or maybe a bunch of carp all pointed in the same direction. I could hear growls deep in throats and I've never seen so many teeth at once. Without much thought, I ankled my way in between the hounds, reached down with my still-gloved hand and grabbed the little mouse.

"Ha!" I said.

Jill caught up to all of us just as the hunt had ended. She still wanted to pet the mouse. I just sighed and presented the little creature while held in my fist. His bewhiskered snout and tiny head with its black eyes stuck out of the ring formed by my forefinger and thumb. Jill extended an index finger and stroked the mouse's head.

"He's so soft!"

"Just don't get bit, I have to take him out back." The mouse was beginning to wriggle in my hand and the dogs had broken formation to jump and paw at my legs. I raised the mouse aloft and out of harm's way; both human and canine.

"Jack?" asked Jill, "Could this be the same mouse?"

"Huh?"

· *The Mouse That Was Saved* ·

Jill continued, "What is this, three in three days? I'll bet you're catching the same mouse over and over. I mean, you just take him out to the woods and that isn't very far away so it could just be the same mouse coming back."

"No way, why would the same mouse keeping getting him self caught in the same trap? That's silly," I argued.

"Maybe it just has a thing for peanut butter," Jill suggested.

I didn't want to admit to my wife that she might be right and that it may have been futile trapping and releasing the same mouse. And all that was really going on was that the dogs were waking us when a mouse was in the trap and after this little "hunt" I was getting tired of the whole thing.

So I said, "Ok, let's experiment. C'mon back downstairs with me."

Mouse clutched in hand, dogs and Jill in tow, I descended once more and approached the bench in the back room.

"See that old bottle of model paint?" I pointed to a quarter ounce jar of Testor's enamel on a shelf. It was probably left over from a project one of our kids had worked on a while ago when they were still kids. "Open it up, would you? I can't use both hands, I don't want to let go of the mouse."

While Jill struggled with the cap and the dogs stared up and bristled, I grabbed a small brush with my free hand. Jill opened and then held the small jar out for me. The color was neon pink. Using the brush and paint, I proceeded to give the mouse a pink punker hairdo.

I thought this little trick might put the issue to rest. "Ok," I said to everyone, "if this mouse is stupid enough to come back, we'll know. We can't miss it."

Jill had a question about whether the paint might hurt the mouse but I dismissed it. However I did wonder if I was not

The Mouse That Was Saved

marking the little thing as a target for the local hawks and other predators. I shook off that thought knowing I could not tolerate another indoor hunting party with a pack of wild dachshunds. The paint was the quick-dry kind, so the mouse was deposited then, pink head and all, in the back woods.

The next morning, promptly at five o'clock, Roller found a pink-headed mouse in the live trap. When I went down to see, I immediately took the whole trap, still mouse-inhabited, into the garage so as to avoid a repeat of the previous day's festivities. Jill joined me for coffee in the kitchen. I told her about the pink-headed mouse.

"I told you," she said.

I was waiting for that and said, "Yeah, I'm going to have to take it out far away somewhere where it can't find its way back. I was thinking of Korsi's farm down the road."

Jill cautioned me, "I don't know if the Korsi folks would be too happy with you just dropping off some little mouse without asking about it. Can you call them?"

"Nah," I said. "What's one little mouse? Farms are full of mice."

Jill was not convinced of my plan. "What about the barn cats? They'll get the little thing!"

"Look," I said, "We can have a wild herd of dachshunds hunting in our living room while we run out of peanut butter, or the mouse can go and fend for itself. I'll put it in one of the sheds at the farm, ok?"

I knew what coming after that.

"Can I pet it before you go?"

I thought about that for a moment and started to phrase a couple different replies, but I took the conservative way out and just said,

· *The Mouse That Was Saved* ·

"No."

I left the kitchen and went to the garage to place the mouse, still in the trap, into the back of my Blazer. The two of us drove out and headed down the mile to the farm. I pulled over, removed mouse and trap and headed through a field to an old utility shed. The door was latched but not locked, and I stepped in, trap under my arm.

The place smelled rusty and dusty and was full of farm tools, old bags the print on which had faded away, and a lawn tractor in the corner that listed on mostly flat tires. A couple of old canvas tarps rotted in the corner. It looked like a regular high class mouse resort in my view. I held the trap up to eye level.

"Ok, little punk rocker. Here's your stop. Hope you like it. There should be some new friends here and I think it will be a lot quieter." (Here I was going again, talking to animals!)

The mouse didn't say anything but through the wire of the trap I could see him using his back foot to scratch the top of his pink head. I said to him, "Don't worry, that stuff will wear off." I put the trap on the floor and opened it. The mouse didn't leave the trap.

I figured the little guy would vacate his prison eventually, so I left the trap in the middle of the floor and took a few steps away to inspect the stuff stored in the shed. There were scythes and rakes and shovels of all shapes and sizes. There was even a bushel of old dried corn against one wall. It was all of only mild interest until I toed over one of the tarps and what looked to be nearly twenty mice began scooting for new cover. They were everywhere.

"This is good," I thought. "Lots of mice must mean this is a good place." I turned to the trap to see that it was now empty. Okay, mission accomplished. I headed for the door.

At the door, my hand on the latch, I paused, thinking for just a second. I felt I had to say something so I turned back and called

· *The Mouse That Was Saved* ·

into the shed. "Hey. All you mice in here! Make this new guy feel at home! And don't be put off by that pink head. Just figure he might be from London."

The Real Christmas Story

(or, What Happened to the Gold, Frankincense and Myrrh)

THE MOON ROSE in the eastern desert sky to illuminate three resting camels and three supine human figures sleeping on the ground nearby. A fire had died to embers. The three figures stirred and then rose and stretched in the moonlight. Their coverings fell down to the ground as they rose and the rich fabrics glittered on the edges where gold and silver threads had been woven into the cloth.

These three men were kings, travelers in search of something important. A bright star in the sky at night had guided them for some time to their ultimate destination. One man spoke to the other two.

"Akim, Jelode, I can still see the star. The sun has gone to earth and we must continue."

The others answered, "Yes, I see it. We must go." and "I see it as well, Rahjem, I shall go and kick the camels, stubborn beasts as they are."

The three men packed their things, clambered up unto wooden saddles on the camels and continued their journey east under the evening sky. Each had a special package tied to his saddle.

· *The Real Christmas Story* ·

A two hour's march away, a man and women woke to the same moon and same star. As they were poor, a single donkey would carry the woman. The man and the three dogs that traveled with them would walk. The woman, seated on a rough blanket on the back of the donkey would allow the dogs, one at a time, to rest, draped in front of her over the back of the pack animal.

The man, Joe, silently wondered why the dogs should get such treatment. He felt that the woman's willingness to share her ride might compromise the donkey's endurance. After all, the woman was pregnant, very, and he thought the dogs should have been walking along on their own.

Joe was a carpenter. And he often received payment for his work with food or clothes or other things than coin. The three dogs had been such a payment. They were small, short haired and built long and close to the ground with short legs. Rumors held they had been bred centuries ago by the Egyptian Pharaohs. Other thoughts belied this and claimed their breed came from the north. No one knew. Centuries later, a country called Germane would take credit for what would be called the "badger hounds", "dachshunds", or "teckels", in the language of the people of the region. For the moment, out on that desert, the dogs just ambled along, jumping up and nipping at the donkey's legs for a chance to ride. Joe just trudged. The woman clasped hard with her knees to side of the wobbling donkey and prayed her time would not come while out in the wilderness.

Hours later, Joe and the woman and the three hounds came upon a small village. The woman's time was very close and Joe begged shelter in a barn for the night. The dogs burrowed down in straw and hay kept there in the little structure to absorb the excretions of the pigs, goats, sheep and unseen little animals that shared the shelter. The woman lay back on the same carpet of straw and waited. Joe fidgeted and the dogs slept.

Akim, Jelode and Rahjem were only miles away. The camels plodded and the three riders were sweating into the cloths wrapped around their heads in spite of the cold desert night. Their gilded traveling clothes were covered with fine dust.

"Akim! Jelode!" shouted Rahjem. "I think we approach our destination! See the star? It is there above our heads. We must indeed be upon our goal."

"About time, I would venture," said Akim, "My sitting parts are well worn."

"Ah, indeed, I am so pleased to agree," said Jelode."

As the three camel riders drew closer, the woman's baby was being born. Joe jumped up and about, prancing through the straw and scattering braying sheep and goats and pigs in all directions. "Get back, you! Out of the way!" he shouted. The three dogs, of course, rose up, sniffed the air and approached the woman, who was lying down on the floor of the barn. Two began to lick her feet and one started on her face.

Joe was not amused. "Away, all three of you little beasts! Leave her be!" The dogs, admonished, shrank away and cowered back under the hay, only three brown heads with black eyes glittering sticking out to watch and sniff.

The baby was born in due time just before midnight. A boy, he was cleaned by Joe with rough cloth and wrapped in one of Joe's shirts to then be placed in the woman's arms. The three dogs approached and were petted by the woman and allowed to snuffle and lick the new baby. The three travelers arrived on their mounts and jumped down.

The Real Christmas Story

Rahjem was stopped by Joe at the entrance to the barn, "Hey, wise guy, what do you want?"

"Actually, dear honored sir, we are *three* wise guys. We have come a long way to see the baby and bring him gifts. We have seen it in the stars and have been guided here. This baby can bring peace to our troubled world. May we enter?"

The three dogs were intrigued. They joined Joe at the entrance to the barn and began to bark and jump and howl while wagging tails so hard one might think they would fly loose from their little bodies. "Um, Okay," said Joe. "The dogs seem to like you."

The men entered, leaving the camels to fend for themselves among the barn animals that had wandered out during the exchange between the men. "Ah," said Akim, "We have gifts for the baby." He peered over at the mother and child and motioned to Jelode. "Place them down, Jelode, there, near the dogs."

Carrying the three satchels from the camels, Jelode produced a small chest. He opened it and it was full of cold coins. He reached again and produced an ornate urn, and then another. All three items were placed on the ground next to the baby and its mother.

"Behold," exclaimed Rahjem, "We bring gold and rare anointments of great treasure. Please accept our gifts on the eve and morning of such a great day!"

"Well, my, thank you," said the woman, babe in arms, "I don't know what to say."

While Joe watched, nonplussed, the dogs knew what to do. They all three descended on the containers. The first pushed its nose into the chest and bit into and swallowed two small gold coins. The other two dumped the urns into the straw and began to roll; eyes wide and feet in the air.

"Ah, no!" shouted Jelode, "For the baby! Not for the dogs! Curse you, all three!"

"Leave my dogs alone, you camel-driven fool!" exclaimed Joe. "I did not invite you here!"

"Please, peace to you all," admonished Rahjem and then held out a hand, palm up. "It is the journey and the future to which we aspire, let the dogs be. Are they not creatures on our earth as well as we?"

The three dogs sure thought so.

They stopped their antics and trotted over to the woman and baby. She said, "Oh, you stink so!" What are we to do?"

The three dogs just sat, shook their heads, ears flapping, and stared up with eyebrows raised. Their biggest concern was dinner but that was handled by Akim who produced hard dried meat for the little dogs and placed it on the straw for them.

Joe had many questions. The woman did as well. The dogs did not; they were full of Akim's dried treats. After a time, Rahjem announced that all should sleep and each person drew a rough blanket over their shoulders and lay down on the straw floor. The woman was given one of the gilded robes to cover herself and the baby. The three dogs each chose one of the travelers with whom to sleep and all was right with the world.

After the spills, the barn smelled really good.

In the morning, Joe would be checking dog droppings for gold.

But that night, three wise guys, three dachshunds and a man and woman and child slept all dreaming of the future of the world.

Another Redstripe, Please

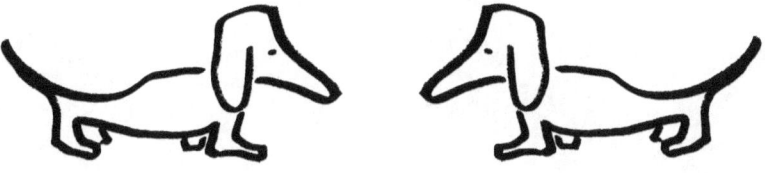

Dachshunds in the Midwest

Another Redstripe, Please

Dachshunds in the Midwest

By Jack Magestro

Unlimited Publishing
Bloomington, Indiana

Copyright © 2004 by Jack Magestro

Distributing Publisher:
Unlimited Publishing LLC
Bloomington, Indiana

http://www.unlimitedpublishing.com

Contributing Publisher:
Jack Magestro

Cover and book design by Charles King. Copyright © 2004 by Unlimited Publishing LLC. This book was typeset with Adobe® InDesign®, using the Myriad® and Adobe Jensen® typefaces. This book makes use of one or more typefaces specifically licensed by and customized for the exclusive use of Unlimited Publishing LLC.

All rights reserved under Title 17, U.S. Code, International and Pan-American Copyright Conventions. No part of this work may be reproduced or transmitted in any form or by any means, electronic or mechanical, including photocopying, scanning, recording, broadcast or live performance, or duplication by any information storage or retrieval system without prior written permission from the author(s) and publisher(s), except for the inclusion of brief quotations with attribution in a review or report. Requests for reproductions or related information should be addressed to the author(s) c/o Unlimited Publishing LLC. See www.unlimitedpublishing.com for mailing address.

Unlimited Publishing LLC provides worldwide book design, printing, marketing and distribution services for professional writers and small to mid-size presses, serving as distributing publisher. Sole responsibility for the content of each work rests with the author(s) and/or contributing publisher(s). The opinions expressed herein may not be interpreted in any way as representing those of Unlimited Publishing, nor any of its affiliates.

This is a work of fiction. All characters, products, corporations, institutions, and/or entities of any kind in this book are either the product of the author's imagination or, if real, used fictitiously without any intent to describe their actual characteristics.

First edition.

Copies of this fine book and others
are available to order online at:

http://www.unlimitedpublishing.com/authors

ISBN 1-58832-094-4

Unlimited Publishing
Bloomington, Indiana

For my wife, Jill,

my best fan.

Negril Beach, Jamaica—
2000 and Something

WE WERE back in Negril, one of our favorite places, and I was wandering alone along the seven miles of beach on an early June morning. The sun was just up and casting shadows of trees onto the sand as I strolled along in the ever-perfect air under a clear sky. The ocean was still calm and had not yet woken to cast any waves up onto the beach. Shirtless and shoeless, I wore a loose pair of old cotton shorts; superfluous, actually, other than to have pockets for my lighter and cigarettes. It was, to steal an often-used phrase, another perfect day in paradise and I was already thinking of my first beer.

Not many people were on that stretch of beach so soon after sunrise, but there were a few diehard young women lying atop towels spread on lounges, their skin soaked in tanning oil, doing their best to acquire skin cancer. I believe that they did not think or believe that some day, after thirty years of basking in the sun, they would all look like horse saddles. The bottles of designer water, stuck in the sand next to each one may have been able to keep them hydrated, but in the end, the sun would win and their youth would fade prematurely.

Besides a few wild dogs, some arguing birds and the leftover litter from the late partying of the night before and me, the only other things on the beach were some sleeping young men, curled on their own lounges or even just lying in the sand and sleeping off the excitement, ganja and high proof rum from the previous evening. I thought back thirty years to when I was twenty, as many of these reclined bodies seemed to appear to be, and wondered if I'd missed something by working so hard at odd jobs during that time of my own life just to pay for school and find a career. I didn't remember snoozing on a beach back then. The memory of my career was a little fuzzy that morning. I concluded that I *had* missed something, shrugged to my self and continued strolling.

While my wife was sleeping late as usual under a simple single sheet back in our rented cabin and dreaming her early morning dreams, I remembered the Redstripe tales told to us nearly a decade ago on that same beach in Negril. Over some time and several trips to the area, we met and continued to meet a local rastamafarian named Cirtron. He'd told us the story of Redstripe, a little dachshund, his girlfriend Sheila and his adventures with the little dog. The stories were somewhat unbelievable. He'd told us of sneaking the dog through international airports, how the dachshund wreaked havoc with the locals and how tiny Redstripe had charmed everyone she met in both Jamaica and the United States. My wife Jill and I often thought that maybe these stories were the product of the overuse of a certain prevalent drug in Jamaica, usually inhaled through the lungs, but the stories have remained with us for years. Thinking about them, I began to laugh out loud as I continued down the beach. No one cared that I was laughing at seemingly nothing, most everyone around was somnolent anyway and there are much weirder things to be seen on the Negril Beach than some middle-aged man walking along and laughing to himself.

I stopped for a moment to light a cigarette and to contemplate a pile of discarded conch shells. The pile was under a palm tree just outside a little shack that had a crude, hand painted sign stuck in the sand. The black letters listed conch, conch soup, jerked pork and chicken, and breakfast. One did not know what the *breakfast* really was, but the place apparently was selling it. The pile of discarded shells must have been three feet high and would have been worth a fortune back in the United States; the larger intact shells to be sold to adorn expensive coffee tables in affluent homes sporting the latest in interior design. To the Jamaicans, it was just a pile of refuse waiting to be buried in the sand.

The sun was beginning to make its way higher into the morning sky and I could feel it begin to sting my unprotected shoulders. I figured it was time to head back to the cabin and my sleeping wife and maybe find a cup of blue mountain coffee. I dug a hole in the sand for my cigarette with my bare foot, covered it and turned to make the trek back. I had only taken a few steps when I was confronted by a wandering beach vendor. He was selling aloe leaves and I, being one of the only moving objects on the beach, was his target.

The man, a very dark Jamaican—yellowish whites of eyes, enlarged feet from a life of pounding sand barefoot and wearing a only simple pair of khaki shorts—carried a large net bag over his shoulders crammed with aloe leaves. Actually, a better description of these would be aloe *branches*. These plants, the juices of which were applied to sunburn and were quite effective in relieving pain, grow to be six feet tall in Jamaica. The bag of branches looked like a bunch of truncated, handless green arms. The man stopped in front of me, placed the bag on the sand and made his pitch.

"Ya, mon. Your shoulders be getting' de red, mon. I have de aloe for you. Good for de burn. Very good."

I stopped and then realized I'd made a mistake. The word "no" or "no thank you" only works to decline an offer from the beach vendors if you keep moving. And one should never say "maybe later." The vendor will take that literally and pursue you "later" for the rest of the day or even the next. But regretting my error in stopping, I had only the second option left in order to remain polite and respectful.

"Maybe later," I said.

"Ya, mon. Irie. Y'come to our place and we rub in de aloe for you later. Come, I show you where t'go, come on, mon. Den you come back later." He picked up the bag.

Darn it. I was going to have to be rude in order get out of this one. I had no intention of going to "his place", wherever that was, just to be pressed to buy who knows what. I opened my mouth to say that I just needed be left alone but I stopped on the inhale before I spoke. I looked a little more closely at the man as I held my breath, wary and surprised at what I saw.

The Jamaican's beard and dreadlocks held some grey. And there were some new lines and crinkles around the eyes. Some gold adorned an ear and eyebrow that I did not remember. But I did remember the face, wiry frame and accent. It had been a couple years, but I would have recognized Cirtron anywhere.

"Cirtron!" I said.

"What? How be it dat . . . Ah! Ya, mon! Jock and Jeel! No! Can't be so!"

"It's me, Cirtron, remember? Jill's back sleeping at the cabin."

Cirtron actually did a little dance. He pumped his arms and stomped from one foot to the other while I thought about coincidences. "Jock and Jeel! No! Cannot be! Ya, mon, I remember. Redstripe!"

"Redstripe indeed, my man. What the heck are you doing here trying to sell me aloe when I can take two steps off the beach and break off a piece by myself for nothing?"

· *Dachshunds in the Midwest* ·

"I dunno," Cirtron grinned at me. "I do de stuff on de beach, mon. Sheila; she does de stuff in de house.

"Sheila?" I asked. "Sheila is here? What house?"

"Ya, mon. We have de guest house and all dat. De people come and stay and we make de living so. Ah! Happy times, mon!"

While my mind was awash in the waters of deja vu, I tried to concentrate on that last part. Cirtron had a house? And his girl friend, Sheila from New York was taking care of it? Something didn't fit here. I could feel invisible antlers, nourished by curiosity, growing out of the sides of my head. I wanted to go back and tell Jill that I'd found Cirtron. But I also wanted to know about Sheila and this "house." Was this just another story woven in the smoke of Cirtron's favorite vice?

"Cirtron, can you show me?"

"Ya, mon! Day all be dere. Sheila and Redstripe and Paris. I be take you, c'mon mon. Say, mon, have de extra cigarette?"

I reached into my pocket, shook out a cigarette from my pack and handed Cirtron a lighter. Nothing changes, really, over time. Cirtron was still bumming and I felt grateful that it was too early for him to have me buy him a beer. I would have gladly if I thought I could get explanations out of him in any hurry. Instead, we headed up the beach together and I had a feeling that the Redstripe stories would begin again and I would find the answer to the puzzle.

Another Redstripe, Please

Letters and Lawyers

CIRTRON, SHEILA's friend who she met in Jamaica, had left New York. Sheila, and the two little dachshunds, Redstripe and Paris remained after the airport adventures. The DEA would never forget the mess they had experienced with the little dog Redstripe. The confusion created when the long little hound took a liking to a drug dealer because he had gravy on his pants had caused a series of events to unfold. The ensuing events had become troublesome to all in the government agency. Most of the people at the facility in the hills ended up having to own up to questions that were tough to answer. Early retirements were in order.

Redstripe had been a stowaway with Cirtron, who was on his way from Jamaica to visit Sheila in the big city. But the little red miniature dachshund and Cirtron the rastamafarian parted company when Cirtron left New York and left Redstripe with Sheila. But they were only separate for a little while. The reunion would have its own set of complications.

Sheila spent some quiet times with Redstripe and her mom, Paris, in Sheila's little brownstone apartment. Sheila's days were spent at work at the insurance agency while Redstripe and Paris did whatever it is that dachshunds do in the house when no one is around. Most times, Sheila returned to peace. Many times, she did not.

Paris and Redstripe had one favorite habit in which they engaged. Sheila was not always diligent in securing the trash. Boy, there is nothing better for a dachshund than to have several uninterrupted hours with the kitchen garbage. There were days that Paris and Redstripe "trashed" the place. They really did. And they did it well. Everyone, including dachshunds, should have a hobby after all.

But usually, after the leftover spaghetti, the regurgitated vegetable scraps and a couple of things best left unmentioned were cleaned up, Redstripe and Paris and Sheila spent most evenings curled in a pile on the couch watching television.

Paris liked the police shows. This certainly had something to do with the squad sirens and she loved to bark when the police cars howled down the streets in hot dog pursuit with their lights flashing. Redstripe liked the educational channels; anything with animals. Sheila began to think she should get a second television. She never seemed to get to watch what she wanted: Dachshunds have a way of getting their way and the television channel selections were no exception.

One early evening a call from the doorman came over the intercom. "Miss Sheila?"

"Miss Sheila?" The tiny speaker played the doorman's voice into the apartment. That set Paris and Redstripe to barking their fool heads off. "RRRwoof! RRR WOOF WOOF. RRR WOOF!"

Sheila rose from the couch and keyed the intercom switch.
"What?"
"Rrrwooff! WOOF WOOF WOOF, RRWOOF!"
"Miss Sheila?"

· *Dachshunds in the Midwest* ·

"Yes? What is it?" she answered again and then, "Paris! Redstripe! SHUT UP, both of you!"

"Miss Sheila, what was that? Is everything all right?"

"Yes. Never mind, what is it?"

"There is a gentleman here for you. He has a package—looks like some papers—says it's real important."

"Ok, send him up."

Sheila turned to her stereo dachshunds. "Go on. In your bed. We have company."

Neither dog moved.

"Honestly! Would you ladies go?!"

Predictably, they didn't, wouldn't and couldn't. After all, Paris and Redstripe were dachshunds.

The man with the package arrived, knocked, and Sheila opened the apartment door. What the fellow had in the package would change things in a major way for Sheila, Redstripe and Paris.

To begin with, the package had information indicating that a distant uncle of Sheila's had passed away. The rest of the details were lengthy and complex.

Guess which lady (with two dachshunds and a friend from Jamaica) was the only heir?

Yup and Ya, mon!

In the little town of Wautoma, Wisconsin, Sheila's distant uncle had spent his most of his days making his living on a small farm. He raised, bred and tended to a herd that was sold for meat and hides. John Armstead had held the farm during the last forty years of his life. He had raised a family with his wife, the late Clara Armstead. His four sons, but one, had taken off for various other pursuits as time had gone on. The last son, Peter Armstead, had stayed on. He took care of the books, made the purchases for feed and hired the help to take care of the herd as his father had aged and had become unable to manage the farm on his own.

The two men had fought, as sons and fathers do. Peter had never really wanted to farm to begin with. Numerous arguments speckled the history of their relationship. John had written Peter out of his will. Clara, Peter's mother, was already gone when John Armstead died so the older man's will stood as contrived.

Peter was actually relieved to be quit of the farm. He was not surprised at all when he received a call from the family attorney who quietly explained that his father had left him nothing.

Yet in some ways, it was still hard for Peter to pack and leave the farm. In spite of his reluctance to be a farmer, he did have affection for the herd, the barn cats and the various woodland creatures that would come to the back porch of the old farmhouse seeking food. He even had some thoughts about missing the local human characters that populated the bars, gas stations and feed mill of the little town. But Peter did leave. He left the farm with hopes of some better futures while still mentally packing a few regrets.

The papers that were brought to Sheila in her apartment did not really explain all of this business between her distant cousin Peter and his father. When the man with the package brought out all the paper work, he only told Sheila that she now owned a farm in Wisconsin. He suggested that his law firm could take care of disposing and liquidating the property should Sheila desire this. He said that he could take it out her hands and she would not have to worry herself about the entire affair. A sizeable check would be delivered when all was said and done.

Easy. Just sign here, please.

Sheila, being Sheila, wanted a second opinion.

"Hey, girls!? You want to live on a farm for a while? Paris, Redstripe. What do you think?"

Paris and Redstripe came galloping into the room. The man with the suit stood up and said, "Do they bite?"

"No," said Sheila, "At least not often."

Redstripe and Paris were sniffing at the man's cuffs, "Would you like our firm to handle this for you?" the man asked with a little tension in his voice. He stared down at the circling hounds.

Sheila said, "I'll tell you what. You leave all the papers here and I'll read them and talk it over with Paris and Redstripe."

"Excuse me?"

"I'll decide after I talk with the dachsies."

The man left, confused. Redstripe, Paris and Sheila settled on the couch. There was no peace until Sheila clicked the television remote to "Rescue 911" so that Paris could watch. She asked the two again. "Want to see some cows?"

They both looked up, raised those dachsie eyebrows as if to say, "Cows? What Cows? Why would we be interested in cows?" They stretched their little jaws in wide yawns.

Sheila looked through the papers that night while sitting on the couch; a dachs under each arm. As far as she could tell, the man was correct; she now owned a farm in Wisconsin and there was enough money invested by her distant uncle that would provide returns to make a decent life on the old place.

Could she leave New York?

You bet.

Maybe she could even get a second television out of this. Sheila was really tired of not being able to watch the ten o'clock news.

Sheila, after phone calls she made to the offices listed in the papers she had received, decided to plan a trip to the farm in

• Another Redstripe, Please •

Wisconsin, "just to see" before she made any drastic decisions. But before she had thought this all out, she received a phone call asking her to come to the law offices of Merril and Fich to "Please help us bring closure to this issue, if you may?" A moderate retainer had been afforded the law firm by Sheila's uncle's estate so they were moderately polite.

Sheila did make the trip to Merril and Fich. So did Paris and Redstripe. The elevator ride up was quite a travail for both dogs. As they little car began to rise, the dogs felt the upward motion and squatted down in nervous anticipation of what would come next. They both expressed their discomfiture in liquid fashion on the elevator floor.

The dogs and Sheila entered a room with dark wood paneling. Lots of books filled shelves and a vague smell of cigar smoke hung throughout the room. This was after a receptionist said in most certain terms that the two dachs could NOT be allowed in the back office and she did not even understand HOW those two CREATURES could have ever been allowed in this building to begin with and . . ."

Sheila said "Sweetheart, these dogs are with me, they are dachshunds and they do as they please. Why don't you chill out and get a date who gives you something else to think about other than to give your bosses' clients a hard time?"

"Well, I never!" exclaimed the receptionist disgustedly.

"That doesn't surprise me, honey." Sheila replied. The dogs started to attempt to excavate the carpeting.

After that, all was explained to Sheila about the farm in Wisconsin by the attorney in a back, cigar- and leather-smelling office. Redstripe and Paris had made certain that they left their impression in that office as to what they thought about the whole thing. Sheila signed all that needed to be signed.

· *Dachshunds in the Midwest* ·

When Redstripe, Paris and Sheila returned to brownstone apartment, Sheila made a final and brave decision; they would go to Wisconsin.

"Redstripe, Paris!"

The dogs looked up, eyebrows in little tents of anticipation.

"Woomf?"

"What do you say we get in touch with Cirtron? You know, YA MON!"

"Woof, rrooff wwwooff!"

"Yes, I thought so. You two are suckers for a good looking man! I am too."

For Sheila, there was a lot to do. She had to make plans to pack up the dogs and their toys and their bed (not that they ever really used it.) She had to get hold of Cirtron, sub-lease the apartment and deal with her furniture. Moving from the east coast to the center of the country was more of a job than Sheila had really thought about when she had made the decision to go to her late uncle's farm.

Cirtron was first. She wrote a letter to a post office box in Negril. It read:

Dear Cirtron,

> *You always told me you loved animals. Well, guess what! I have a FARM. You know, like cows and pigs and chickens and stuff; just like you have back home. And it is MINE! Redstripe, Paris and I are getting ready to go there. Want to come? The girls are excited to see you again and I think it would be fun. Write or call me collect and I will make the arrangements to get you there.*

Love, Sheila

• *Another Redstripe, Please* •

Cirtron called a few days later. The phone rang in the evening and Sheila accepted the charge. "Hello?"

"Aie, Sheila, m'lady. Waht be happn', girl?"

"You got my letter?"

"Ya, mon. De letter, she be wid me here now. Waht be it wid de farm, girl? Since when be it dat you know how to take care of de animals and so? Big job, de y'know?"

"Well, I thought you could help. I mean, how much work can a couple of old cows take? Are you going to come or not?"

"Ya, mon! I come. You send de ticket again and I be dere. But, m'lady, know what you do. De farming, she be a lot of work, mon. Ah, my uncles, day say as much, mon. Y'know?"

"Cirtron, I'll send the ticket and some money. Pick it up at the airport in Montego Bay, ok? When you get to Chicago, you can take a bus up and meet me in Wautoma. I'll get a reservation at a hotel and put that detail stuff in with the money and ticket. You don't have to worry about bringing the dachs this time. It should be an easy trip. So you'll you come?"

"Ya, mon. I be check at de airport for de ticket and such in a few days, Irie."

Sheila finished the conversation, "Redstripe, Paris? Say hey to Cirtron." She held the phone down to the two little dachshunds. They just stared at the receiver. "Common guys, bark for Cirtron. It's CIRTRON ! You know, ya, mon! Irie!"

Paris snorted and Redstripe wandered off. They wanted to make sure Sheila knew who was in charge. *Gee whiz,* they thought, *where does she get off telling us when to bark? Really!*

After all was said and done, Sheila decided to let the apartment go and gave notice to her landlord. He only asked if the dogs were leaving too and then said we would be glad to let her out of the

· *Dachshunds in the Midwest* ·

lease. She made arrangements for her furniture to be removed by a firm that bought and resold furnishings as complete sets to those moving into new apartments and had come with little in the way of chairs and tables and such when moving freshly into the city. The losers in recent divorces made up most of the firm's clientele. Two men came to the apartment one day to inventory the contents and to get a signed contract. The furniture would be sold on consignment.

After being allowed upstairs by the doorman, they knocked on Sheila's door. The dachshunds responded in full voice, of course

Sheila opened the door but one of the two men said. "Hang it a minute, lady, we don't do dogs much. Hey? And not especially viscous ones! Ya, know? My gawd, whadayou got in there?" The guys had heard the howls and barks and snorts and snarls of Redstripe and Paris through the door and now that it was opened, the full force of the righteously indignant hounds blared out into the passage where the men stood.

"Baby Dobermans. Is that a problem?"

The first man, Jake, turned to his partner Milt, rolled his eyes and turned back to Sheila. "Oh, well, yeah. Y'got puppies? Um, yeah, well ya know, they sounded like big dogs. Hey, I mean, they won't like pee on our shoes would they? They don't bite, do they? I mean, we could come back, y'know?"

"I don't think that's necessary," said Sheila. "I can lock them in the bathroom if you're afraid of puppies if you want."

"Hey Milt, you afraid of puppies?"

Milt shook his head no but he was not too sure.

The men entered the apartment with their clipboards and forms. They intended to complete the inventory quickly but Redstripe and Paris had other ideas.

• *Another Redstripe, Please* •

The dogs barked and they pranced and they darted at cuffs. They ran from room to room, constantly under the two men's feet. They made certain to make noise. They made a lot of it. Neither man could hear the other over the constant din of barking dachshunds.

"HEY, MILT, YOU GOT THE COUCH?"
"ROOF" and "WWROOF!"
"WHAT?"
"THE COUCH, YOU GOT IT ON YOUR LIST?"
"ROOF, WWROOOF!"
"I'M NOT A SLOUCH, I'M DOING MY BEST!"
"NO! THE COUCH!"
"I'M NOT A GROUCH, IT'S THESE DAMN DOGS!"
"ROOF" and "ROOF" and "WWROOF!"
"LOGS? MILT, THERE'S NO FIREPLACE. DO YOU UNDERSTAND?"
"ROOF," *scamper*, "WWRROOF!"

Things went on like that for a while. Milt and Jake continued the inventory including Sheila's O'Keefe prints while Sheila let the dachshunds do their thing. She thought the whole process was a stitch and celebrated her opinion by pouring herself a glass of wine from a half full bottle in the fridge. Beverage in hand, she continued to watch the festivities with great amusement.

Finally, when Milt and Jake left, Paris and Redstripe jumped unto the couch, lay down on their backs, feet in the air, and feel asleep.

They were thinking, *Gosh, they had helped a lot, hadn't they?*

On the Way to Montego Bay

CIRTRON'S TRIP to Montego Bay was much different than his last. This time he did not have Redstripe with him to act as a foil to solicit favors. Most of his trip was made on foot and the free food and drinks were scarce and hard to find. But Cirtron did make it to Mo Bay and, as Sheila had promised, found money and a plane ticket in his name at the airport.

When he was preparing to leave his family home in the mountains of Jamaica, his uncle Basi approached while Cirtron was packing.

"Hey, mon, whaht you be doing now, mon?" asked Basi.

Cirtron stopped stuffing things into his gym bag, looked up, and answered. "Ya mon, I gonna be de farmer. I am go to raise de cows and such with Sheila. I will go to Wascoonseen."

Basi turned his head to one side and laughed. "Ah! Now when do you change to be de mon dat works so hard? You would not know on which end of de cow does de business. Stay here, cousin, you can be help me in de shop. Dere is plenty work, mon."

"No, mon, I already made de decision and promise. Whad I need is de ride down and out to de road. Ga will tell me 'bout de cows. Sheila has told me day would not be so much trouble."

Basi shrugged knowing there was no hope of ever arguing and winning with Cirtron. "Okay, collect de stuff and we go down again to Negril. From dere, you be on your own, mon."

Basi went to start the old tan Chevy. Cirtron joined him at the car, climbed in as passenger, and placed his gym bag in the back seat. Over the hot and dusty and narrow roads to Negril, Basi piloted the way with Cirtron and finally deposited him near Alfred's', the beach bar and grill so popular with both the locals and tourists. Basi turned the car and started the return trip to the enclave, family and his machine shop in the mountains. Cirtron, once again, stepped on to Norman Manley Boulevard and stuck out his thumb to find a ride to Montego Bay. Within the seven miles of road and beach that make up Negril, Cirtron had plenty of friends. It was only a minute or so before someone picked him up. The driver took him from Alfred's up to the small airstrip that marked the north end of town.

"Dis be as far as I go, mon," the driver said. "Luck and go with Ga, respect."

"Tank you, mon," replied Cirtron. He climbed out of the car and began the trek to Montego Bay.

Two days later after a couple of short rides and after sleeping on the roadside, with his gym bag as a pillow, Cirtron was still a third of the way away from Montego Bay. He was dirty, hot and tired. He almost did not notice the car that pulled to the side of the road in front of him. It was a taxi. It had the red plates issued by the Jamaican authorities that legitimized the owner's right to charge fares for transport. Cirtron did not have much hope for a ride in this case even though the car had stopped for him. He had no money to pay a fare.

The taxi had a passenger who leaned out the window and called back to Cirtron.

"Hey, guy, looks like you need a ride. Get in. It's on me."

Cirtron looked and saw a tallish, slender black man in the passenger seat of the cab. As the rastamafarian approached, the passenger could be seen to be of Jamaican descent but with close cropped hair and western style clothing. He wore a freshly pressed blue shirt, creased white trousers and his sockless feet were clad in expensive looking leather sandals. The sandals showed no sign of wear. A simple gold chain adorned his neck. He smelled of some lime-based cologne.

Cirtron said his thank you and climbed into the back seat.

The driver steered the car back on to the road and took off, a rush of gravel escaping behind the rear wheels. The passenger turned in his seat to face Cirtron in the back. "So, my man, where are you going? I'm on my way to the airport, so we can take you that far. The cab is paid for and I figured you needed a ride just by seeing you trudging along there."

"De airport, ya mon. Dat is where I go," said Cirtron.

"Good. That works fine. What will you be doing there?" asked Cirtron's benefactor.

"I be get de ticket and take de plane to Wascoonseen. Gonna be de farmer, d'know?"

"Wisconsin?" returned the slim man, "Yes, I know that. It's a state in the Midwest of the United States around the Great Lakes. Actually I know the United States pretty well. I went to school there. I graduated from Yale a while back."

"Yale?"

"Yes," the man explained, "That's a big university in the United States. But I didn't like it there and came back here. I opened a Jet Ski rental business on the beach in Negril and right now I have to go back to the states to do some business with the manufacturing people. They've been sending me some units that just are not up to par so I need to go and speak with them."

Cirtron was intrigued. "So, mon, you be Jamaican? You d'not sound so. But you did de big school in de United States? Why come back here again?"

Another Redstripe, Please

"Like I said, I didn't like it; too many people that are too selfish. I've found I would rather live here and make what living I can and enjoy my life with the people here. Let me tell you something. I have seen both sides of a lot. And compared to the Americans, I prefer our own countrymen. Jamaica may not have all of the things that are in the United States, but I believe our people are better, simpler and therefore actually more civilized. I don't mean to be negative about the states; I just prefer to be here. And let me tell you something else. I have come to understand that using one's head and not expecting more out of life than one deserves is the key to a good life. The Americans don't generally understand that. They can't think straight for worrying about wants they do not need. On our island, my friend, that problem is not so frequent. It's all about an attitude, really.

And I have learned this as well. It applies everywhere, here and in all of the other places to which I have traveled. It is this, *Common sense is not common.* Remember that."

The man and Cirtron continued their conversation during the last miles of travel to the airport in Montego Bay. Cirtron carried very little of the exchange. The man had lots of opinions to share. At one point, the man extracted a pack of Marlborough Reds from his shirt pocket and offered a cigarette to Cirtron.

Cirtron accepted reluctantly. "Ah, mon, jus de one. Day c'make you sick, mon. I be stick with de Ganga. Irie." He accepted the cigarette regardless and then a light and sat back in his seat, blowing smoke to the side and out the window of the car.

A bit later, the cab pulled up to the entrance to the terminal at the airport in Montego Bay and allowed the passengers to get out onto the hot pavement. The man and Cirtron shook hands, touched closed fists, respected and took off on their separate ways.

· *Dachshunds in the Midwest* ·

Cirtron would remember to tell Sheila about common sense. In the meantime, he made his way into the terminal, collected his ticket, cashed in Sheila's Western Union transmission at the bank exchange and made his way to the gate for his flight back again to the United States.

A Plane and Bus with Little Fuss

THE PLANE trip to the United States was without problems for Cirtron. He slept most of the way, snoring and missing most of the scenery viewable from his window seat. With a brief layover in Newark, New Jersey, the trip ended peacefully at O'Hare in Chicago. From there, Cirtron would need to find a bus to take him up to Wisconsin and the rendezvous planned with Sheila and the hounds in Wautoma. Once off of the plane and through customs, (no need to stop at baggage claim as all he had was the gym bag) he stopped the first official looking person he could find.

"Excuse me please. Can you tell me t'find de bus dat take me to Weescoonseen?"

Cirtron's person of choice turned out to be a janitor. He answered Cirtron. "I don't know much about busses, buddy. I just swing a broom and empty the trash. But you might ask at one of the information desks."

Ah, I tank you, sir. May I ask de question on how to get dere?"

"Oh, let me see. Follow this hallway, about fifty yards, take the second right after the *Newstand and Skyway Book Shop* and then the next escalator down. I think there is an info place at the bottom. Just ask there."

"Esculatar?"

The man looked at Cirtron, puzzled. "Yeah, buddy. You know. Those moving stairs things."

"Ah, yes. Ya, mon. I know of dese from before. Tank you. Go with Ga. Irie."

· *Another Redstripe, Please* ·

The man stood a moment in front of Cirtron hoping he'd been understood, but surprised by the answer. "Say, you're not gonna hand me a flower or something, are you?"

Cirtron did not get this, but just said, "No, mon. No flower today."

The rastamafarian followed the janitor's directions. As he passed the *Newstand and Skyway Book Shop*, a small book in the window caught his eye. The brown cover had a caricature of a dachshund on it below the title. It reminded Cirtron that he was on his way to meet up with Redstripe and Paris, and of course, Sheila at the end of his trip. He passed the window and quickened his pace, in a hurry to find the bus.

As promised, Cirtron found an information kiosk at the foot of the escalator. After some discussion, (the Jamaican dialect and the Chicago accent make communication difficult) he had enough information to be able to proceed to a bus route for Milwaukee and where to buy a ticket. Route number and ticket in hand, he left the lower doors of the airport concourse and stationed himself beside the correct sign as explained by the lady behind the desk. When a bus with the correct number hissed to stop in front of him and the doors opened, he climbed on. He handed the driver the requested ticket and then asked. "Ya, mon? Dese bus, she go to Weescoonseen? To Wautoma?

The driver answered. "No, not actually. But I turn around in Milwaukee. When we get there, you come and see me and I'll be sure to get you to the next route. Go sit down. I'll be sure to watch for you. OK?" The driver looked at the ticket. "Look, you've got a transfer in Milwaukee, piece of cake."

"Ya, mon," said Cirtron. And then, "I do not have de flowers, mon."

The driver had no idea how to respond to that so he just repeated, "Go sit down. I'll get you where you need to go." A few other passengers clambered on, the driver looked out to see that the curb was empty, he turned the wheel, applied the gas and left the airport.

An hour and a half later, in the bus terminal in downtown Milwaukee, the bus stopped and the driver directed Cirtron to the next route with a new driver both bound for central Wisconsin.

The Highway of Harrowing Hounds

SHEILA HAD packed her little white Toyota Camry, installed Paris and Redstripe into the back seat of the car and began the road trip to Wisconsin soon after the apartment was emptied. The lease papers had been signed and turned over to the landlord, the attorney's documents concerning the farm were in the trunk and a map, the route marked in pink, lay on the passenger seat. Sheila had called ahead to find some dog-friendly motels along her route to the Midwest. She planned to leave the city on Interstate 495, cross New Jersey and then pass into Pennsylvania. She would then take Interstate 80/90 all the way to Wisconsin. Redstripe and Paris had ideas about traveling of their own. The back seat was not part of them.

The trip became torture. The two dachshunds insisted on climbing into the front seats and to compete for Sheila's lap as she tried to drive and watch traffic. When shooed back into the rear seats, they tried to dig holes into the upholstery as if to hollow out holes in dirt to make comfortable dachshund beds. The windows became smudged with nose marks, nearly opaque in places and passing truckers blowing their huge air horns to warn the distracted Sheila out of the way only served to bring on the howling and baying of the hounds. Paris and Redstripe scrambled about the interior of the car, got under Sheila's feet and their claws punched holes and tears in the road map at her side making it useless.

Sheila was becoming frantic. She glanced down at her trip odometer and was dismayed to see she'd traveled only fifteen miles.

• *Another Redstripe, Please* •

Rather than become one human and two dachshund fatalities, an accident just biding its time, Sheila knew she had to do something. She pulled off the expressway and into the first travelers' rest stop she could find. As she decelerated down the ramp to the stop, she noted a sign:

NO PETS

This was not turning out to be a good day, no, not at all.

Sheila parked the Camry and climbed out, careful to shut the door without pinning curious dachshund noses but closed firmly to keep the hounds inside. Stepping back around to the trunk, she opened it and then opened one of her suitcases. Extracting bulky items like sweaters and heavy jeans and leaving the light shirts, underwear and such behind, she took the items forward and opened the passenger door. Shoving the two dogs into the back seats with one hand, she used to clothing to stuff into the spaces between and around the seats. She was trying to construct a sort of dachshund dam. She remarked to herself that the interior of the car looked a little like a Chinese Laundry, but she hoped the barriers would hold.

With the trunk closed, Sheila returned to driver's seat, keyed the ignition and rolled out of the rest stop and back on to the highway. The dogs were not amused by the new arrangement and proceeded to whine and paw at the barriers of Sheila's wardrobe.

"Damn!" said Sheila.

"Woof!" said the dogs.

"Redstripe, Paris! Knock it off! You two need valium or something. Settle down!"

Humming down the highway, dogs trapped, for a while anyway, in the rear, Sheila knew she had to take another step. She adjusted the rearview mirror downward so that she could see the hounds still scrambling around in the back. Maybe some music would help; but nothing too exciting. Sheila reached over and fumbled in the glove compartment for a CD she was pretty sure had been tossed in there and forgotten. It was an album given to her by a long-ago cheesy date of hers who was a bank teller who thought he was a high-roller investor. She plucked the CD from the box, flicked open the case and chucked it into the player on the dash. The voice of John Denver filled the car. Either soothed by the ballads or just bored, the hounds settled down. The music worked but Sheila would be able to write down every word of every song from every track from memory by the end of the trip.

Crossing the rest of New Jersey was peaceful. Sheila continued and made it all the way to Pennsylvania, crossing over into that state near Stroudsburg. She stopped to feed and water the dogs and let them stretch at another traveler's stop near White Haven that did not have the dreaded *NO PETS* sign. Just before the stop, Sheila had seen a billboard that advertised an up class restaurant named *Casa Belle*. She thought the add looked nice. But the name seemed to have struck a memory somewhere within her mind. There was something about the word *Belle* that seemed familiar and she thought maybe it might be from something told to her by Cirtron when he was visiting in New York. But the feeling faded.

White Haven was near the edge of the Pocono's, a famous spot for romance and honeymoons. Sheila thought, ruefully, that the dachshunds were probably not the right company with which to enjoy the area. But even with her map destroyed by the marauding canine occupants of the car, she recalled that she had found a *Days Inn* in New Columbia that allowed pets. The three of them made it there in the early evening of a June day. She stopped the car in the motel lot, killed the engine and John Denver was mercifully silenced. Redstripe and Paris were not silent at all. They were suddenly up and ready for more adventures. The next adventure would have to be a walk on leashes on some of the grass on the edge of the parking lot.

Redstripe and Paris relieved, Sheila did the best she could to untangle the leads and headed the dachshunds into the lobby and up to the front desk of the motel. The two dogs pulled at the leashes in two directions as Sheila made her way across the carpet as they were both interested in a different potted plant decorating the edges of the lobby. With a little coaxing, all three, Sheila, Redstripe and Paris made it to the registration desk. "Excuse me?" announced Sheila to the clerk behind the counter, "I need a room for the night and I understand you take dogs. I have two."

"Yes mam, we can accommodate you but there will be an extra deposit for the dogs. Let me check. I think we have a room available for pets on the first floor. Would two double beds be alright?"

Sheila replied; one arm still extended as the dogs tugged. "That's fine, where do I sign?"

The clerk, who probably did not need to shave more than twice a week, produced some papers after clicking on his keyboard for a bit and then peered over the counter at Redstripe and Paris.

"Are these the dogs?" he asked.

Sheila, the tired captain of the good ship of two dachshunds with the Chinese laundry cargo could not help but say, "No. I just borrowed these two so that I had something to hold on to while I checked in. My dogs are still out in my car."

"Oh," said the clerk. "But there are just the two?"

"Just give me a pen, here's my credit card."

Sheila made one more trip to the car. She retrieved her lightened suitcase and the dog dishes and steered the dachshunds to their night's lodging, room key in hand. Most of her clothes remained stuffed between the car seats.

The room was not bad. It had two big beds, a TV and a clean bath. The pictures on the wall would have sold at some sort of starving artist type art auction, but the place was livable. Sheila lifted the dachshunds onto one of the beds with her, lay back, clicked the remote for the television and tried to relax for a little bit. Paris took about two minutes before she padded to the edge of the bed and asked to be let down. Redstripe followed suit. Sheila lifted the hounds down only to have them paw at the edge of the bed a few moments later to be hoisted back up. And then down again. The hounds would not settle. Having spent most of her patience during the drive, Sheila rose, extracted the three pillows from the second bed, tossed them on the floor and said, "Here, you two. Make yourselves comfortable and stay put for a while, please?" The two hounds must have heard the edge of exasperation in their caretaker's voice and plunked down between the pillows. Even Redstripe and Paris knew that certain limits were not to be exceeded. Shelia reached for the phone book in the nightstand.

She found a pizza delivery place not far from the motel, phoned in and ordered a pizza and some soda and then paged through more of the phone book looking for pet stores. Someone, somewhere, must be able to advise her about safely securing the hounds in the car during the remainder of the trip. As things were going, Sheila, with her long blond and attention-getting mane of hair, would be bald by the end of the trip if she did not get things under control. She worried that John Denver might lose his effectiveness in the next several hundred miles of highway 80. A pet store on page 175 caught her attention, not far from the motel, and she decided to visit it in the morning while the hounds were snoozing. The pizza man arrived a little later with Sheila's order.

There was a knock on the motel room door and a voice filtered through, "Giovanni's, got an order here for room 115." The two dachshunds broke into open throttled voices; a cacophony of canine sounds, Sheila opened the door, purse in hand. As she tried to juggle the offered box in one hand and extract money to pay the guy, Paris made her way out between Sheila's ankles and out into the hallway. The pizza guy took the money and tip, turned and left. But Paris was loose.

Sheila hurriedly placed the pizza box on the floor, glanced back to make certain that Redstripe was still secure in the room, and took off after Paris. Paris was streaking down the hallway, a mimic of a furry brown space shuttle flying at weed top level aiming to leave the planet as soon as possible. Sheila was in desperate pursuit in a flash; pizza forgotten. *"Paris!"*

Breathless, Sheila caught up with Paris ten doors down as the dachshund was pawing and barking at the door of room 125. As Sheila slowed to a stop, the door opened and a fat woman wrapped in a towel stood in the opening. "Can I help you? Is this your dog? Is there a problem?" The smell of fast food, greasy burgers, wafted into the hallway which explained Paris's interest.

Sheila really wanted to say, "No, I just found the dog in the parking lot and thought I might get some exercise by chasing it up and down the hall."

But she restrained herself and just said," Yes, I'm really so sorry. She just got loose and took off before I even knew it. Please let me apologize, we've been traveling and I guess I am tired and was not paying attention. I am so sorry."

The fat woman told Sheila not to worry about it, it was ok, and that the little dog was sort of cute. Sheila grabbed Paris in a football grip, left as quickly as she could; the lady's towel was beginning to slip and Sheila did not want to be around for that. Walking back down the hall to her own room she was dismayed to realize she'd left the door ajar (lucky as she did not take the key) but where was Redstripe? Had she taken off through the open door? No, Redstripe had already chewed through some of the cardboard box containing the pizza and was happily lapping at the cheese and sausage on one side. Sheila's dinner would be limited.

"Damn!" said Sheila.

"Woof!" said the hounds.

The next day would *have* to be better.

The hounds and Sheila did make it through the night without further incident and although Sheila had to switch beds halfway through the night to get some room to sleep while the hounds controlled the first bed; the sun came up once again and the world looked ok. Sheila revisited the phone book in which she had been researching pet stores and snuck out of the room while the dogs were still snoozing under the covers of the first bed. The pet store was just blocks away and she figured the hounds would not rise; exhausted from traveling and from a little extra pizza from the day before. It was a three block jaunt and Sheila entered the doors of the pet store.

"Excuse me?" she approached the first person she found. "I need a crate or a grate or something for my car for my two dogs. They are just bouncing all over my car and I'm afraid they will hurt themselves or get me into an accident. Do you have something?"

"Oh, sure," replied the clerk. What you need is a couple of harnesses. We have a bunch. What kind of dogs?"

"Dachshunds. Little ones."

"They come in more than one size?"

"Just show me, could you?"

"Oh, sure," the clerk led the way down one of the isles crammed with dog toys, leashes, collars and rubber chew thingys. "Here you go."

The clerk took a jacket like looking thing off of a hook and showed it to Sheila. It had a strap for around the chest of the dog and another for around the middle. The closures were of Velcro and there was a sort of a strap on the back. "See? You put this on the dog and the straps keep it in place, then the loop on the back is for the seat belt and keeps the dog from wandering. These are very popular."

Sheila did not hesitate, "I'll take two. Two small ones."

The items paid for and wrapped in a plastic bag, Sheila returned to the motel. When she entered the room, she could tell that Redstripe and Paris had never moved. Maybe the next leg of the trip would be better. She rustled the hounds out of their warm covers, took them outside for a bit, fed and watered them and then packed the Camry. The dogs bristled a bit when she applied the harnesses and clipped the dogs to the belts, but then she was back on her way to the west on Interstate 80. She'd grabbed a coffee, bagel and cream cheese from the motel lobby and munched as she drove, the dogs secure in the back seat. Just in case, Sheila started the John Denver CD once more. Ohio was not too far away.

Redstripe and Paris remained calm and quiet, secure with their safety harnesses and lulled into oblivion by the music coming from the dashboard CD player. Sheila herself felt pretty numb as she drove and listened to the CD. It may have been some sort of Rocky Mountain High thing influencing her as the sounds played into the car. The three of them crossed into Ohio near Youngstown and

· *Dachshunds in the Midwest* ·

Sheila figured she might still make it to Toledo if things went well. Then they hit the toll way. A road sign warned of the first set of toll booths coming up and that those without exact change should bear right. Sheila did.

As the Camry slowed to thread its way into the payment booth for the toll, Sheila felt a cold poke on her right elbow. She glanced down and right to see some of her clothes that had been used as a dachshund dam on the passenger seat and then at Paris who was trying to get her attention via nose signals. Paris was loose and in a moment Redstripe came scrambling up between the seats and over the broken clothing barriers as well. The two dogs, seemingly so quiet for so long during this current leg of the trip, had taken turns chewing at each other's back straps and broken themselves free while Sheila had been the victim of highway hypnosis. Redstripe and Paris were actually pretty proud of their accomplished jailbreak. Tails were wagging.

"Damn!" said Sheila.

"Woof!" said the hounds.

They pulled up to the toll booth. Sheila held the wheel with one hand and fumbled for her purse under the paws of the escapees and managed to grab some single dollars to pay the dollar and five cent toll. Paris and Redstripe began to howl, bark and attempted to cross Sheila's lap to get at the stranger in the toll booth. She nearly flung three dollars at the poor man and stepped on the gas to leave the booth while trying to shoo the dogs into the back seat. The barricade for the booth did not rise and the Camry, with Sheila's foot suddenly on the brake, lurched to a halt. The toll keeper leaned out of his window and shouted, "Lady! Your change!"

"Forget it!" Sheila yelled back. "Keep it and pay for the next car! Let me out of here!"

The barricade rose and Sheila, while still attempting to shoo the hounds, glanced in the rear view mirror to see the car behind her pull up to the booth and the toll keeper flinging his arms about while apparently trying to explain to the next driver. No matter, the Camry with all three occupants accelerated forward.

The Camry was low on gas, the hounds were loose and Sheila took the next exit off of the interstate to fill up and to find some way to re-secure the hounds. There was a "FEED AND FILL" just off the end of the exit ramp and she pulled in. Sheila climbed out of the car, careful to close the door on the hounds while leaving a window down enough for air and stepped back to the pump to fill the gas tank. Fifteen gallons later, purse over shoulder, she crossed the parking lot to the "FEED AND FILL" store to enter and pay for the gas.

At the counter, as she was paying, she asked "Do you have a stapler?"

"Staplers?" This very young clerk behind the counter was female and while shaving was never going to be an issue, she appeared as though it might be some time before she needed any underwear above the waist. "Uh, no. We don't carry staplers." She handed Sheila her change. "Sorry."

"I don't want to buy one. I want to borrow one. Do you have one or not?"

The young clerk replied, "Uh, yeah, I s'pose so. Let me check." She bent down and rummaged under the counter a moment and rose again and handed Sheila a stapler. "You're gonna bring it back?"

"Yes I will. I just need it a sec to staple my dogs. I'll be right back."

Sheila left the store while the clerk stood transfixed.

· Dachshunds in the Midwest ·

The stapler did a nice job of rejoining the chewed straps for the two dachshunds and within in a few moments Sheila had the disgruntled hounds re-installed safely with their harnesses in the back seat. She'd have to keep an eye on them to make sure they did no more chewing so she adjusted the rearview mirror once more so that she could see them from the driver's seat. Stapler returned, the two dogs and Sheila turned to the interstate in the Camry once more with the CD playing. Toledo seemed a long way down the road.

Sheila and the two dogs did make it across Ohio, then Indiana and further into Illinois before they turned northward toward Wisconsin. Rest stops, fast food places and motels all blurred into one collage over the next days. Thankfully there were no more escapes and no more motel fat ladies in towels or chases down unfamiliar hallways. But the trip took its toll on all three of them. They were tired. Even John Denver was beginning to sound a little weary although that may have been because the CD, playing on and on, may have been begun to wear. There was, however, one last problem that occurred at a fast food place somewhere in Indiana.

Sheila stopped at a burger type place, a chain, wanting to walk the dogs and use the facilities inside her self. A little food was in order for her and she figured she would share a little with the hounds even though it might be a little unhealthy for them. She paced the dogs on their leads on the grass on the edge of the parking lot and then secured them back into the car. She headed for the glass walled restaurant's doors. After using the ladies room, she approached the front counter and ordered a large hamburger and fries for herself, a drink, and a small hamburger she figured she would split between the two dachshunds as a treat. Returning to the car, she let the two dogs out, leashed, onto the parking lot, placed her own stuff on the driver's seat and then unwrapped the smaller hamburger and tore it into two halves. She placed it on the ground for the two dogs.

They nosed and just stared at the two halves of burger. They looked up at Sheila with quizzical expressions on their little faces.

"Oh, sorry, I forgot!" Sheila said. She reached down, removed the tops of the hamburger fragments and removed the pickles, popping the offending condiments into her own mouth. Dachshunds never eat pickles. The pickle less hamburger halves disappeared in about four bites each. It may have been less. It happened too fast to see. Sheila reached through the open window of the car for her own food and realized she did not have her purse. She'd left it on the counter when she paid for the food. "C'mon ladies, I have to go back inside or we won't have money to get to where we are going." Sheila, with the dogs still on their leashes, headed back to the restaurant in pursuit of purse intending to disregard any *NO PETS* rules in her haste to retrieve her purse.

She had not taken more than a few steps back inside the restaurant, dogs in tow, when an employee approached her and was holding her purse for her. "Ma'am? This is yours? You left it on the counter."

"Oh, thank you, thank you!" responded Sheila, "I don't know what I would have done . . ."

The person started to hand her the purse and said, "Don't worry, it happens all the time. We're just glad we caught you. But, um, the dogs? They really shouldn't be in here. Health regulations and all that."

"Hey, we are on our way. Thanks again." Sheila reached for the purse and somehow dropped Redstripe's leash in the process.

· *Dachshunds in the Midwest* ·

Redstripe, free of the constraint, took off and paddled after a man headed for the restrooms. The man pushed open the door and the pneumatic closer held the door ajar long enough for Redstripe to bound inside. Alarmed, not thinking, Sheila followed the little dachshund right inside the tiled room.

The dog skidded to a halt and Sheila, inside the men's restroom, reached down to grab the little hound. Two men, their backs to her and facing the wall doing what men do in men's restrooms swiveled their heads back and over their shoulders in unison to view the intrusion.

"Hey!" shouted the first. "What do you think you're doing?"

The second exclaimed, "Lookatthat! It's a wiener dog! Is it yours lady?"

Sheila replied, "Yeah, it's mine. Sorry." She left as quickly as she could, Redstripe in arms.

The employee with her purse was just outside the door and handed it to Sheila without a word. She retrieved Paris and the three of them left the site as quickly as possible. There might have been a little rubber from the tires of the Camry that was left in the parking lot.

Eventually, after passing through the maze of expressways around Chicago and then Milwaukee and then passing the towns in Wisconsin of Port Washington, Fond Du Lac and Oshkosh and even bizarre places like Omro, they arrived at a final motel in Wautoma. The three of them checked in and sleep was in order.

Bus Stop at the Lakeshore Family Diner

THE DRIVER turned his huge bus off of the county highway and into the parking lot of a medium sized diner. The sign, in neon, read "Lakeshore Family Diner——EAT." Cirtron rose up out of his seat, grabbed his gym bag, and made his way to the front of the bus. The other passengers ambled forward too.

At the front of the bus, Cirtron addressed the driver.

"I tank you, mon."

The driver looked back over his right shoulder at the rasta man. Cirtron chucked him on the shoulder with a closed fist. "Respect, mon!"

The driver just nodded and Cirtron climbed down the steps of the Greyhound bus and onto the asphalt parking lot of the diner. He took two big lungs-full of air, cold to him, and then looked at the entrance of the diner. In he went.

Once inside, he glanced left and right at the narrow passages lined by booths. A counter was right in front and he stepped toward it. He seated himself on a chromed, floor-anchored stool with a red vinyl seat. Cirtron thought the stool looked like a shiny red mushroom. Color notwithstanding, he was reminded of the much darker "shrooms" his uncles cultivated in the mountains of Jamaica.

One of the bustling waitresses came up to Cirtron right away. The plastic tag on her short sleeved shirt read "Mary." She was tall, dark haired and large shouldered. Her thick hair was pulled back by a single barrette. She smacked a green and white order form on the counter in front of Cirtron, placed her hands, palms down, on the counter and asked, "What do you need, Bob?"

Cirtron was confused and replied, "Ah, no. I'm not Bob. I be Cirtron."

"Well," said the waitress, "Ya' do look like Bob Marley."

Two stools down, a young man dressed in jeans and a flannel shirt glanced over and laughed, "Bob Marley! Ha, Mary, that's a good one!" He continued to chuckle as he clutched his fork with grimy fingers. "Bob Marley, yeah, that's good."

Startled, Cirtron chose to ignore the joke and looked up and down the waitresses' forearms. The left was hairy. The right had been shaved. On that right forearm he noticed a beautiful tattoo. The image of an eagle, peering out from some sort of multi-colored foliage, had been stenciled on the skin on the back of her lower arm.

Cirtron was intrigued. "Preety picture on de arm, mon! Where did it come from?"

"Oshkosh," stated Mary.

"Oshkosh?"

"Yeah, town about thirty miles from here. It hurt like hell when I was getting it done. Lots of bleeding."

"Ah," said Cirtron. "Sorry to hear dat, but it is de pretty thing t'see."

Mary leaned over the counter and said, flatly, "I've got nine more, what will it be for you?

Cirtron did not see the other nine tattoos and did not ask about them.

"Coffee," he said.

Check In and Check Out

While Cirtron was sipping coffee, Sheila, Redstripe and Paris were pulling into the motel right next to the diner. By the time he paid the bill and said goodbye to the waitress, Mary with her tattoo, Sheila and the dogs were already settled and ready for an evening's sleep. Cirtron left the diner and made his way just next door to the motel.

Standing at the registration desk, gym bag in hand, Cirtron asked for a room for the night. The hotel manager eyed him a little longer than normal and then said, "Yes, we have rooms available. It's not a busy time. The spring fishermen have left and the summer tourists haven't showed up yet. Just one person?"

"Ya, mon. Just me."

"Okay, then, we'll put you in a room with two kings but we can just charge you for a single. That alright?"

"Ya, mon. Dat be fine. Not to worry 'bout the kings, though. I jes need to get de sleep alone, mon."

The manager blinked and paused but then recovered and said, "No, I meant the beds, the sizes. Never mind. Here," he handed a form to Cirtron, "just fill in your name, home address and the plate number on your car. I'll get you keys and a property map."

"Don't have de car, mon. The bus, she be de one dat bring me."

The manager took a breath and then explained, "Fine, just fill in the name and address and we'll get you all set." Cirtron took a desk pen, filled in Negril, Jamaica, West Indies and his name.

The clerk wasn't quite finished when he took back the form. "Do you have a last name?"

· *Another Redstripe, Please* ·

"Ya, mon," answered Cirtron. The last one I be using be Cirtron and still it be so. Does not change, mon."

"Right, ok, fine. How will you be paying, sir. We take Master Card, VISA, American Express and the Motel 'Merica credit card."

"Wid de money, sir. I use de money, irie?"

"You mean cash?" The manager looked down at the form and the address that Cirtron had filled in and asked, "You don't mean Jamaican money, do you? I'm afraid we might not be able to . . ."

"No mon, I have de YOU ESS DEE money from Sheila, d'you see?" Cirtron plucked a handful out of the gym bag.

"Do you mean U.S Dollars, sir? Is that what you have there? That would be fine." Cirtron paid, collected a map and key and a list of the amenities for the motel which included breakfast off the lobby in the morning and then made his way to his room. With the gym bag plopped down on the second king sized bed, Cirtron lay down on the first king sized bed, flicked through the cable channels on the provided television and fell asleep still clothed. The television remained on, casting stroboscopic colors on the motel room walls the rest of the night. Cirtron snored his way into a deep sleep. Sheila and the hounds snoozed away in another room just a ways down the hallway. While neither party realized the other had arrived in Wautoma, they would meet, accidentally, in the morning.

Cirtron was the first to rise. His internal clock was still set in Jamaican and it was always his habit to rise early. As the next morning's bright June sunlight began to sneak in around the edges of motel room's curtains, Cirtron was up and ready for a shower. Once clean, dried and dressed in clean clothes from the gym bag, he headed to the lobby to seek out some breakfast.

· *Dachshunds in the Midwest* ·

Sheila woke not too much later. It took her a while longer in the bath than Cirtron. She dressed, fussed with her long blond hair, and then shook the hounds awake so that she could get them on leashes and walk them. While Cirtron was piling toast, bagels and fruit on a plate at the breakfast buffet off the motel lobby, Sheila was out in the back of the establishment with Redstripe and Paris hoping they would get things over with quickly. They didn't; too many smells to investigate, but the three finally headed back in. The outside door near their room was locked. Sheila had to guide the hounds up front to the main doors to gain entrance. It was a bit of a walk around the building but the two dogs pedaled their little legs willingly all they way up to the main entrance.

Once indoors, of course, the dogs smelled breakfast. They began to try to drag Sheila by their leashes toward the side room with the buffet. Having inhaled most of his food quickly, Cirtron was just leaving the room. All four, two humans and two hounds, literally bumped into and tangled with each other at the doorway.

"Sheila!"

"Cirtron!"

"Ya, mon. It be good t'see you m'lady. See, I told you I would come t'here!"

Sheila let go of the two leashes and threw her arms around the rastmafarian and hugged him; her long blond hair tangling with his dreadlocks. She spoke into his shoulder. "You made it!" You found everything? How was the trip? Did you get the ticket and, well, I guess you must have, huh?"

"Ya, mon. But de dogs, mon. Day are in back to find dere breakfast. Maybe we go an catch de two?"

Sheila had not realized that as soon as she'd dropped the leashes, Redstripe and Paris, dachshunds that they were, had taken off to follow their noses to the closest food. They could be seen in the next room and could be heard whining around the chairs of a young couple with two preschoolers all seated at a table with their morning munchies. Alarmed, she entered the room to corral her hounds. Cirtron just dropped to the floor, crossed his legs and called out, "Hey, dere, you dogs, Redstripe, Paris! C'mon here you little ones. C'mon!"

Redstripe and Paris froze just a moment after, looking in Cirtron's direction and, amazingly, streaked right for him, loose leashes flapping behind. "Doggy?" said one of the little ones at the table. The mother shushed the child.

"Redstripe, Paris. Ah! Be it de good ting an see both of you both again, here!" The two dogs climbed onto Cirtron's lap and he embraced the two little hounds. They rose up on their hindquarters and began to paw at the front of his shirt in order to gain purchase and rise up to lick at the remains of recent breakfast still stuck in the Jamaican's beard. Sheila looked on and had to wipe one eye. Cirtron laughed while the hounds licked.

The woman with the Jamaican, two dachshunds and farm to be discovered in Wautoma, knelt down and tried to hug all three of her dearest friends. She rose, turned to the front desk and called to the day manager.

"Miss? I think we'd all like to check out now."

Realtor's Office

WITH CIRTRON and the two dogs in the car Sheila, in the driver's seat, started the engine. She drove the little Camry out of the motel parking lot and out onto the county highway. The office for Egan's Realty was only a couple of blocks north. Sheila turned the car into the small lot in front of Egan's, parked it and shut off the engine. The lawyers in New York had told her that this agency was where she could complete forms and pick up the keys to the farm buildings on the property she had inherited.

Sheila, Cirtron and Paris and Redstripe piled out of the Camry. It was a bit of a leap from the back seats for the two little dachshunds. But they were excited and were down and out of the car before the humans had a chance to help them.

Paris and Redstripe scampered across the asphalt and up to the glass door to the realtor's office. It was trimmed with cheap-looking aluminum. Their little heads craned up, waiting for the door to be opened. Their tails were wagging. Dachshund eyebrows were raised and eyes were bright.

Cirtron looked a little worried. He asked, "Will day let de dogs into da building?"

"If we don't ask, they can't say no," said Sheila, and she stepped toward the door.

"Come on girls." Sheila opened the door and the dogs rushed over the threshold and into the small office. Sheila and Cirtron followed them in.

A woman in her late forties sat at a desk. Plastic-rimmed glasses lay against her chest, secured by a beaded string that was slung around the back of her neck. She wore a business jacket and skirt.

"Oh my goodness!" said the woman. "You can't bring those dogs in here! Please!"

Sheila looked at her and said, innocently, "I can't?"

Cirtron said, "Irie, it be okay, mon. Day jus' be de little dogs."

The woman seated at the desk sniffed and then reddened. Redstripe and Paris had already made their way behind her and both of the dogs were snuffling at the woman's nylon clad ankles.

"Oh my goodness!" she said as she lifted her feet from the floor and away from the dogs. She pushed her chair back from the desk, nearly rolling the wheels over dachshund ears. Leaning back, she raised her feet even further and away from the inquisitive hounds.

It was too far a lean and she went over backward in her chair. When she and the chair hit the floor behind the desk, the impact made a loud thump and the two dachshunds scrambled back toward Sheila. The woman lay on her back in her chair on the floor behind the desk. . Her skirted legs were spread, immodestly, toward the heavens. Cirtron looked up and concentrated on a spot on the office wall. As amused as he was with the entire situation, he did not want to seem disrespectful or too interested in the view.

The dachshunds began to bark.

"Hey, little dogs," Cirtron said, "be still, mon. be still."

Sheila walked around the desk and bent down over the woman.

"Are you okay?"

The woman's eyes were wide and she said, "Yes, I'm fine. Can you please hold on to your dogs? What was it you wanted?"

"Let me help you up."

"Uh, no, I'm fine. What was it I can help you with?"

Sheila said, "I was told your office has the keys to the buildings on the Armstead farm. I guess I am the new owner so I sort of need them. And I was told there were some papers I had to sign and deal with here in your office."

The woman remained on her back in her tumbled chair behind the desk and the dachshunds came back to investigate. Cirtron crossed his arms and looked at still another spot on the wall. The woman made no move to try to get up but eyed the two dogs. "Can you please get these dogs away from me?"

Sheila shooed the two dogs. "Go on, let this lady alone! Behave!" Paris and Redstripe looked up with an offended expression on both of their little faces. But they retreated.

The woman on the floor seemed relieved when the dogs moved off and then said, "The Armstead Farm? Um, I don't know much about that. Mr. Egan would, but he isn't in right now. But the caretaker? She could get you into the buildings. She has keys I think. That would be Ms. Carson. She lives right next door to the property and has been watching over things for a while. Just go see her, I'm sure she can let you in today and then you can see Mr. Egan about things tomorrow."

Sheila had one more question. "Where exactly is this place, the Armstead farm?

The woman, still on the floor, lying back in her overturned chair, gave directions.

Then Sheila asked, "Please, can I help you up? Are you going to be alright?"

The woman said, "Oh no. Oh yes, I'm fine right here. Please, if you come again, please leave your dogs outside. I'll get up after you leave if you don't mind"

· *Another Redstripe, Please* ·

Cirtron and Sheila left the office. The dogs followed them out and over to the car. Everyone clambered in.

As Sheila started the engine again, she was thinking that maybe things would not be so simple. Cirtron was wondering why the lady in the office, seemingly so stiff and formal, had been wearing thigh-highs with lace undies. Redstripe and Paris decided they would both rub their wet noses all over the back windows as they peered out of the car.

Dachshund nose painting on glass is a much underappreciated art form.

The Armstead Farm

SHEILA FOLLOWED the directions given by the secretary in the Egan Realty office and together with the dogs and Cirtron, she made her way north. The Armstead farm that she had inherited was described as being only about a mile north of town. She found the gravel drive leading to the house easily by identifying the fire location number; a red sign with white letters on a steel post driven into the soil near the entrance to the property. She steered the Camry up the long stretch of drive and stopped. She did not think the place looked like much. Cirtron was ecstatic. He burst from the car while Sheila pushed open her own door slowly and stepped out to get a better look. Cirtron was nearly bouncing and the dogs climbed down and out onto the front lawn with no help, all on their own. Sheila grimaced. Those dogs were going to hurt their backs one of these days.

"Big house!" yelled Cirtron.

"Looks like it could use some work," said Sheila.

The house had been stained a brown color and looked in need of repair. While flowers grew against the foundation and the roof looked tight, gutters hung from the eaves at unhealthy angles. A section of fascia was missing at the edge of one part of the roof and the rafters stuck out like bad teeth. The window screens looked torn and rusty. A leaning shed adorned one side of the house, open on two sides and the grounds looked like they could use some cutting. The dachshunds were thrilled to be quit of the confinement of the car and galloped forward to explore.

Another Redstripe, Please

Sheila and Cirtron became aware of a soft hum, rubber tires on soil, and the dachshunds stopped, turned and looked. A powered golf cart was approaching; a woman at the wheel. The cart was traversing a double rutted lane leading from the next property and quickly came to a halt near the drive on which the Camry was parked.

The driver, once stopped, stepped out slowly, the caution of age governing her movements. She wore a wildly printed house dress that ended at mid calf; the pattern looked like it had once been copied from a curtain in a Caribbean resort. She had a full head of white hair, short, cut off half way down her neck, thick glasses and a pair of clean Nike running shoes on her feet. She looked as though she must have weighed 180 pounds and could not have been more than five feet tall. "Well, hey there. 'Been expecting you. I'm Rose Carson, they call me Carson, and I'm the sorry wretch that has had to be watching over this place till someone showed up after old Armstead died and his son took off. Pleased to meet you." She extended a chubby hand and Sheila shook it.

"Hi, I'm Sheila, and this is Cirtron. We just got here. How did you know we were coming?"

"You're gonna want to corral those two little hound doggies of yours before they go too far. They could get out in the back and get stepped on by the herd. How did I know? Girlie, word travels around here like the flu. I just heard you were coming. Cirtron?" Carson regarded the rastafamarian and clasped his arm with both hands. "Welcome here, my friend. And don't let'm call you Bob!"

"I see," said Sheila. Cirtron went to catch the dachshunds.

"Well, girlie," Carson looked up at Sheila, noted her blond hair and looks but kept silent on what she thought about this would be rancher/farmer, "we'll see what you see. Let me take you into the house, I got the keys and some papers here for you in the go cart and we can get you acclimated. Better get your friend too. If he's staying, he's gonna have some work to do."

Sheila called to Cirtron who had a dachshund under each arm and the five of them headed for the front door. At the front entrance, Carson pulled some keys from a folder she had taken from the golf cart, opened the screen door, propped it with an ample hip and unlocked and opened the main door. She waved Sheila, and the hound holding Cirtron into the front room. "Welcome home," Carson smiled.

Sheila was not smiling but Cirtron's eyes widened as he looked around. Redstripe and Paris were wriggling to get free and sniff the place out.

Entering the front room, Cirtron squatted down and released Redstripe and Paris. They took off to examine the first area; noses snuffling around the edges created by the walls and floor while inhaling deep noisey breaths and snorting out short wet sounding exhales. The two of them moved almost too fast to be seen. Sheila gazed at the walls and the furniture.

The furniture, left behind by John Armstead, was bad enough: dark brocaded chairs and couches well-stained and with claw feet legs. It looked as though bears had been living in there and had used their claws to rearrange some of the fabric. Cushion material stood out in tufts and the fabric of the furniture was pushed up in wrinkles here and there like badly thrown bedspreads. The walls were worse. They had not been acquainted with a new coat of paint in what looked to be generations. As time had gone by in that front room and pictures had been added, moved and subtracted, large faded patches decorated the walls. A myriad of unused nails, pounded into the plaster, poked out nearly everywhere. The rugs on the floor had lost their colors and patterns long ago.

The dogs headed for the back room and Cirtron plunked down in a chair that was loosing its stuffing. "Ah, mon! Soft! Good!"

Sheila just stared. The two dachshunds could be heard scrambling and snooting around in the back room, the kitchen.

Carson looked at Sheila's expression and laughed. "Heh, heh, heh! I told you Cirtron would have some work to do, hey? And I haven't even taken you out back yet. That'll be a treat, let me tell you."

"Oh my god," said Sheila.

"Ya, mon, be it so cool!" said Cirtron.

"Heh, heh, heh," chuckled Carson.

At least the place did not smell as Carson had aired it when the weather was good, as it was now, and the summer breezes made their way into the house through the opened windows and rusted screens. The curtains were useless; so aged and thin that they were virtually transparent. But the air did flow. The hounds scampered back into the front room and leaped up to join Cirtron on his chosen seat. "Ya, mon, little dogs. D'you like?"

The two dogs woofed in excitement, expressing their approval of the new home. There would be lots of corners and things to sniff and explore but they were content for a moment to rest on Cirtron's lap.

Sheila was thinking that New York was a long ways back.

Rose Carson looked at Sheila who was frowning and looked at Cirtron, his yellow smile wide in his black face and thought for just a moment. She did want these two newcomers to be comfortable and to take over the farm; she was tired of looking after things. After all, an old lady had other things to do than watch over the neighbors and their animals and house. "Tell you what you two, you must be hungry. I wouldn't be surprised if the little doggies were too. I can take you out to the pasture later or in the morning and you can take a look around at the rest here when you're ready. Let's go into town and get some lunch. The best place is Tilly's. I'll drive."

Sheila liked the offer. So much at one time was so much. She asked Carson, "Sure, where is your car? Are you sure we can't just take mine?"

Carson grinned, "No, girlie, no need for your car, we take the go-cart. It's only a mile. I do it all the time. Come on back out and you two can climb in. Bring the doggies."

The three adults and the two dogs left the house and walked (and padded) out to the golf cart. Cirtron looked with interest at something that was bolted to the back of the cart. It was an aluminum half barrel; meant to hold beer. "Ya, Mon! Ya, take de beer right t'along. Dat be an idea, ah yes, mon."

"Sorry, my curly headed friend, that's not beer. It's a tank for propane gas that one of my buddies made up for me. He attached it to the go-cart and it's got a fuel pipe welded on for the engine and a special valve to fill it. I can go for days with this baby," Carson explained with a little pride. "But don't worry Cirtron, they've got plenty of beer at Tilly's. Just get in. Sheila? You take the doggies and sit in back."

"Ah, mon. Not to be so," Cirtron raised one hand and pointed up with his forefinger and continued. "D'lady, wid de respect mon, she be de one t'sit up in de front, mon."

Sheila was about to intervene but Carson spoke first. "Trust me, let Sheila and the doggies get in back, you and I sit up front and you'll see why."

Sheila said, "Cirtron, go ahead, it's not a problem. Just get in. I'll take the dogs."

Cirtron shrugged, Sheila picked up Redstripe and Paris, each under one arm, climbed in and Carson stepped in and lowered her

· *Another Redstripe, Please* ·

pudgy frame into the driver's seat. Cirtron took the passenger seat in the front of the golf cart. Before they rolled off, Carson reached under the dash and pulled out two pair of clear safety glasses complete with side protectors. Settling one pair on her own face she handed the other to Cirtron. "Put 'em on. You'll need 'em. We got no windshield on this little buggy."

"My god," said Sheila, "How fast does this thing go?"

Carson answered, "Its not speed, girlie. You'll see."

Taking It to Tilly's

THE LITTLE golf cart, dogs and passengers aboard, beer keg bearing propane on the back, wheeled down the driveway to the road. Near the Fire Identification Number sign, Carson stopped and looked both ways. Seeing things were clear from both directions, she pressed on the accelerator and made the way across the asphalt and unto the gravel shoulder on the opposite side of the road. She turned left and headed south. The moving golf cart began to jostle and shake and Cirtron grabbed the dash with one hand to steady himself. Sheila was not so lucky. She had the dogs each under one arm and no hands left with which to brace herself. Redstripe and Paris began to pant and shake and the sitting end of Sheila began to bounce and slide from one end of the back seat bench to the other. Sheila and the dogs remained attached to her sliding backside but it was a near thing.

"Yeah!" shouted Carson, "Here we go folks! Hang tight!"

Sheila had no comment. She was too busy balancing. The dogs just shook and panted. Cirtron managed a grunt and the unlikely entourage proceeded down the gravel shoulder. Carson leaned over the steering wheel and peered forward. The toothy grin on her face could not be seen by her passengers but would have competed pretty well with the gleeful expression of a fourteen year old on a roller coaster. After only a few hundred yards of gravel shoulder passed under the golf cart wheels, the first semi-trailer passed them. The golf cart rocked as the wind of passage of the semi hit the little vehicle. The sound of the diesel engine and the buffeting air were deafening in the windowless golf cart and the dogs began to bark while Cirtron gripped, Sheila continued to slide and Carson kept grinning. Road dirt and gravel and chunks of this and that flew up from the sixteen wheels of the semi and hit the rocking golf cart like shrapnel. It all bounced up and hit making loud clicks on the side of the cart and then unto the chests and faces of Cirtron and Carson sitting in the front. Sheila and the dogs, still in the back, were spared the onslaught.

The safety glasses Carson had donned and the ones she had given to Cirtron held. Unseen little projectiles bounced against the plastic lenses and fell into the foot wells. Cirtron yelled, "Ah, NO MON, de stone! Watch for de stone, mon!"

Carson just cackled, "Heh, Heh, Heh! I told you it wasn't speed! Cirtron, keep those glasses on. Girlie? You three all okay back there?" She looked over her right shoulder into the back of the golf cart at Sheila and the dogs while letting the golf cart weave dangerously close to a ditch. The cart tilted sharply and Sheila slid hard to the right while hanging on to the hounds and banging her hip.

"We're fine! Watch where you're going! My god!" Sheila yelled.

"Yeah!" shouted Carson, "It won't be far, folks! Hang tight!" Hanging tight was most definitely the order for the day. Redstripe and Paris were not amused.

What is this? the dachshunds were thinking— *that car trip was bad enough but there isn't even a decent place to lie down in here. Dachshunds like us should not have to put up with all of this. Really, this is just not acceptable. We will certainly have something say about this later.*

A car passed. The passengers stared at the golf cart with two dachshunds, the dreadlocked adorned Jamaican and Sheila and the still-grinning Carson. Another semi truck passed, launching more gravel onto and into the cart. The truck driver sounded his air horn, a blast loud enough to rattle the tympanic membranes of humans and hounds. Sheila shouted forward. "What was that!?"

"Just a friend of mine, he pulls a route from Milwaukee to Wautoma every day. His rig carries a load for the big grocery store. Frozen food mostly. That truck has a Thermo King refridge system. Nice guy. Sometimes he drops some overstocks off at my place. Remind me to ask him if he ever has any doggie food. They make some of that stuff you keep in those little pouches. Stays moist like cat food." Carson had been talking again back over her shoulder and the cart wove to the right once more.

"Would you *please* watch where you're going?" Sheila was beginning to tire. Her arms holding the dachshunds were feeling numb. Cirtron, stoic, just hung on to the dash.

"Oh, yeah, not a problem, we're almost there." Carson

The dachshunds had perked up at the mention of food and cats. *Cats? We hate cats. Food is okay, but how much more of all this do we need to put up with? And, by the way, we are dachshunds, not doggies! Let's hear more about those pouches. It's only right.*

After only a mile of travel in the golf cart that had no business running along the side of a busy highway, the crew of the Carson go-cart made it into the town of Wautoma. Carson swung the cart off of the shoulder and onto the paved surface of the main street. A few blocks later, she pulled up and parked the cart just outside Tilly's bar. A broken and crumbling concrete sidewalk led to the entrance for the place and the door looked heavy enough to need two hands to pull it open. Neon signs with beer logos decorated small windows.

"Here we are, folks," announced Carson, "Let's go. I know you all must be hungry."

• Another Redstripe, Please •

Sheila, Carson and Cirtron climbed out of the cart. The two dachshunds were placed on the sidewalk, leashes in the hand of Sheila. The hounds had only one thought between them. *Food? There's gotta be. We can smell it.* The dachshund noses had already picked up the odor of French Fries, greasy burgers and all sorts of unhealthy things wafting out and around the edges of the thick door of the bar and grill. Tails began to wag and noses were twitching. The phenomenon was not limited to the hounds. There is nothing like risking one's life in a speeding golf cart to encourage the onset of hunger for any species, be it canine or homo sapiens. The three homo sapiens and the two canines entered the establishment, ready for food and libations.

Tilly's Bar and Grill had been established and owned by a man years past by the name of Attilio "Tilly" Delora. The place had originally catered to the many itinerant workers in the area that came to harvest corn, pickles and peppers in the local fields. Most of that business was now gone, replaced by tourism for folks who came to fish the local lakes in summer and skid across those same lakes in winter on snowmobiles when everything was frozen. Now his granddaughter Sue owned and managed the place as well as the property next door, "Just Rusty's". The two places were nearly as one; a short indoor hallway joined them. Tilly's had a dining room (fish fry on Friday's, chicken on Saturday) with a large, brooding stone fireplace and Just Rusty's had an upstairs electronic archery range that had been installed to bring in business when the local economy began to fall off. The White River, the main water flow feeding the lakes in Wautoma, meandered just behind the two bars. The water passing by ended up in Little Cedar Lake, Irogami Lake and Silver Lake, all mainstays of the local tourism industry. The mainstay of Tilly's Bar and Grill was an oval shaped bar with beer taps scattered here and there. Sue, the owner-manager, greeted Carson and her guests as they pulled back the heavy door and entered the dimness of the bar. "Hey Carson! How are you?"

"Oh, I'm fine, hi Sue," replied Carson while she used her hands to dust off the road grit clinging to her dress. "I just brought in some friends today. Is the kitchen goin'?"

"Yup, ready to go. Hector's cookin' today," answered Sue. "Park yourselves. I'll be right with you."

Lunch at Tilly's

CIRTRON, SHEILA AND CARSON seated themselves on stools at the bar. Carson took Redstripe and Cirtron took Paris. Both dogs planted their back legs in laps and used their front paws to brace up on the bar so they could see the sights. The first thing they saw was a cat. It was stepping arrogantly along the varnished oval surface with a haughty look that only cats can portray. Redstripe and Paris showed interest by making ears go perpendicular to little skulls while lips curled back to show the tips of teeth.

Sheila, the one without a lap dog, asked the bartender. "Uh, Sue? Do I have your name right? What's with the cat? Should we be in here with the dogs?"

Sue laughed. "Don't worry about it. We always have dogs in here. The cat? That's Joe, he's our patrol cat. He just goes in circles around the bar all day and night and picks up scraps. We never have to feed him cat food. Just watch your stuff when I bring it out. He'll snatch it before you can wink. By the way, what are those little guys? Are those like wiener dogs? They're cute. I'll find something for them."

Redstripe and Paris listened and thought, *Things are NOT getting better. Can't that person tell we are ladies and not guys? Really! Besides, that cat needs a good bite.*

Not realizing she was interrupting the dachshunds' thoughts, Carson told Sue, "Get us three cheeseburgers and fries and the usual. Do you have some of that deer sausage for the dogs? They'd like that, I'd bet."

"You got it." Sue wrote an order on a green slip of paper and then fixed up three bloody Marys with beer chasers and placed them in front of Cirtron, Sheila and Carson. "Be right back. I'll take this to Hector. I'll get the wieners some sausage. Hey, get it? Wieners? Sausage? Ha! I can't stand it!" The dogs sniffed at the drinks from their vantage points on Carson's and Cirtron's laps. The spicy smell was not of much interest to them. Both snorted with dog disgust.

Redstripe and Paris continued to watch Joe the cat parade around the bar top. Their little heads moved back and forth, eyes focused on the feline. The cat circled around and the dogs followed its progress with wide eyes and widened nostrils. Swiveling heads in synch, the hounds looked like two slow-motion spectators at a tennis match. Cirtron took a moment to look around as he balanced a hound with one hand and used the other to reach for the spice- and vodka-laced tomato juice on the bar in front of him.

Cirtron saw that the dark stained walls had posters pinned to them. Many were of racing cars and some were of bikini clad young women holding bottles of beer. A pinball machine and some sort of long table strewn with white dust and little bowling pins on one end occupied some of the space not given over to the bar and stools. A music player with a rack of shiny compact disks behind glass sat at the end of the room. Redstripe and Paris were still eye locked on and tracking Joe the cat.

Besides the two dogs, Cirtron, Sheila, Carson and Joe the cat, only two sets of other people were at the bar. Two were men in tee shirts and jeans and baseball caps. Two were senior women whose white hair had turned a little greenish purple from cheap hair treatments. Both pairs were alternately slurping from mugs of beer, using French fries to shovel ketchup out of their red oval plastic basket look-a-likes and biting off chunks of hamburgers. It was slurp, shovel and bite. Place the burger back in the basket and slurp and shovel once more. The gastric-based performance was rhythmic. Joe the cat stopped in front of each pair in turn and was shooed off with the waving of hands each time. The eaters did not even have to look up.

While the eaters ate, the cat patrolled and the dachshund heads swiveled, Carson was talking to Sheila. "You're gonna love these burgers. And the fries are great too. Lots of grease. Anytime I'm feeling a little slow I come in here and it all gets me going right away. There's nothing like a burger at Tilly's to get an old lady's insides moving again, if you know what I mean."

Sheila was dismayed to realize she knew exactly what Carson meant. She began to think of salad.

Breaking the choreography of the slurp, shovel and bite show, one of the men paused and peered across the bar at Cirtron. He reached down and tapped his knuckles on his lunch partner's leg. "Hey! It's Bob Marley! How ya' doin' Bob?" He leaned back a bit on his stool, his partner clapped him on the shoulder and they both began to giggle.

Sheila thought that grown men should never giggle. Carson sipped at her drink. The dog's ears perked up, two sets of fuzzy radars aimed at the source of the new voice. *Now what?* they were thinking, *We can smell food! Let's get on with this.*

All that went through Cirtron's mind was, "*Ah, no. Not again, mon!*"

Sue returned from the kitchen with just two plates. Each had a little pile of sausages cut into thin slices about the diameter of a quarter. She clanked one down each in front of the two hounds. "Eat up guys!" Redstripe and Paris were too interested in the plates to be concerned about another gender insult. Sue turned to the two men. "You two can just shut up. These folks are with Carson here, leave the guy alone and go find your brains somewhere, would you? You wanna a couple more beers? Or do you want Carson mad at you?"

"C'mon Sue, I was just kidding," said the one man. "Ms. Carson, I didn't mean anything. Me and Bobby here were just having fun, okay?"

Carson nodded and sipped more of her drink. The two women with the purple green coiffures whispered to each other. Sue returned to the kitchen. Redstripe and Paris were already licking the remnants of sausage off of their plates. Cirtron looked down, hoping for peace and covering his feelings by adjusting Paris on his lap, her paws still on the bar while she lapped at the sausage plate. The man was not admonished. He returned one more comment. "But, anyway, shouldn't this guy like maybe comb his hair once in a while?"

Sheila looked down, placed both hands flat on the bar and turned her head. "Okay, boys and girls, that's it." Carson placed a hand on her arm but Sheila shook it off and rose to step to the other side of the bar where the two men sat with their unfinished food and greasy napkins. She stopped as the men hiked themselves around to see her.

"I have a question for you," Sheila said, her arms folded across her chest. "Do you have a belt buckle?"

"Well, yeah, I sure do. Did you want to see it?" The man grinned impolitely.

"Sheila explained, "Well, what I really want to do is just borrow it a minute."

"What? For what?"

"I notice you can't hear very well. The bartender told you to leave my friend alone. So could I just borrow that buckle a minute so I can use it to clean out your ears? I'm only trying to help." Sheila stood and smiled. The man's friend covered his mouth with his hand and started to snort the snort of held in check chuckles. The first man lost his grin and looked over at Carson.

"Don't look at me, buddy. The girlie can handle herself it seems to me. Maybe you might want to just be nice?" Carson did not raise her voice at all.

The man rolled his eyes and said, "Yeah, I'm sorry. Hey there guy," he addressed Cirtron across the bar, "We were just kiddin, no harm intended."

"Ya mon, no problem mon, Irie." Cirtron raised a closed fist. "Respect."

Sue came back with the burgers and fries in red plastic baskets and the two dogs and three humans finished lunch at Tilly's in peace. Sheila was really wondering just what place Carson held in this community.

Seeking Supplies

THE THREE humans and the pair of dachshunds left the bar and grill and stepped back to the golf cart. The three of them fitted with two legs clambered in while lifting the dogs up and into the cart. Redstripe and Paris immediately began to pant and shake, anticipating another rough ride. Sheila's thoughts were back in the bar.

"Carson? Who were those two guys? What a couple of wastes of oxygen!"

"Ah, don't worry about it, girlie," Carson answered. "Those are Mike and Bobby. They're harmless. Actually they're sort of friends of mine. They work for Tom's Roofing and replaced the rain gutters on my place for me last year for just the cost of the supplies."

"You mean they did it free? You didn't have to pay them?"

Carson looked straight ahead and said, "Not exactly, we made a trade. I'll explain sometime."

Sheila didn't pursue with more questions after hearing Carson's rather mysterious answer. Cirtron was listening carefully. Carson said brightly, "Tell you what you two. Before we go back, I'm gonna take you over to Copps.

Cirtron spoke up right away. "Cops? No, mon. No need for de cops, mon. Have no done any ting. Why we need de cops, mon?"

Carson laughed. "Heh, heh, heh. No, Cirtron, it's Copps; two p's, and that's a big grocery store here in town. It's just down the road. I expect you need some supplies back at your new place; gotta eat, you know, and so do the doggies."

"Ah, Irie. Yes, mon. Be it okay den, mon."

• Another Redstripe, Please •

Redstripe and Paris, hearing the "doggie" name again, began to bark; a duet of protest over the offensive label. Sheila sat back, gripping the dogs in anticipation of another rock and roll ride. Cirtron settled back and Carson pressed on the gas pedal while steering the cart out onto the street and down the way to Copps.

Copps Foods was part of a chain of superstores scattered around the middle and north of the State of Wisconsin. There was nothing remarkable about it, a large building set back from the road behind a parking lot that could hold hundreds of cars. A fast food restaurant and a gas station occupied space in the out lot. The windows were plastered with handwritten signs proclaiming specials on price for everything from beer to smoked hams. Carson pulled right up to the front doors with the cart and stopped it on the concrete apron. "Ok, here we are. Sheila, you come with me, I'll show you where everything is and Cirtron, you stay here with the doggies. We won't be long. Let's go girlie." Before Cirtron could protest and before the hounds could respond to the hateful name once more, Carson had climbed out and was waddling toward the automatic doors with Sheila following obediently.

Inside the store, after directing Sheila to grab a grocery cart, (the kind of which the wheels don't work and cause it to travel in all directions but the chosen one) Carson pointed out the aisles that held fresh fruit, vegetables, bread, meat, eggs and the rest of the things needed to stock a refrigerator. The two women passed the liquor shelves and Sheila eyed some bottles of California wine. Carson grabbed a twelve pack of Blatz beer instead. The food run went well, all in all, the cart was half full, and the checkout lane was the next stop. Outside things were not running quite as smoothly. Cirtron and the dogs had left the cart to stretch. Cirtron was pacing with the dogs on their leashes up and down in front of the store.

· *Dachshunds in the Midwest* ·

Not far from the main doors, the store management had placed a mechanical pony. Electric motors in the base holding it up caused the little horse to rock back and forth while circus music played. The little contrivance was there to amuse children and collect seventy five cents from their parents for a two minute ride. A five year old boy was on it while his mother waited in front of him, her grocery cart loaded and overflowing. Cirtron and the dogs needed to investigate.

As the three of them came up to the pony, mother and child, Redstripe and Paris began to bark. They reared up on their back sides, vertical, and began to paw at the air around the moving hooves of the little horse. The little hounds mimicked two noisy furry brown self powered pogo sticks. It may have been they wanted a ride. It may have been the music hurt their ears. The little boy looked down, delighted and shouted, "Heeee! Puppies! Mommy, puppies!"

Mommy was horrified. She could not decide which presented the greatest danger, the black rasta man or the horrible hounds. "Get these wild animals away from my son! What's the matter with you!" Her head jerked back and forth to first look at Cirtron, then the hounds, then her son and then back at Cirtron. "Get them away!" She grabbed her son from the still rocking horse, plopped him in the back of the grocery cart and made a hasty retreat to the parking lot. She called back over her shoulder, "Something should be done about people like you!"

"Puppies!" shouted the little boy.

Cirtron did not know what to say. He reached down to pet Redstripe and Paris. "Not to worry, my small friends. De people, many are without de respect mon."

The dogs, subdued after the woman's outburst thought, *Wild animals? Us? We just wanted to play! Besides, we didn't bite anybody or knock anybody over or anything. There was some good food in that cart, though.*

Cirtron straightened, sighed and wondered if he was going to get used to this new town. The little horse continued to rock as Sheila and Carson came out through the doors to see Cirtron with the two dogs still standing near the little mechanical horse. "Cirtron?" asked Carson. "Aren't you a little big for that?"

"Yes, mon. Ah, no, mon. See, de woman, she not have de respect for de little dogs."

"What woman?" asked Sheila.

"Ah, not to mind, m'lady. Be it okay. Irie. Now we can go, mon?"

"Yup," replied Carson. "Let's dump these bags in the cart and blow this popcorn joint. It's about time we got back. I'll show you the rest of the farm."

Where the Deer and the Antelope Play

THE GOLF CART ride back was not much better than the ride into town. Gravel flew. Winds stirred by passing trucks rocked the little vehicle and all hung on as best they could. Carson whooped and grinned, an aging pilot leaning over the controls of an old biplane. A long silk scarf wrapped around her neck would have completed the picture. Sheila collected another hip bruise and Cirtron's collection of road dirt grew. The dogs shook and panted.

Back at the Armstead farm and after the groceries were stuffed into the fridge and into cupboards, Sheila asked Carson, "So, can you show us the herd? I promised Redstripe and Paris they would get to see some cows."

Cows? Where's the cows? Can we chase them? Dachshund ears perked up.

"Cows?" asked Carson.

"Yes, you know, like 'moo.' Cows," said Sheila. "Where are they?"

"Cows, huh? Well ok, better come with me out back." Carson led the way out the rear door.

Behind the farmhouse, a tract of nearly eight acres spread out covered with some sort of grass, muddy areas and two double acre sections enclosed by heavy duty fencing. The fence posts were nearly six feet high, made of eight by eight inch beams and connected by heavy wire mesh. Piles of baled hay were placed in spots here and there just outside the enclosures and a couple of water troughs could be seen along the inside edges of the fencing. More than a good dozen animals milled about in one of the fenced areas. Grass and hay stuck out from their mouths as they chewed.

· *Another Redstripe, Please* ·

Sheila froze. Cirtron put one hand to his beard. Carson began to chuckle. The dogs stood still, pointed and their hackles rose in strips down their backs.

"Oh ... my ... god. They're buffaloes!" Sheila could barely get the words out.

"Bison." Carson corrected. "This is a bison ranch. I expect you didn't know?"

"Bison," said Sheila. It wasn't even a question.

"Ah, ya, mon," said Cirtron. "Day look like no cows I have been to see. Lot's of hair, mon. Like mine."

Indeed the high shoulders that sloped down to the lower and smaller hindquarters of the bison were covered with thick mats of hair, not unlike Cirtron's dreadlocks and tangled beard The two dogs began the backward dachshund dance. They each lifted their little heads, let go one bark, took a step back and then barked and stepped again. They'd reversed about three dog lengths before Sheila asked, "What in the world do you do with buffalo—bison I mean?"

Carson was enjoying the surprise of the situation and answered, "Oh, 'bout the same as with cows. You feed them and water them and in the end you can eat them and wear them. They bring a good price if they are cared for well."

Sheila had not recovered. "Oh ... my ... god. Bison." And then she thought about the dogs. "Cirtron, grab Redstripe and Paris. I don't want them running under that fence."

"Ya, mon." Sheila should not have worried. The hounds were still dancing backward.

"Good idea," remarked Carson. "Those dogs are already long enough, we don't want them flat too. What do you say we go back into the house, open some of that beer we brought back, and I'll explain some of this?"

"Ya, mon."

"Lead on, Carson, I can't wait to hear."

Inside, the humans sat at the kitchen table with the twelve pack of Blatz torn open in front of them. The dogs scampered into the front room, hopped up onto a worn couch, placed their heads on paws and began to snooze. Carson began her lecture.

"First of all," started Carson, "you might remember I brought over some papers for you. They're over there on the counter top. The bank books, check books, deeds, tax records and all the things related to this property are in there. There should be a survey in there too and a list of all the contacts for things related to the bison like feed suppliers and the processing plant and all of that. I know there's a ledger book with all the expenses as well and the records are pretty good. Actually, while I was taking care of the place, the last entries are mine. I ended up with all the papers when old Armstead's son finally left."

Sheila asked, "This son, I guess he would be my cousin, did he give you all that?"

"No, he didn't. I needed it all to take care of things so I got it from one of the suits at the Midland Bank. Tom Pederson; nice guy but a little old for me. I don't why he's still working. He should be in a rocking chair."

"He just gave it to you? Should he have done that?"

"Well, girlie," answered Carson, "If I was gonna take care of this place for a while, I needed to pay the bills and such. I suppose Tom broke a little rule or two, but he was just being nice. Besides, we made a trade."

"A trade?" asked Sheila. This was the second time she'd heard about trading.

"Ah, mon. What did you make wid de trade, mon?"

Carson gave the same answer as before. "I'll explain later. Let me tell you about bison. You really need to know this stuff."

"Now then, you two. There is some stuff you really need to understand. Just let me jabber on a bit and try not to interrupt. Bison are creatures that deserve a great deal of respect. They're sort of the ghosts of a lost culture. But they will take care of your needs over time if you take care of them. They will provide you with a livelihood. This thing is really a partnership between you and them and that partnership between the bison and people goes back a very, very long way. It is one of the great sinful tragedies in time that people did not honor that relationship so well in the past centuries."

Sheila and Cirtron were riveted. Sheila realized they were about to receive a philosophical history lesson and was trying to revamp her impression of this chubby little neighbor, the pilot of golf carts and caretaker of the farm. Cirtron settled back with his Blatz beer and prepared to just listen. Patience was one of Cirtron's better virtues.

Carson continued. "Round about two or three hundred years ago, there were tons of these creatures stomping around on the western plains of the United States and Canada. They were the biggest creatures around and few predators messed with them very much except for the young and the sick. I've heard that there were somewhere between thirty and seventy million bison milling about, mostly west of the Mississippi river. I don't suppose they had any white shirted accountants out there counting bison on their handheld computers back then, but most accounts tell of so many bison that herds of them could be seen to stretch clear to the horizon."

Sheila was startled, stared at Carson and said, "Seventy *million?*"

· *Dachshunds in the Midwest* ·

"Don't interrupt. You see, these big hairy critters were the main thing needed by most of the plains Indians out there in the west before our ancestors went out to settle it. Tribes like the Sioux and the Dakotas and lots of others depended on the bison for their lives and their societies. This is where the respect thing comes in. The Native American folks used the bison for clothing, tools, weapons, shelter, food and everything else. They ate the meat, dried some for later, took the hides for shelter, blankets and clothes, and carved up the bones for all kinds of things. They even munched the innards and used the left overs to make things. Of course being dismantled into all these parts was rather tough on the bison. But the native people had great respect for life and realized they were taking a bison life in order to keep their own selves alive. They were in the habit of thanking every bison that was killed for letting them live another day. And they didn't waste anything. That's not like today's folks. Just check the trash anywhere."

"Ya, mon. Respect. I know how dis be true and must be for all de tings under Ga."

Carson looked at Cirtron and smiled. "Yeah, Cirtron, I've heard you use that word; respect. Good for you. But let me keep going here before I forget something. Old ladies don't always think so well."

"I'm beginning to get the impression you think pretty well, Carson," said Sheila.

"Don't interrupt. Now, where was I? Oh yeah, trash. See, there was a time when the people trying to settle this country out in the west did not do so well by the bison. By the end of the eighteen hundreds, most of animals had been killed. There were only a few thousand left and the original millions all died for the wrong reason. In a manner of speaking, the white people wasted them. The bison were killed by the thousands by hunters, the army, explorers

Another Redstripe, Please

and folks that were just heading west. It got so bad that when the railroads went through, people paid to ride the rails and just shoot the bison through the open windows of the trains. The worst part was most of the animals were killed just for their horns or hides or the pure sport of things and the carcasses were left to rot. The bison were all gone after a while and their deaths went for nothing."

"Now then, not only did the bison lose out, but the Native Americans lost big time. In spite of what you might read about the soldiers and the settlers, it wasn't really them that did in the Indians and other native people. It was really the lack of the bison herds that destroyed those cultures. The source for food and shelter and clothing and all that just was gone; wasted by stupidity." Carson reached for and raised a beer can to her lips and gulped. She wiped her mouth with the back of her hand and said, "You can interrupt now."

"De people, day had no respect, mon?"

Sheila was silent.

Carson clunked her beer can back on the table. "So, okay. Here's the deal. Bison are not cows. Sorry you are disappointed not to have any here. But these bison beasts are not to be ignored. Did you see those fences? They're better than six feet high. A full sized bison can jump one up to four feet. They can hit forty miles an hour on a dead run without a lead more than ten or twenty yards and they are big. Most of the time they just stand around and chew but when they get into a mood, they're dangerous. Don't go out there and think you're gonna pet them or rub their noses or something. But if you feed them and water them, that's about all they need and maybe some corn before they go for processing, they'll provide you with a living. They don't even need a barn in winter. The snow just builds up on their backs. Let me tell you, a snow fall on a bison herd looks like something from a Currier and Ives print; very pretty. But you need to understand the respect thing. You have to understand they are the ghosts of a lost culture."

"It's a funny thing. People in this country and in Canada are bringing the bison back. There's herds in some parks out west and there are ranches all over. Last I heard Wisconsin had about seven thousand bison residents. What's funny is that it's the descendants of the people who wiped out most of the bison hundreds of years ago who are trying to bring them back. Odd, hey? A bunch of organizations have sprung up here and there that have people as members who try to promote the bison and bison ranching. In fact, because bison don't have a history of folks messing with their breeding and health and meat production and all that over time like with cows, the animals are pretty healthy and don't need much in the way of veterinary attention. No antibiotics or hormones or that stuff. They do just fine on their own."

Carson finally wound down and Sheila asked, "So, let me see if we have this straight. We raise the bison, and then send them off to some processing plant? Sell them for the meat and hides?"

"Yup," nodded Carson, "just so that you have some respect for them. That's my whole point."

Cirtron was quiet, sipping beer and thinking but Sheila had another question. "Um, how do we get more bison? I mean, I noticed all the animals inside the fences had horns. Don't we need some girl bisons? I mean, well, you know?"

Carson looked up at the ceiling and started laughing. Her stocky body shook as she tapered off into a snicker and then took a breath and said, "Oh! I'm sorry! I forgot! There is one bull out there. You'll get calves when the time is right. Usually 'round April."

Sheila did not get it, "But . . ."

"Girlie..Sheila, with bison, both the males and the females have horns. You gotta look down, not up, to tell who's who."

Cirtron spoke. "De lady bison have de horns, mon?"

Carson, snickering again, opened her eyes wide and said solemnly to Cirtron, "Well, yes, my dark friend. After all, don't lady people get horns sometimes?"

The rasta man opened his mouth to ask another question but Sheila got the pun and said, "Forget it, Cirtron, Carson is joking. Don't go there."

"Where would I go? I not be going t'anywhere."

Sheila was getting too tired to try to explain and Carson just smiled and said, "Tell you what, you two, let's have another beer and then I'm off to my place. I'll leave you alone and you can get some rest. God knows these old bones of mine need some too. I'll come see you tomorrow and show you where more things are out in the shed. If that's alright?"

"Sounds good. And thank you, by the way. I don't think I said that," replied Sheila.

"Irie," said Cirtron.

Beer tabs clicked, they drank and Sheila excused herself to walk the dogs, on leashes this time, out in the front. Dachshund noses were more interested in sniffing the evening air than in taking care of business, but things did get done and Redstripe, Paris and their mistress returned to the farmhouse. Inside, her second beer can empty, Carson said good night and left by the main door. Sheila and Cirtron could soon hear the hum of the golf cart fading as it followed the path to the old lady's place next door.

Thunder in the Grass

On the first morning that Sheila and Cirtron and the dogs rose from sleep in their new home, Sheila cooked breakfast. "Don't expect this will become a habit," she said to Cirtron. "I'm no morning cook and I don't get up early if I don't have to."

"No problem, mon," Cirtron answered. He studied the burnt toast and runny eggs on his plate. "I can cook d'next time. 'Like t'do so."

"Fair enough. Look, I'm going to go take a shower and then we can go out and check on the bison. Feed the ladies, would you?" Cirtron nodded and when Sheila left he scraped his breakfast in two portions into the dog dishes. Redstripe and Paris were very appreciative; dachshunds *never* waste people food and the sounds of slurps and dachshund grunts and the banging of dog bowls filled the kitchen. Under the circumstances, the two dogs were hoping that Sheila would cook breakfast often.

With breakfast finished, the hounds sated and Sheila cleaned up, it was time for the four new resident ranchers to go out back and meet the bison. Cirtron splashed some water from the kitchen faucet on his face, dried with a dish towel and Sheila, down from the upstairs bath, opened the rear door. The hounds darted out before either of the two humans had even set a foot over the threshold. Redstripe and Paris, a matched pair of furry brown blurs, catapulted themselves at grass-top level straight across the lawn separating the house from the pasture. The two stopped at the fence, noses extended through the wire mesh. Both were busy inhaling bison smells and stood rigid, aimed at the big animals. Dachshund chests were pumping like little bellows to power their snouts and Redstripe and Paris were ready for trouble. Trouble there would be. It usually comes when dachshunds are in the picture. Sheila and Cirtron caught up to the dogs.

"Cirtron! Grab the dogs!"

"No, problem, mon. Not t'get true de fence, mon. Irie."

"Well," said Sheila, "maybe. But I don't want them in there. They'll get hurt or flattened. Cirtron, you know the ladies. They'll go anywhere. Silly things."

"Ya, mon. Silly. Hah! Day ha' none of d'sense. Maybe put dem 'pon de leash?"

Sheila, worried, tried to think reasonably, "No, let's just see what they do. I think you're right. It would be tough for them to get through that wire fence. They wouldn't like to be tied so let's just keep an eye on them, ok? Redstripe! Paris! Get away from that fence! Those things in there would as soon stomp you as look at you!"

The dachshunds were not interested in advice and remained at the fence; long low bodies on the outside with noses sticking through to the inside. The smells could not be ignored and twin tails twitched in tandem. The dogs began to wuff and whine. *Bison! How cool is that?* they were thinking.

Sheila had her own thoughts. "Cirtron, what do we do here, do we feed them or what?"

"I tin we do de feed, mon, not d'what. Seems dere be de hay on de sides for de beasts, water in is de tanks, so we need t'trow it over de fence where d'beasts kin eat it, yes?"

"Sounds right to me, let's go lift some bales I guess. That fence looks pretty high to be tossing over, but we can try. I wonder were Carson is? She said she'd be over. Maybe she has a better idea. I suspect she does."

• Dachshunds in the Midwest •

"Ya, mon. Be it for now we toss, yes?"

Cirtron and Sheila made their way around the to the first pile of hay bales while Redstripe and Paris found a way to scramble under the fence and into the bison pasture.

The first pile of hay reached nearly to the top of the fence. Sheila and Cirtron climbed up on the stack and pushed the first couple of rectangular compacted bales over the fence and into the pasture. Some of the bison looked over and made their way to the forage. Sheila and Cirtron pushed four more bales over and in but the pile was getting lower and the bales were so heavy that the next was going to be a problem to lift and toss. Both of them were beginning to sweat from the effort. Three bison arrived to chew at the fresh chunks of hay. They began to eat the stuff, restraining twine and all.

Redstripe and Paris had moseyed across the pasture, moving slower and more cautiously than on the run from the house, and began to bark and howl and snort and do the backward dachshund dance at the first bison they came near. The big hairy bovine, the subject of their attention, was not amused. She turned her huge head sideways to get a look at the two little irritating canines and bellowed. Bison are herd animals. They seek protection as a group. While Redstripe and Paris were barking at the single bison the bellowing summoned her friends. They came quickly. And the weight on their hooves shook the ground in their haste to come to the support of their herd mate. The two humans on top the hale bales could feel the thumping of the bison through the ground and even up through the pile on which they were perched. Both of them look up, concerned.

Sheila spotted the dachshunds and screamed. The bison gathered in a tight group to confront the dogs. The bovine heads were

Another Redstripe, Please

lowered. They were not happy. Redstripe and Paris continued to slowly back but they did not know whether to stand their ground or run. *This was not in the plans*, they thought. Sheila was in a panic. "Cirtron! The dogs! Get the dogs!"

Cirtron did not hesitate. He leaped off the pile of hay bales and over the fence landing hard after the six foot drop and dropping to his knees. He recovered quickly and headed for the hounds but the first bison beat him in the race. She lowered her head even further, stomped forward toward the hounds and used her nose to give Paris a little push. Paris weighed in at about ten pounds. The bison tipped the scales at about a half ton. The bison won simply by the laws of physics and Paris was rolled over and over in the grass, a hair-covered tootsie roll without a wrapper. Redstripe figured this was time to exit and headed toward the edge of the pasture where Sheila was still screaming and waving her arms. Cirtron got to Paris and bent down to grab her, ignoring the bison.

"No! No! You dog, not to worry at the hairy cows, they will . . ."

It was too late. The bison, still aggravated, bumped Cirtron with his dachshund burden and sent both of them down and into the mud and grass of the pasture. Bison manure is supposed to be rather clean but some of it coated Cirtron and Paris as they lay there trying to catch their breath. The bison stopped. Perhaps it had had enough fun for the moment but it remained hovering a few feet away. The rest of the herd just stood by.

"Cirtron! GET OUT OF THERE!" Sheila had gone over the fence to retrieve Redstripe and was trying to climb back out to safety. "Cirtron! Get up! Get out of there!"

"Ya, mon," said Cirtron from his place in the mud and manure. "Be right dere, mon." He got up and made his way quickly to the fence, handed over Paris and climbed up and over to the pile of bales. "Maybe d'fence, n'work so well?"

Sheila did not answer at first, she only was checking on the two hounds. She found them sound and then turned to Cirtron. "You stink. And so do the dogs. What a mess."

"Ya, mon. De smell. But de dogs, day be okay. Irie."

Sheila immediately felt bad. "Oh, Cirtron, I'm sorry! I was so worried and scared. You saved Redstripe and Paris! How can I thank you?"

"Ah, no problem, mon, m'lady. I just go to wash. But now, maybe put d'dogs 'pon de leash?"

"Yes, mon," smiled Sheila. "I promise."

The hum of the golf cart slithered into Sheila's and Cirtron's awareness. They looked over to see Carson in the cart around the corner of the pasture. Even from a ways away, Carson could see that things were a bit amiss and that Cirtron and Paris were filthy.

"Hey! Good morning!" she shouted, "I told you not to try to pet the bison, didn't I?"

"We'll meet you in the kitchen," shouted Sheila. We've got some cleaning up to do and we have some questions about this hay."

Carson waved and turned the golf cart toward the house.

Cirtron and Sheila, each with a dog under an arm, made their way back to the house. Carson was already waiting in the kitchen. "My god, man," she said to Cirtron, "You really stink! Paris, is that Paris under all that goo? She won't get prizes for cleanliness either."

"Ya, mon. We go up for de bath. Irie."

While Carson and Sheila seated themselves at the table in the kitchen, Cirtron went up the stairs and to the bathtub. He filled it, undressed and plunked himself in right along with the two dogs. While Paris was the one that really needed the bath, he figured that it would do no harm to dunk Redstripe too. Once the three of them were soaped and scrubbed, the water looked pretty bad but most of the bison smells left down the drain. Afterward, two wet and indignant dachshunds shook themselves dry and scattered water all over the floor and walls. Cirtron dried off with a towel.

Redstripe and Paris were thinking, *What was that BATH all about? We hate water! And actually if anyone would have cared to ask us, we LIKED those smells.*

Cirtron looked down and said to them, "No more under de fence. Not safe for d'little dogs, ah?"

Redstripe and Paris, still miffed, just turned and left the bathroom. They gallumped down the stairs and climbed on a couch in the front room to pout for a while. The Jamaican just sighed, dressed and went down to join the women in the kitchen. He entered the room as Carson was talking.

" . . . so you see there's no reason to try to lift all that hay over the top. Oh, Cirtron! You're clean. Good. I was telling Sheila about the little bobcat machine in the shed. I'm sure the two of you can figure how to work it. It's got a set of spiney things on the front and you can use it to lift the bales over the fence and drop them in. You don't have to work so hard with the hay.

"Speaking of hay, now that the next crop has been cut, the feed company will deliver the big bales and dump them in the pasture in a day or so. I don't know if you've seen those things in the fields around here, they're big and round and better than six feet across. They've got these machines that cut and then roll the stuff into these huge wheels. That'll last the bison for a while and you can just watch and order more when you need it. You'll pay for it, of course. But then all you need to do is make sure the water troughs are full, there's a pump in the shed that pushes the water through underground pipes. You just make sure it always has power out there. Ok?"

"Ya, mon. I understand de ting."

Sheila said it sounded simple even though she had some doubts about lots of things after living through the last couple of days. As she spoke, two of the objects of her most serious concerns trotted into the kitchen. They approached the table and each gave a little bark.

"Cirtron?" asked Sheila, "You did feed them, didn't you?"

Cirtron answered, "Ya, mon. Day finished while you were in d'shower." He was hoping Sheila would not ask *what* they were fed. Dachshund meal times basically coincide with all of their waking hours so the two dogs stayed to pester down under the kitchen table. Carson grinned down at them and told them to be still.

The old lady began again, "Now then, the dogs. We can't have them crawling under that fence, although god knows how they did it, and hurting themselves or disturbing the herd. You're gonna have to do something about that and . . ."

Sheila interjected, "I know, I know. I just hate to see them tied. What do we do, build a big fence just for them?"

"Girlie, you've got to do something about that interrupting habit of yours. Let me finish. I think I know what you can do. Just listen."

Admonished, Sheila fell silent and sat back but she was wondering precisely who was supposed to running this place. She knew she needed Carson's help, but the woman was so commandeering. Cirtron, being Cirtron, knew when to be quiet and he did so. He was thinking more of what fun it might be to drive that bobcat around. Under the table, the two hounds sensed they were the subject of the conversation and went quiet. Ears were perked. Tails were still.

Carson continued. "Building a new fence would not be a bad idea. But I have a better one. What you need to do is install fencing on the *outside* of the pasture fencing. You need strong stuff with small openings in the mesh. Tack it on about three feet up and that should do it. But there is a trick. You see you need to dig that new fencing down into the ground. I'd say another two feet down should work and then the dogs can't dig under it. It's the same way we protect gardens so the rabbits and such can't in around here. The trick is to get that fencing deep in the ground where nothing can dig under. In this case, your doggies. Actually, some people dig a three foot trough and fill it with concrete and stick the fencing down into that. But this should work and the concrete is expensive. This isn't a set of vegetable gardens; this is a big area." Carson stopped and leaned back, smiling, proud of herself and her idea.

"Ya, mon. Lot's of work and maybe d'money too?"

Sheila broke her silence and said, "It doesn't matter. We have to do this. This morning was way too close for my nerves and if it isn't the dachshunds that get hurt, it will one of us chasing them like fools through a stampede. I can pay what is needed."

Carson had still another answer. "In this case, you don't have to worry. I happen to have a friend who installs fencing, has the materials and tools to do this quickly, and not charge a thing."

"What?" exclaimed Sheila. Cirtron was coolly interested and did not speak.

"Well, I can work it out. See, it just so happens this fencing friend is ready for a trade."

Trader Carson

Sheila and Cirtron had been hearing about this trading business for two days. This time Sheila was determined to press for an answer from Carson even though the woman had demurred several times before when asked. "Carson," demanded Sheila, "what is all this trading business? I've asked you two or three times and you said you'd explain later. I think it is later now, don't you?"

Carson exhaled slowly. "Yeah, I suppose you're right. But I think it is easier to show you than tell you. We need to take a little trip out the back of my place. Let's go climb in my go-cart and I'll take you there. You can take the doggies if you want."

"Fine. And they're dachshunds, not doggies." Sheila's impatience was beginning to bubble just a bit.

Carson shrugged, "Fine yourself, girlie, and bring the dachshunds. But leash 'em and don't let 'em loose. Come on then, you too, Cirtron, I think you'll like this."

The four left the house and boarded the little golf cart for another ride. Sheila sat in front this time and Cirtron took the back with the two hounds. Redstripe and Paris were ready for another adventure; noses sniffing and tails wagging. Undaunted that they'd nearly become bison stepping stones, they were hoping for more fun. *More cats? More of those hairy cows? Food? What's next?* Jaws opened, tongues dangled out, and they began to pant.

Carson drove the golf cart over the track that led between the two properties and then around the back of her house. Another worn, double-rutted path ran from the rear of her home and out to what was nearly two acres of corn growing in neat rows. The plants were not quite three feet tall, had not produced their distinctive silklike tassels yet, but they looked healthy and deeply green. Carson took the four of them out over the little path and pulled up just a few feet away from the field of corn. "Ok, you guys," directed Carson, "climb out and have a look."

"What are we looking at?" Sheila was confused. "It's just a bunch of corn for pete's sake. What do we do, build a fence out of corn stalks?" Sheila just stood there, staring at the corn rows wondering what nonsense she would hear next.

Carson took Sheila gently by one elbow. She said, in an uncharacteristically soft voice, "Honey, look closer, look between the rows. It's not the corn we came out here to see. Cirtron? You look too, you'll see it, I'm sure."

Sheila took a couple of steps forward and aimed her gaze between one the rows. Where she expected to see dirt, the lanes between the stalks seemed crowded with weeds. Cirtron took a closer look and just froze, his lower jaw dropped, threatening to take permanent residence, whiskers and all, in the middle of this chest.

Sheila said, "Yeah? So what? Somebody needs to get out here with a hoe or something. Or one of those machines that the farmers all have. Aren't you supposed to keep the rows clean of weeds so the corn grows better? What a mess!"

Cirtron broke out of his stupor, closed his mouth and began to grin. Before he could say anything he dropped with a hard sounding plop on the edge of the field, sitting with his elbows on his knees and his head in his hands. Sheila was alarmed. "Cirtron, are you alright? What's wrong? Did you get hurt out with those bison?" She was frightened and then maddened because Cirtron began to laugh.

Cirtron sat there, head in hands with chuckles coming out from the back of his throat, a hoarse sound, almost as if he was coughing. He raised his head, looked up and let go a loud peal of pure laughter that set the hounds to barking. Carson was trying to hold back giggles and that made Sheila even madder. She turned to the giggling old woman and shouted, "What is going on here?! What is so damn funny?!"

Carson continued to try to suppress her laughter, only squeaks and giggles escaping and said nothing. Her hand was clamped over her mouth. Cirtron rolled onto his side; still laughing so hard his breathing was coming into question. Redstripe and Paris barked and added to the din. Sheila looked again at the weeds, saw Cirtron laughing in the grass, glanced at Carson and some switch clicked closed in her brain.

"Oh . . . my . . . god!" Once more, she could hardly get words out. "Carson! *This* is what you trade with!"

Carson took a deep breath, calmed herself and said, "Yup, the corn isn't the real crop. The weeds are. You sort of couldn't see the forest for the trees, girlie, but I figured Cirtron would, him being from Jamaica and all that."

Sheila looked at the weeds, the corn, the old fat and dumpy woman who drove a golf cart and began to feel dizzy. She just could not grasp this, on top of the bison, and get it all into one coherent picture she could understand.

Carson saw this and said, "Tell you what, let's go back to my place and I will explain all this. It really is not that complicated. It's okay. Really. Come on, bring the dachshunds."

Sheila glanced over to where Cirtron had been laying and was about to tell him to get into the golf cart, but he was not there. She turned to the cornfield and saw him a few rows over, bent down,

Another Redstripe, Please

pulling at weeds and stuffing his pockets. "Dammit, Cirtron! Get out of there!"

"Sheila?" Carson said sternly. "Don't worry. He's welcome. There's plenty."

Cirtron, Sheila, Carson and the two dogs finally climbed back into the golf cart. In the back, Redstripe and Paris sniffed at Cirtron's pockets and then snorted and looked away. They were not interested. The little cart hummed its way back down the rutted path and then the five of them entered Carson's house. Sheila was completely distracted by what she had seen but did have a moment of clarity to look around inside. The place was obsessively neat with no clutter and the kitchen was immaculate. Carson noticed Sheila's glances and said, "Hey, you know? When you live alone, you have plenty of time for cleaning. Go make yourselves comfortable in the living room. I'll get some coffee." She pointed. "Its right through there." Sheila, Cirtron and the hounds made themselves comfortable on brocaded furniture with carved wooden legs kept company by end tables topped with doilies. The room was open through several windows to the morning light and everything was bright and smelled fresh. Anyone's grandmother could have occupied the place. Sheila's head was still spinning; the dogs had climbed into Cirtron's lap for a morning snooze. Cirtron absently patted his pockets. Carson came in with three mugs on a tray. The coffee was spiked with anise seed.

Carson seated herself and started talking after the mugs were handed around.

"Now then, first off, I suppose you're wondering: I don't use the stuff. Not much anyway unless my arthritis is kicking up. I use it to trade for things I need. Mr. Carson did not leave me much in the way of insurance or a pension and our dear government does not give me enough of that social security stuff to keep up the place. So I trade for the shortfalls like the roof and maintenance and all that. You'll get that dachshund deterrent fencing out of it. Fall is not that far away and most years I have the boys plow most of what is not used under anyway. Drives 'em nuts. Sheila, are you going to interrupt?"

Sheila just waved a hand and then put a finger to her lips. She was listening.

Carson said, "Good." And then continued.

"Here is how it all works. You should realize my grandfather was a judge in this county. My family, most of them gone now, all got to know all the politicians and the law folks and such, most just through social connections, but the ties stayed in place. You would be surprised about all the people in high places around this area that know me and I trade with. There's lawyers and bankers and county people and even people that work in good old Washington of the D and C. By the way I use that way of naming our capitol for a reason. Figure it out. Wanna interrupt, Sheila?"

"No."

"Good enough. So I trade with them all. But I never take money. Only service and materials like for your fencing. And those that are not one of the big folks are related or have made themselves useful with their votes or some such thing or another and they have nothing to fear if they get involved with a trade with me. They are all pretty much protected unless they get stupid and try to sell some stuff elsewhere, not for their own use. That has happened now and then and the results are always pretty sad. For me, I just have to make the field look nice, cosmetic I guess, so no one gets embarrassed. That's why the corn is there."

"I told you I made a trade to get the bank things for your uncle. That worked because the banker Tom Pederson's wife is suffering terribly from some sort of muscle disease. I don't understand it but I do know she would have put herself into her own grave a while back without my trading. The guy who is going to do your fencing is just trying to get his business going a little stronger. He will be able to say he did the work on the Armstead Ranch and use that to promote things. Besides, he'll have to do the work on a weekend and that will keep him out of Tilly's and his wife will be pleased. I think she uses a little of the trade herself. The fellows who did my roof and gutters still had to buy the supplies for the job. They paid for those and one of the local suppliers got the sale, See? I am really an underground community service. I add to the economy."

Carson paused so Sheila asked, "Don't you worry about that stuff out there in the back?"

"No. I don't. See, the people that trade with me are all over the county. I am pretty much the only game in town, so to speak, and I am honest and generous. I don't talk when I don't need to. If someone would go out there and steal, the rest of the traders would sort of take care of things if you know what I mean. I do worry that some animals get in there and get sick but you may have noticed that your doggies, the dachshunds, sorry, just turned up their noses. I don't worry too much. But one time, as a matter of fact, when old Armstead was moving the bison from one pasture to another, one of the bison got loose and wandered into the cornfield. It ate down a whole row of corn and munched up the weeds at the same time. Boy, I gotta tell you, that bison got such a case of loose stools it was dangerous. The stuff that was coming out beneath the tail of that beast was so strong and furious the stream could have knocked a cat off a fence post from six feet away. The animal got better but old Armstead was not too happy. I just told him to watch his gates."

During Carson's lecture, the dachshunds had become restless. Cirtron handed each down to the floor and they ambled over to Carson where she was seated in her chair. They pawed at her legs and Carson leaned down, grabbed each one in turn and placed them in her own lap. "I could get used to these little... what do you call them, ladies? They're cute." Then she settled back with the dachshunds in her lap and closed her eyes.

Sheila looked over at Cirtron. "I think she fell asleep. What should we do?"

"Ah, we go back to t'other house. Leave d'little dogs with her. Come back later and let dem all sleep a while. She be d'good lady, I tink."

"I suppose that's okay," Sheila was still in a state of slight disorientation. "I suppose you just want to go back and play with that bobcat, huh?"

"Ya, mon. Dat too."

The Wautoma Flute

Two months went by and life for Sheila, Cirtron and the hounds, with the help and support of Carson, settled into routine. Carson had "traded" for the extra fencing and there were no more bison-dachshund confrontations. Huge bales of hay in rolls had been delivered to pasture while Cirtron continued to move the smaller bales around with the bobcat. He always found an excuse to drive it out to the pastures if for no other reason than to just check on things. Redstripe and Paris were pretty much free to just wander about and sniff the grass and chase the fall butterflies or to make an occasional visit for shaking and smelling at the edge of the fencing for the bison. More evenings than not, the three humans shared dinner at one house or the other while the dachshunds begged scraps. With the group dinners and table scraps, the smelly old bison, the ability to wander about freely and the abundant gophers, the hounds found themselves in their own version of dachshund heaven; an endless vista of freedom, smells, fun and food.

One typical afternoon, the two dachshunds were lying in the shade of the back of the house, recovering from an almost-successful gopher hunt. They were tired. But a half hour snooze brought Redstripe up and into alert mode. She nosed Paris who was still sleeping with half closed eyes. *Paris, wake up! I see butterflies!* Paris stirred. *Go chase them yourself, I'm busy.* Paris went back to sleep. Redstripe wandered off to harass butterflies.

Carson had taken Cirtron into town on supply runs on many occasions and one of the first ones was to the "Coast to Coast Do-It-

Another Redstripe, Please

Best" hardware store. Sheila had directed Cirtron to buy some paint and cleaning things for the inside of the old farm house. Carson parked the golf cart outside the hardware store and told Cirtron she would wait for him.

The rasta man entered the store and approached the check out counter. "Ya, mon. I need d'paint and d'brushes and d'tings ta clean d'walls, mon." He'd addressed two men standing behind the counter. Each had a shirt with a name stitched above the pocket; one label read Kelly and one read Robert. Robert turned to Kelly.

"Go help this gentleman out. He needs paint and maybe some ammonia and maybe a box of Borax. Don't forget a paint tray and the brushes. Get him a bucket, too. And a scrub brush."

Kelly seemed affronted. "Why do I have to go? Are your feet painted on?"

The two men glared at each other. Cirtron held up a hand and said, "Ah, no need to have d'arguing. Jus tell me where t'go in d'store?"

Robert looked away from Kelly and then at Cirtron. "Oh, don't worry about it. We were just giving each other a hard time. It passes the day. We've had this store for nearly forty years and we need to have a little fun now and then. Here, come with me, we'll find your stuff." Robert led Cirtron toward the back of the store down and between rows of shelves crowded with nuts, bolts, tools, endless widgets and garden supplies and most things seen under the sun. He stopped at a row of shelves with cans of paint; a floor mounted mixer was bolted down nearby. "What color?"

"I tink d'white, she be okay."

"We've got clamshell white, eggshell white, frost white and, let me see, yes, we have glacier white and I believe some storm cloud white. What will it be?"

"No need for de clams or de eggs mon, just need d'white. Do ya' have d'white?"

Robert smiled. "Yup, it's called white. Let me grab two cans and then I don't have to mix nothin', just give you the base. You can always come back for more and we won't have to worry about matching it."

Cirtron said thank you. Robert led him out to the front and pointed to the other supplies for the rasta man. The pile of purchases was placed on the counter and Kelly rang it all up. Once the paint and supplies were bagged, both Kelly and Robert helped carry the things out to the golf cart and the waiting Carson. Kelly raised a hand. "'Lo, Ms. Carson, have a good day, hey?"

"I'll see what I can do with it, Kelly. You too."

Carson started the golf cart, Cirtron, paint and supplies on board, and headed back to the farm. Cirtron was thinking that he had not been insulted or teased even once. Kelly and Robert were nice guys.

The rest of that day, Cirtron spent his time cleaning the walls of the front room at the old farmhouse and painting with the white, not eggshell, not clamshell, not frost, just plain white. Redstripe and Paris naturally wanted to help and made sure they each had noses half covered with paint after investigating the roller pan. At the end of the after noon, the cleaning included the brushes, paint pan and dachshund noses. Carson arrived and announced that dinner would be at Tilly's that night. No cooking.

"It's on me," declared Carson.

Sheila said, "Oh, no, don't tell me this is another trade of yours, is it?"

"Nope," answered Carson. "Just got my social security check, we'll use real money. Respectable and all that. What a concept, huh?"

· *Another Redstripe, Please* ·

"Fair enough, then. But let's take the Camry. What does Tilly's have for dinner?"

Carson explained the soon to be divulged menu at Tilly's. "Well, you see, you're in Wisconsin here. They have what they call fish fry on Friday and today is Friday. Most places do a fish fry, some are better than others, but Tilly's is pretty nice. They've got slaw and potato pancakes and all that. Little lemon wedgies on the side. Good stuff.

Cirtron had a question. "Potato pancakes? How t'get de potatoes flat, mon?"

Redstripe and Paris had trotted in to where the humans were discussing dinner and knew they were hearing about food. *Ah, this sounds good. Fish, yeah. Slaw? Is that a vegetable? Not sure about that.*

Sheila had her own question. "What's this about a fish thing on a Friday? Is that some sort of local tradition, like clam digs or lobster boils or something? Where do they get fish around here big enough to eat anyway? Sounds a little odd."

Carson tried to answer both questions. "The potato pancakes, they grind 'em up and then fry them in little patty shapes. The fish comes in from other places, cod and haddock and all that, maybe a little perch from around here. But the Friday thing, that's a leftover from the Catholics. You'd have to live here a long while to understand it so, yes, I suppose it is a sort of local tradition. But the food, it's good. You'll like it. Get the ladies and we can take your car and go into town."

The trip to Tilly's was smooth. The air conditioning system in the Camry kept the humans and the dogs comfortable and no trucks or other vehicles on the road could throw stones in and upon the occupants. Sheila parked the car along the broken sidewalk in front of Tilly's and they all sauntered inside. Once the three were seated on the bar stools, the dachshunds let loose on the floor,

· *Dachshunds in the Midwest* ·

Carson called to Sue who was on duty for the dinner rush. "Three fish frys and three mugs, Sue. And something for the little ladies if you have anything. You'd better, or I'll let them loose on the bar top and they'll be sure to eat your patrol cat."

Sue reached for three mugs and began to fill them with beer from a tap. "Hey listen, Joe the cat can take care of himself. You watch he doesn't scratch those little dog's noses right off their little faces. Have I told you lately that you're impossible, Carson?"

Cats? Scratch US? No way. Let us at 'em! We'll get any cat around. Just tell us where it is. Cats are just disgusting. Yuck!

"Nope. You haven't. Have I told you lately that your burgers are better than a good laxative?"

Sue frowned a moment and then her face relaxed as she realized Carson was trying to get to her. She handed three beer filled mugs to Sheila, Cirtron and Carson in turn and replied. "No, Carson, you didn't tell me that. But that's a good thing to know as you are so full of it anyway. Nice to know we've been of some help."

Sheila tensed, waiting for some sort of outburst. Cirtron looked off in another direction. Sue and Carson were silent for just a second and then each laughed. "Sue?" said Carson, "You're all right, dear."

"So are you Carson. You're okay," Sue answered back.

Carson was not done. "Well, yes, I know that. I'm actually quite fine, thanks."

Sue laughed again, "Oh, enough! Shut up, you. I'll go and order up your fish. How about some bison jerky for the hounds? I'll get that myself."

From the floor, Redstripe was listening. *Jerky? That sounds a little dangerous.* Paris heard the offer as well but was thinking, *Bison? Yup, I could get into that.*

Cirtron, Sheila and Carson sipped their beers while the dachshunds craned their necks up to watch Joe the cat pad round and round the bar top. It was only a few minutes before the fish dinners arrived and Sue came out with two plates of bison jerky for the hounds. She placed them on the floor and the dogs each grabbed a strip in paws and jaws and began to chew. Above them, the humans dug into their own dinners. Carson watched Cirtron pick up a lemon wedge and bite into the entire fruit, gnawing it and peeling the rind off and away from his teeth.

"Cirtron!" admonished Carson. "You're supposed to squeeze that on the fish."

Sheila just held her hand to her eyes.

Cirtron said, "Ah, ya, mon. Not so as sweet as does back home."

As the dachshunds chewed and the three humans worked on their own plates, Sheila looked up and across the bar to notice the two men, again, with the baseball caps that had teased Cirtron during the last visit to Tilly's. They were snickering and pointing once more over the pizzas they had in front of them. They were not loud about it and had not yet made a nuisance of themselves, but Sheila worried about what might come. She decided to stem things quickly and said so to Cirtron and Carson.

Cirtron, the permanent pacifist, urged her to stay still. Carson told her to go ahead and knock herself out. Sue saw what was about to happen and leaned back, arms crossed, ready to be entertained. Sheila, once more, made her way around the bar and approached the two men.

"Hey. Remember me? I thought I'd come over and tell you I was sorry to give you a hard time about that belt buckle. I'm sure you understand I was just sticking up for my friend."

The first man looked up and said, "Uh yeah, that's okay. We didn't mean anything anyway. No harm, no foul, you know?"

The second man was quiet. He was worried about what might be coming.

"Well, anyway," said Sheila, "maybe you could give me your phone number? Would that be all right?"

"Oh! Yes! I can do that! Sue? Give me something to write with, would you?" Sue was quick to supply a pen and a clean napkin and the first man carefully wrote some numbers down and handed the paper to Sheila. "There you are. I hope to hear from you!"

"Oh, I'm sorry. Maybe I didn't explain. You probably won't. Not directly. I thought I'd give your wife a call. I'm new here and am always looking for friends. But I'll be glad to tell her you were so nice to give me the number. Thank you so much." Sheila turned away and returned to Cirtron and Carson.

The second man, Sue the bartender and most of the other patrons in the bar erupted in laughter at the expense of the first man. Those that had not heard the exchange looked over and wondered what all the excitement was about. Redstripe and Paris began to bark, temporarily ignoring the bison jerky, and Carson was smiling. Joe the cat paused in his rounds. Cirtron gazed down at his potato pancake and wondered again how it had become flat.

Carson, wiping laughing tears from her eyes, told Sheila, "Honey, that was pretty good. I'm impressed. But you might want to go stick some money in that music maker over there and maybe take some of the pressure off. A little music always helps." Carson pointed at the machine holding CD's at the end of the room.

"Good enough, good idea." Sheila pulled a pair of dollar bills from a pocket and walked over to the player. Most the titles listed on the display were country western or light rock but she found a selection by Loggins and Messina called "The House at Pooh Corner." She let the machine suck in her bill and punched in the numbers on a pad. The lilting music filled the bar but it quickly became obvious that the other patrons were not impressed by the selection. People frowned and murmured as Sheila returned to her seat.

Cirtron noticed all of this and put a hand on Sheila's arm. "I can make dis better, mon. Here." He reached into a deep pocket of his pants and pulled out a wooden flute. Sheila had never seen it before. It was beautiful. A simple long hollow cylinder of wood with eight holes on top and two underneath, it had no apparent mouth piece. Both ends were open but a notch near one end was there to split blown air apart to make sound. The wood was multi grained with dark streaks like mahogany and lighter ones like teak. It appeared polished.

Sheila was awed. Carson leaned over to look. Sheila whispered, "What is that? Where did you get it? What are you going to do?"

"Be it my flute, m'lady. Made it in d'mountains. It be of d'wood of the hart of a tree called lignum vitae. It means d'wood of life, mon. Very good. Heavy and strong. Carves well, like iron but can be cut wid d'knife. I will play it, ok?"

Sheila could not find words but Carson said, "Play away there, Cirtron. Let's hear it."

Cirtron held one end of the flute to his lips and began to play. He used his fingers deftly over the holes to match exactly along with the music playing on the CD. The crowd in the bar, even the two men with the baseball caps, fell silent and listened. Cirtron's notes followed the tune precisely and when the CD track ended, he repeated the melody, only his flute making any sound in the room. Sheila was certain she saw his music carving clear notes in the smoke near the ceiling of the bar.

Cirtron finished, Redstripe and Paris began to howl from their spots on the floor and the room burst into the sound of applause. Cirtron pressed his palm to his head and then dropped his hand down, still open, as a salute and recognition. Sheila was stupefied.

Carson looked at Cirtron and said, "My, that was awfully good. But the dogs? I don't think they're gonna get first chairs in the woodwinds at the symphony orchestra."

Us? Don't sell us short, there. We can howl with the best, you know.

Nobody in town ever teased Cirtron again.

Wedding at Webb's

THE REMAINS of a bison roast that had been carved into thin slices lay on an oval plate. The meat was surrounded by a few unclaimed boiled potatoes and lonely fried carrots. Cirtron, Sheila and Carson were drinking the anise-laced coffee after their dinners while Redstripe and Paris busied themselves tongue-polishing their own dinner bowls now empty of dog chow that had been soaked in roast bison juices. The dog bowls clinked as little tongues lapped around them there in the kitchen of the Armstead Farm.

Carson placed her coffee mug on the table and wrapped both of her hands around it. She glanced over at Sheila and said "Say, girlie, 'mind cleaning up for us all tonight?" Carson did not wait for an answer before she continued, swiveling her head around to look at Cirtron. "Cirtron, ah, you know what? I should really show you how to work the frost plugs on the water supply lines for the drinking tanks in the pastures. If I don't do it now, I'll forget about it and come the first freeze, you'll have a problem. Come along, the plugs are in the shed."

Carson pushed her chair back, rose, and walked out the back door. Cirtron looked at Sheila, shrugged and followed the old woman out leaving an annoyed Sheila sitting among the soiled dishes while the two dachshunds looked up from the floor anticipating exercising their rights to help clean the supper plates.

In the back yard, Carson stopped and said to Cirtron, "Listen, forget the shed for now. I made that up. 'Just wanted to talk with you for a bit. And I think we'll need this." She pulled a small pipe, stuffed with trade, from a pocket and lit it with a butane lighter plucked out from the same spot. Placing it to her lips, she dragged on it briefly and while exhaling slowly handed it over to Cirtron. "Ah, then. That's better."

Cirtron took the pipe, inhaled and then, as he breathed back out said, "De talk, mon? Whad to be t'talk 'bout?"

"Cirtron, I'm not a person that usually interferes. Let it all be, that's me."

Cirtron doubted this but did not reply. He just sucked on the pipe again and handed it back.

"Ok," Carson went on, "here's the deal. If you haven't noticed it, your lady Sheila loves you." She held up a hand as if to stop traffic when Cirtron's eyes widened. "What you really need to do here is marry her and turn this double set of people and pups into a real family. It's a simple idea, really, Cirtron. But I wasn't so sure you were going to click on it yourself. So I'm here telling you. Understand?"

"Ah, mon. Not s'sure dis be de good thought. Dinna know 'bout it. Maybe I think 'pon dis."

"Well you *should* know about it and by all means, yes, you should, as you say, think upon it. Cirtron, if the whole idea got any closer to you, it'd bite you on the nose. And I'll tell you what; if you don't bring it up to Sheila, I will. So there you have it. Here," she handed the pipe back to Cirtron, "have a little more of that and just think it through." Carson turned and walked back to the house leaving Cirtron with the pipe and his thoughts.

Back in the kitchen, Sheila was finishing with washing, rinsing and drying the dishes. The hounds, sated finally, had headed for comfortable furniture in the front room. As Carson came back in, Sheila asked, "Did you get those pipe things taken care of with Cirtron?"

"I think so. He'll be back in a bit. I suppose we'll see if he really understood a little later on. I explained things as best I could. Tell you what, pour us some more coffee and let's go into the front room and I'll explain it all to you too."

THERE HAD BEEN a little bit of discussion about the clothing Cirtron and Sheila should wear at their wedding at Little Hills Lake. In the end, things were simple. Carson took Sheila up into the attic in the Carson farm house and pointed the tall blond to an old chest full of clothes. The two of them chose a long white muslin gown with wide, cuffed sleeves that smelled a bit of dust and mothballs. When Sheila tried it on she remarked that she felt a little bit like Shakespeare's Juliet. Carson commented that Cirtron did not look much like Romeo, but he would do and that Sheila looked just fine. The chest may have dated back to the Civil War and likely would have brought a better price at an antique shop than the entire contents.

Cirtron would choose sandals, a flowered shirt from home and a pair of long and stiff cotton pants he had found at the local hardware store. They were really painter's pants with big pouches and straps for tools, but they were clean and bright. Carson would weave wild flowers into wreaths for them both and that would complete the outfits. The trader planned on a sacky looking knee length cream colored smock and would wear her usual Nike running shoes. Her dress likely had started its life colored snow white but had aged to the darker shade over time. But it was one of the best things she had.

The dogs presented a more complex problem. Dachshunds do not dress up in their finest church- and go-to-meeting clothes with any cooperation. But a simple set of daisies, woven by Carson

· Another Redstripe, Please ·

into collars for the hounds and barely to be noticed by the little prospective witnesses, would do just fine, thank you very much.

Previous to all of this wardrobe planning, one evening found all three of the humans at the kitchen table in the house on the Armstead Farm. It was just after dinner and the dachshunds were busy licking the remains of people dinner off of the plates that had been put down for them. Sheila was asking questions.

"Okay, if we are going to go through with this, there's some things we need to get straight. Where are we going to do this? Can we use some church around here? I suppose we'll need a minister and then there has to be some legal paperwork and all of that."

Carson had answers. "Camp Webb, Father Champaign, and I'll have one of my lawyer friends take care of the license and all that. Piece of cake."

Sheila was not convinced. "Camp Webb? Who is this Father Champaign guy? What about a marriage license, don't we need that?" The dachshunds continued to lick down below.

Carson sighed and Cirtron remained quiet. "Listen," said Carson, "Here's how it'll work. Camp Webb is a church camp on Little Hills Lake. The place is run by the Episcopal Church and it's over on that lake. Kids come up for the summer and they live in little cabins and get to swim, ride horses, make stuff and sail and canoe. They have a great time and come from all over, even as far away as Chicago. Father Champaign runs the place. They call him Father Champ. He'll be glad to do the ceremony, he owes me a favor anyway, and I know all the camp kids would be thrilled to be around for the festivities." The hounds had pretty much licked the dinner plates clean and Redstripe was pawing at Cirtron's leg and Paris was nosing against Sheila's. Out of habit, the two dogs were lifted up unto two laps.

Cirtron, holding Redstripe asked, "Dis man, de Father Champ? He owes d'favor mon?"

Sheila, holding Paris, opened her mouth to ask another question but Carson beat her to it. "Oh sure, Father Champ has been trading with me for years."

"Ya, mon, irie," replied Cirtron.

"Carson, I just give up," said Sheila.

Carson simply smiled and said, "Cirtron, how about you plan something to play on that flute of yours. I think that would be nice."

The next few days were filled as usual with the engine noises from the bobcat as Cirtron drove it around, more than really needed, and used it to lift the remaining hale bales up and over the fence for the bison. It really was not necessary as the big hay rounds had been delivered and the bison were chewing on those big wheels. But Cirtron did enjoy the bobcat. Carson had obtained the needed paperwork for the wedding, only the witness signatures were missing and of course Cirtron and Sheila would have to sign as well just after the ceremony planned at Camp Webb. At the end of the next week, on a late afternoon, Sheila, Cirtron and Carson dressed in their wedding day clothes and climbed into the Camry with the dachshunds for the short trip down the road to the camp.

At the camp they were met by Father Champ. He wore his black priest's shirt with the little bit of white showing out from his collar, black shorts and sandals. His hair was cropped short and close to his skull and a wide smile balanced a set of aviator sunglasses that covered his eyes above. He was tall. Very. "Hi! How are you Carson? This must be Sheila and Cirtron? Peace be with you all." He shook hands all around. The campers had gathered already, kids of the ages of eight to eighteen and looked on at the arriving wedding party. They pointed and whispered among themselves and a few of the older girls took a long look at Cirtron. A few older boys were staring at Sheila. Two of the younger girls approached and one handed Sheila a bouquet of wild flowers, the stems bound together with rough string, and the other reached up and placed a daisy in Cirtron's shirt pocket.

Once the hounds were lifted from the car and down onto the pine needle covered ground, Father Champ directed everyone over to the nearby amphitheater. It was simply a cleared circular area, the edges defined by rocks, and furnished with wooden benches. The campers seated themselves on the benches and Father Champ brought Cirtron, Sheila and Carson to the front. Redstripe and Paris, necks circled with their daisy chains, trotted along beside. *Lot's of people to play with here; maybe some have food.* Dachshund noses tested the air.

Hands placed on their shoulders, Father Champ gently turned Sheila and Cirtron to face the little crowd of campers. Carson turned as well and Champ stood towering at least a head over Cirtron and Sheila, two heads over Carson, and addressed the crowd. "God's afternoon, everyone!"

"God's afternoon," the campers recited back in unison.

"Ya, mon," said Cirtron.

"Hi there," said Sheila.

The priest called out to two of the older kids in the crowd. "Marylynn, Mike. You two come up, you can be witnesses and hold the two dogs, okay?" The teenagers rose, went forward and bent down to grab the hounds. *Ah, what's this? We were busy smelling things.* With Cirtron and Sheila in the middle, the two campers each on one side, dogs in arms and Carson standing as the matron of honor, Father Champ said quietly to Cirtron and Sheila, "You ready?"

· *Dachshunds in the Midwest* ·

"Ya, mon."

"Hi there," Sheila flushed a little, "I mean..yes."

Father Champ began. "We have been honored today to be able bear witness under God's eyes the joining of two into one. As we have all come to be here from different places, holding different ideas and dreams, so have these two people done. They seek to go forward, not as two different people, but as a pair bonded by trust and aspiring to live in concert under God. And also under *Ga*, as I understand it. Ask that they be blessed."

"Be blessed!" repeated the group.

Father Champ turned to Cirtron, "I believe we have some music?" Cirtron nodded, pulled his flute from his pocket, held it up to his lips and began to play. The notes began to be heard, they were slow to leave the flute and began to fly upward through the trees, butterflies in motion and rising toward light. It was a moment before Sheila recognized the melody but she did. It was an old song from the sixties. Where Cirtron had found it she had no idea, but Cirtron's wooden instrument was breathing out the song, "A Whiter Shade of Pale." The piece itself held little interest to the campers, they were too young to know of it even though they were fascinated with Cirtron's skill. But Sheila and Carson had to wipe at the corners of their eyes. Cirtron ended his performance with a long, low last note. The entire group stood awestruck and silent.

"All right, then," said Father Champ. "Everyone sit down, not you," he grinned at the wedding party, "let's go on." He had no paper, book or copied verse, he just began to speak. "Marriage is called a sacrament. It is a present from God, one that lets us be bound together in pairs, man and woman, and travel forward in life in such a way as to share the best of each other with one another. Over time, we also have the responsibility to take that sharing, that strengthening, and pass it on to others. This is what Cirtron and Sheila, Sheila and Cirtron, are promising today under the eyes of God and Ga. Yet this joining, this partnership, should never diminish the single spirit of either. A man and woman, a woman and man, should be like trees growing in the sunlight. They must thrive, bear their fruit, shelter those below them on the ground, but never allow one shadow to cast upon the other. Both are equal. But in the case of a strong wind, one shelters the other depending upon from which direction the storms come. So, Sheila, Cirtron, do you understand and make these promises?"

"Ya, mon."

"Yes, I do."

"Excellent," said Champ. "Do you have rings?" Cirtron and Sheila looked at each other and Sheila said, "Uh, no. We never thought of it."

Carson chimed in, "Well, I did. Here, she reached into a pocket and then held out two gold rings on her palm. These were mine and Mr. Carson's. You two should have them."

"Carson? No, we can't do that," Sheila protested.

"Yes you can, what am I gonna do with the darn things, anyway?"

Without speaking, Sheila took the rings, placed one on her finger and one on Cirtron's. He looked down at his hand and said, "I tank you, Carson."

"Now you are married," pronounced Champ, "Most people kiss about now."

Sheila and Cirtron kissed, the crowd of campers clapped and the two hounds, still bound in the arms of Marylynn and Micheal were thinking, *What in the world was THAT all about?*

Sheila and Cirtron stepped back from each other as the clapping faded away. Sheila said, "Uh, now what? Are we done?"

Father Champ laughed and said, "We are just about finished, yes. But we have go to over to the camp office and have you sign some papers. Marylynn and Micheal, you come too; you're going to sign as witnesses. Bring the dogs." He turned to Carson. "As the orchestrator of this marriage, we need you to sign as well so come along now." Champ took Carson by the arm and led the way out of the amphitheater and toward the office. The rest followed behind.

Half way down the path to the camp office, a few steps ahead of Cirtron and Sheila and the two hound bearing campers, Champ leaned over and whispered into the older lady's ear. "Say, Carson? About the trade?"

Looking straight ahead, Carson whispered back, "Hold your peace, Champaign, it's in the car. You know I keep my promises so just be still about it. Didn't they teach you patience at the seminary?"

"Oh, yes. I'm sure." Father Champ straitened up and, turning his head back over his shoulder said to the rest of the group, he proclaimed, "Isn't it a great day for a wedding?"

Inside the office, Father Champ directed the dogs be deposited on the floor and then directed the humans to a desk. He indicated papers and lines for signatures and explained who would need to sign where. Everyone signed as shown by Champ and he ended the process with a signature of his own. He bound up all the papers in a cardboard envelope and handed it to Cirtron. The outside had been pre-printed in black marker with "CIRTRON/ARMSTEAD" and the day's date. The father congratulated Cirtron with a handshake and Sheila with a kiss. "Go in god's peace and in Ga's."

Marylynn and Micheal were watching Redstripe and Paris devour one another's daisy chain collars. *Not bad for vegetables*, thought the dogs.

Carson spoke up. "Ok, I see the dogs have had their salads already so it's time for dinner for the rest of us. I'm taking Cirtron and Sheila to the Silver Bull. Father Champ, I'd be pleased to have you join us. Marylynn, Michael, care to join the party?"

Marylynn answered, "No, thank you very much, Mrs. Carson. We'd better stay here and we can keep the dogs if you want. They're cute and we can get them some of their own dinner. It'll be fun. Do they like hot dogs?"

Carson said, "I'm quite certain they'll suffer through. Thanks a lot."

The party arrived (the bride had to drive again) at the Silver Bull, Carson's choice for the post wedding dinner. Standing in the parking lot, Cirtron regarded the namesake symbol of the place with an open mouth. Facing the road to attract business, the hindquarters aimed at the front doors of the dining establishment, was a large bull constructed from clear, glass-like fiberglass. From inside of the creation, red lights lit the eyes of the bull and the body of the twelve foot long structure showed off white interior light like a transparent full moon. The clever creation looked indeed like a glowing silver bull; horns included. Cirtron recovered from his surprise, closed his mouth politely and then said, "Ya, mon, De big cow, de male, no? If we have such on de island, would not need de candles, lights or lanterns after de sun she sets. Pretty. But, maybe day may have de bison here as well."

Carson chuckled and said, "Don't worry about it, Cirtron. It's just an advertising thing and actually, I don't think the Silver Bull would put bison on the menu. It would upset the tourists." She took Sheila and Cirtron each by an elbow and directed them toward the front doors of the restaurant. "You coming, Champaign?" she asked the father. "Or are we all going to stand in this parking lot and get hungrier?" Father Champ trotted along obediently behind Carson and the two newlyweds.

Once all four were seated at the table that Carson had reserved, their waiter for the evening approached, identified himself as Alan, and proceeded to shake out the linen napkins from the table setting onto everyone's lap. Father Champ accepted the ministrations as did Shiela and Carson, but Cirtron grabbed the napkin and said, "Not to need d'help, mon. I can do it m'self. Irie."

"Very well, sir," said Alan. And then he handed a of menu to each that were expensive looking and nearly eighteen inches tall. "May I bring you a cocktail? A drink? While you look at the menu?"

Carson was the one to answer. "Alan, you can bring us a bottle of champagne. And four glasses. Keep an eye on the bottle and bring another when that one is gone. We're celebrating a wedding here, so make it nice, can you do that?"

"Ah yes, and congratulations to . . . ?" He looked at Father Champ, Carson, Sheila and Cirtron and did not know which were the bride and groom.

"Those two," said Carson pointing, "They just were married today."

"Ah, yes. My best wishes. This is wonderful. I'll bring the wine and then maybe you will be ready to order. No hurry. Please be at your leisure."

As Alan walked off Sheila leaned over to Carson and said quietly, "Carson, this place is very impressive, just great. I mean the linens and the sliver and all; it looks like a high class place back in New York." Sheila turned around and about to eye the brocaded wallpaper, the little lights installed at the top of the walls and the dark and perfectly polished woodwork that decorated the dining room. "But this is just too much. You shouldn't have done this!"

· Another Redstripe, Please ·

Sheila was not completely surprised, probably not surprised at all, when Carson told her, "Don't worry about it, I made a trade."

Before Sheila could say anything, Alan arrived with the champagne and four glasses. He filled them for each and said he would be right back for orders. It was Cirtron who made the first toast. He held his glass up and motioned for his new wife and the minister and their friend to do the same. "Hold on de glasses, m'friends and loves. I do remember today what de father has said 'bout de trees and shadows and storms and winds, mon. So it be for Sheila and me and all t'others so as Ga decides."

After that toast and a refill, the bottle was pretty much gone by the time Alan got back to take orders. Sheila recklessly ordered lobster, Carson asked for steak, and Father Champ politely asked for broiled chicken. Cirtron could not decide and requested chicken, steak and lobster. He ate every bit.

A second bottle of champagne was drained, accompanied by other toasts, and the wedding party toddled out of the Silver Bull over and to the car in the lot. No bill had been brought to the table. Carson had seen to all of that ahead of time. Sheila drove the car back to Camp Webb, dropped off the good Father Champ, and Marylynn and Michael brought out the hot dog saturated hounds to the car. Little dachshund bellies could be seen to be just a bit larger than usual. By the time that Cirtron, Carson and Sheila got back to the Armstead farm and Carson's place, everyone was pretty tired. Carson made her way back to her place and Sheila, Cirtron and Redstripe and Paris, climbed up the stairs to find the bed. Cirtron, who was not accustomed to champagne of any sort, plopped dead center in the middle of the bed. Redstripe and Paris clambered up, with help, and took positions one on each side of Cirtron. When Sheila came into the room, Cirtron lifted his head and said, "Ah, so sorry, m'lady. Dinna mean t'take the middle of de bed, mon. De dogs . . .

It was dark. The hounds were nearly asleep. Even dachshunds can have too much camp food. Sheila said, "You just stay right where you are, Cirtron, don't move. I have plans for you."

Redstripe and Paris woke from their dozing and peered up. *Can we help with something?*

Interlude on the Porch

CIRTRON WAS SITTING on the front porch boards of the house at the Armstead farm. It was nearly dusk, that time of day when the air is stilled and the world waits for the coming darkness. Cirtron could still see the highway at the end of the farm's driveway as he sat. Redstripe was in his lap, a little hound with her head on one of his knees while his legs cradled the little dog comfortably. Redstripe sighed and Cirtron did the same. The sighs had different meanings. Redstripe's was contented. Cirtron's was sad. Sheila came out from the house and onto the porch to see what was up. Paris followed out and began to nose at Redstripe for a spot on Cirtron's lap.

"What are you doing out here?" Sheila asked. Paris found a spot in which to curl along side Redstripe. Cirtron did not answer.

"The three of you are going to get cold out here. Why don't you bring the dogs in with you and we can watch some television or something. Wisconsin is not much different than New York and I can tell you it will be cold out here soon at this time of the year. It's not Jamaica, you know."

"Ya, mon. Is not Jamaica, no."

"C'mon Cirtron, come inside," Sheila urged.

"Ah, I dun know 'bout it, just want t'tink a bit here."

"You miss the island, don't you?" asked Sheila.

"Ya, mon. Be dat true. I tink 'pon dat a great deal while de days go on."

"I'll tell you what, Cirtron, I know Carson would watch after the bison and dogs for a bit. Flights to Jamaica at this time are probably tough to find. How does Hawaii sound for a few days? It would be warm..."

The two dachshunds raised their heads. *Don't you think we are gonna stay here while you two go gallivanting around, you know. We know quite very well how to travel as you should remember. Don't even think about leaving us here with those big hairy things out back!*

Cirtron had his own answer. "No, mon, Hawaii. Is not so good as you see. Takes a lot of de money and de people not so happy as de television says. No."

"Cirtron, are you homesick?"

"Homesick? No mon, no home can give you de sickness. Just miss de island and all dat. De people here, day be different, nice people, but not as so. And de Sun, she not be so warm."

Sheila did not quite know what to say. She simply patted Cirtron on the shoulder, leaned down to kiss his head and said, "Look, I'll get you a blanket for out here and you just stay and think as long as you want. Should I take the dogs in?"

"Ya, mon. De blanket. But de little dogs can stay wid me, mon. Day jus wanna sleep.

"Good enough, Cirtron, I'll get a blanket. Maybe we can talk about all this later, alright?"

"Irie."

Doctor Aspin and Solutions

It was only two weeks after Cirtron and Sheila were married, had created a reasonably official family of two hounds and two humans, when there was a rapid knock on the front door of the house on the Armstead farm in the morning, way before coffee had even been brewed. Redstripe and Paris leaped from their covers on the bed upstairs and rushed down to sound the bark alarm and guard the door. Sheila heard the noises and rose to amble down in her rumpled nightclothes; eyes coated with the excretions of sleep, and opened the door.

"Can I help you? It's awfully early, what is it?"

Redstripe and Paris barked at and threatened a man standing outside the door. He had fresh jeans on and a work shirt. His feet were clad in rubber boots. He appeared to be a young person, slender, but his head of thick hair was nearly white; his complexion very pale. "Hi there!" he said. "I'm Doctor Aspin. I'm here to check on your bison. I can just go around the back but I wanted to let you know I was here."

Sheila, trying to muddle through the leftover numbness of a deep sleep, looked out in the front yard to see a pick up truck parked in the drive. "ASPIN VETERINARY" was painted on the driver's door. "Oh. Well. Yes. Please go ahead. We'll be out in a second after we get dressed." Redstripe and Paris, nudging at the door, continued to bark and scuff. "Would you two cool it!?" Sheila shouted down, "Settle, would you?"

The vet returned, "Hey, are those dachshunds? I wouldn't worry about them; they're fine, doing what they're supposed to. Did you know they were specifically bred for loud barks so that they could be heard when they dig through tunnels?"

"No, I didn't know that, but I'll tell you, with these two, I wouldn't mind putting them down in a tunnel now and then."

The doctor laughed and said, "Good enough, I'll see you out back." Redstripe and Paris gave loose a couple of indignant snorts. *Tunnels? We are not interested in tunnels. What we are interested in is breakfast!*

Sheila climbed back up the stairway, rousted Cirtron out of the bed and told him a vet was there to check on the bison, "We should go out and see what's up." Once dressed and out the back door, the two of them saw the vet inside the fencing and toeing around with the bison droppings. He scooped some samples into little plastic jars. The ever-present Carson was on her way over down the double rutted path in her golf cart. She stopped at the edge of the fencing and called out, "Hey Mike!"

The vet looked over and waved back. "I'm just here to check on things, just met the new owners!" He quit playing with the droppings and strode over to the edge of the pasture, the bison ignoring him, and climbed over and out. Redstripe and Paris approached slowly and snuffled at his rubber boots. "Things look all fine," he said to the assembled crew while looking down at the hounds.

Sheila and Cirtron, Carson at the side, stood in front of the doctor. Sheila asked, "How can you tell?"

The vet explained as he reached down to pat at the hounds. "In the case of bison, it's rather simple. You really can't do much with them anyway. Generally they don't need the injections and other treatments like dairy cows or beef cattle or horses. And it is pretty difficult to treat them. They are so primitive. Even getting them into a trailer is tough, their skulls are so thick and strong, they can dent the inside of a horse trailer like a tornado inside a can of tuna. What I do, unless I see lesions or cuts on them somewhere that warrants an antibiotic, is to check their dung. If it's pretty dry and there aren't any creepy crawlies in it, things are probably okay. It looks like your herd is fine today." He shook off some bison dung that had clung to a boot and the dachshunds pursued it to where it landed in the grass. They gave a new definition for the term "brown nosing."

Cirtron asked, "You take de care of de animals all 'round den?"

Aspin answered, "Yes, the big ones are my specialty. I take care of my clients' horses and cows and, of course, your bison. I like the big ones. It used to be that I shared a practice in a little town called Hartland with my brother. He's a vet too. But I came up here to work with the larger animals and left my brother to deal with all the cats and dogs that the rich people down there would bring in. It has worked out for both of us."

Cirtron nodded. "Ya, mon. You do de big ones, and your brother, he do de small, like de dachshunds?"

"Yes," replied Aspin. "That's pretty much it, although I treat the occasional cat or dog if someone needs me too and can't find another vet. Once, as an example, there was this guy who came in. His cat had gotten into his tackle box and got a fishing lure stuck in the skin around its mouth. The guy put the poor cat in his lap and drove over to see me, but by the time he got to my office, the cat had wriggled around, got the lure that stuck in its face stuck to its paw and then stuck again right into the poor fellow's groin. You had to see it. This man comes in with a cat stuck in his lap. The cat's howling and the guy can't stand up straight. I few snips with pliers took care of it all but that was something."

While Sheila laughed, the dachshunds looked up. *Cats? What's this again about cats?* Cirtron had walked away and took up a position down the fence line and just gazed out at the herd, his arms folded against his chest.

Carson said, "Mike, you keep telling that cat lure story. Aren't you going to get any new ones?" The dachshunds had approached Aspin again at ankle level and used noses to show their fascination with the clods still stuck the to veterinarians boots. Before the man could protest, Carson said to Sheila, "Hey, what's with Cirtron this morning? He off his feed or something?"

Sheila glanced over at her Jamaican husband and said, "No, well maybe. I think he's homesick."

"Homesick?" asked Mike Aspin, "Where is he from?"

"Jamaica, he's a rastamafarian," offered Sheila.

"I know that place; it's in Illinois, right? I've been there I think. Rastamafarian? I remember a pizza place with that name there," said the vet.

"Mike," Carson told him, "you are an unmitigated fool. Jamaica is in the Caribbean south of Cuba and a rastamafarian is someone who holds to certain beliefs. It has nothing to do with pizza. I think you really ought to stick with groping cows, I really do. You'll never make it as a travel agent. Sheila, let's go inside and talk about this homesick thing over some coffee. Mike? If you promise not to tell more stupid stories, you can come along too." Carson headed for the house, Mike and Sheila following behind, and the dachshunds trotted over to keep the brooding Cirtron company. They were thinking that *Cirtron could use a good lick on the nose, or maybe some dog cookies. Or maybe he should just go and bite a cat, yeah, that would be good. There is nothing like biting a cat to improve your point of view!*

Over coffee and while Mike Aspin was preparing a bill for his service to the bison, Carson listened to Sheila explain that Cirtron had told her he was not as happy as could be living on the bison farm and in the little town of Wautoma. Sheila tapped her fingers on the side of her coffee cup while Carson rendered an opinion. "You have to go to Jamaica, girlie. That's just it. Stay here and Cirtron is just going to get buried in resentment. Besides, you like Jamaica, don't you?"

Sheila had doubts. "I do, I really do. I'd love to go back there, but the farm and the dachshunds and all that; I can't see a way to get that all taken care of and just leave. Dr. Aspin? I know it is a problem to take dogs to a foreign country, but do you know of a way to make that happen? I can't possibly leave them here. They're family. And what about the bison?"

The vet answered, pushing the bison dropping samples he'd brought in to one side. "What you need to do is get the right forms filled out and filed, I can do that, and the little hounds would be probably placed in quarantine for a while. It's a tough thing. I don't know about Jamaica, but it could be as much as four weeks or more. There are some exceptions for show animals and all of that, but I am pretty sure that is what you would be looking at if you want to take the dogs. As far as the bison are concerned, there are a couple of other ranches in the state that would be more than happy to buy them from you. That part is easy."

"Mike?" asked Carson, "isn't there another way for the dogs?"

"No," said the vet, "unless you are some high and mighty movie star or some big politician, the rules always apply about transporting dogs from one country to another."

Carson perked up. "Politicians. Yes, that might be it. Let me make a few calls. Sheila, Mike has given me an idea. Let me see what I can do. And I'll call Pederson at the bank. I tell him to take care of selling your place and Mike here can contact some folks about buying the herd. Right Mike?"

Another Redstripe, Please

"Sure, I can do that. Give me a few days, okay?"

Cirtron and the dogs wandered into the kitchen through the back door. "Waz up?" he asked.

Sheila smiled at him and said, "You said you didn't like Hawaii. What do you say to Negril? Carson says she can fix it with a little help from Dr. Aspin here. What do you say we go home?"

Cirtron froze for a moment and then his face broke into a bright smile. "De dogs, mon. Not to leave widout de dachshunds, mon. De bison, though, too big t'take along."

Carson rose from the kitchen table and said to Cirtron, "Well, of course not you hairy thing. Do you think I want to stay here and watch these two little carpet crawlers forever? They are way too much trouble for an old lady." Redstripe and Paris started to bark. "See what I mean?"

In the next few days, Carson had worked her magic, mostly based on trade agreements, and had procured promises from high level government officials to forward papers for the dogs. Redstripe and Paris would be allowed to travel to the Caribbean and enter Jamaica with the quarantine requirements waved. She'd also talked to her favorite banker.

"Tom?" she'd spoken to him over the phone. "I have something to tell you. Your bank is going to buy the Armstead place and issue a check to Sheila Armstead. Pick you price, just make sure it is at least the last appraisal number; you should still have that in your files."

The banker said stiffly, "Rose, you must know I can't do that. I have people to which I must answer. This is just too irregular. I'm sorry, but, no, I simply cannot approve such a thing."

Carson was firm, "Tom, you are going to do just that or I will stop trading with you. It is up to you, it's your choice, so what do you say?"

Pederson was silent for just a moment but said, resigned, "All right. You have a hard attitude, Rose, but I will take care of this. I only hope no one asks me any specific questions. And I want you to remember something. This time you owe me, I don't owe you. Is that satisfactory?"

"Perfect as a peanut, Tom. Thank you."

Later, in the shadow of a waning afternoon, Carson invited Cirtron and Sheila and the hounds over to her place next door. She explained how things would work and that the traveling papers for Redstripe and Paris should arrive shortly. All that needed to happen was to get the check from Pederson. Sheila had one more question. "I can't believe what you've done. And all from trade? You are an amazing lady. I did check the airlines though, the only flight we can get to Jamaica, to Montego Bay, is out of Chicago. I'm not crazy about driving all of the way there, even with Cirtron to help, with the two back seat barkers. Once was enough."

Carson, the virtual encyclopedia of anwers said, "That's not a problem. Wautoma has a little airport and you can charter a single engine plane down to the windy city. It'll be a nice view. Those little planes fly pretty close to the ground, not like the jets."

Goodbye

Sheila and Cirtron and the dogs, Carson in the back seat of the Camry, drove out to the little airport on a fresh October morning. Carson held the dogs on the short trip. The airport was just a wide strip of grass used for landings and takeoffs with a long hanger off to the side. A single wind sock hung on a pole for pilots to judge the local conditions. A dozen little planes were parked on the side, big and brightly colored moths resting in the grass. A quick trip to a small office, equipped with fans, was all that was needed to complete arrangements and payment for the flight to Chicago.

Once outside the little office, the group looked out to the grass runway where a female pilot, her ears covered with headphones, was waving at them as she stood next to a small plane. Sheila thought she looked, with the headgear, a little like a high tech Minnie Mouse.

Sheila was the first to speak. "Well, I guess it's time to go. Rose Carson, I don't know a good way to thank you for all you've done for us. You drive me nuts, you know, but what you've done is . . ."

This time, Carson had the chance to interrupt Sheila, "Honey, it has been a pleasure. It's been loads better than just sitting on my duff out at my place all by my self. Don't give it a thought. You two just take care of yourselves, and take care of the dachshunds." She placed a hand on each of Sheila's arms and stood tiptoe to be able to kiss her on the chin. Carson's eyes were welling up just a bit as were Sheila's. Carson stood back and turned to Cirtron, "And you, my good man, I must say I have never had the joy of meeting anyone like you. Go with God and be happy, Cirtron. Take good care of the girlie here. And don't forget to play your flute now and then, ok?" Carson raised her eye glasses and wiped at her tears with the back of one hand.

"No need for de tears, mon. De parting of de friends is to be a time to be happy to tink on de meeting later on. You see dat it is not sad."

"Those are not tears, Cirtron," Carson argued, "my allergies are acting up. Happens all the time." She sniffed and cleared her throat.

"Ah, so may it be dat. But y'know little lady? From what I learned, de allergies, day not come so dis part of de year, mon."

"Oh, shut up, Cirtron." Carson was embarrassed, a rare thing to have happen.

"Ya, mon. And so." Cirtron smiled a broad smile looking down on Carson. "I have de thought. Y'come and be wid us soon. We find de place on de island, get some ah de chickens and de goats mon, make a place t'live happy, mon. You come soon. Not cold dere. Always hot. Even de rain, she be hot."

This time Carson let the tears flow down her cheeks and reached to hug Cirtron; her head just below his chin. "Thanks, buddy, that is such a dear thought. But I'm too old to . . ."

It was Cirtron's turn to interrupt. "Not to listen 'bout de old ting. No matter. Long as we breath and love under the gaze of Ga, den, young? Old? N'matter. T'tink another way is not t'have de common sense, mon. You tink on dis as I say and you come soon, mon."

Startled by her own feelings, Carson said, "Ok, I'll think about it. You guys will have to tell me where you light anyway. I'll have papers and such from the sale of the farm to send you." She reached down, groaning and gasping just a bit, to lift each one of the dachshunds up. She held first Paris, then Redstripe and kissed each one on the end of their long little noses. "You girls be good. I'll miss you little trouble makers!"

Back on the ground, both of the dachshunds snorted and tried to shake off the moisture from Carson's kisses from their snouts. "You know what you two little furry fiends?" said Carson, "you two just have no respect."

With little left to say, promises hovering in the air and feelings rising up into the cool morning sky, Cirtron and Sheila grabbed the hounds and headed out to the little plane. Carson called out suddenly shouting, "Wait! Wait! What about the car?"

Sheila staggered mentally for just a second. She'd forgotten about the Camry. It certainly was not going to packed in luggage or shipped over seas. She made a quick decision and shouted back, "Keep it Carson, the title's in the glove compartment. Park that damn golf cart of yours and drive like a real person!"

O'Hare International Airport: 3 AM

The Dachshunds Save Chicago

RAINDROPS HIT, clung and then raced downward to the sill on the outside of a window of a hotel room near O'Hare in Chicago. Nearby, within sight of the Helios Winds building, the airport was mostly quiet at three in the morning. The runways and boarding gates and check-in counters would not begin to visibly bustle until just before the sun began to rise. Inside room 356, behind a carefully locked door, two men huddled over a small suitcase that was open on a bed.

"Hey, pay attention," said one of the men to a third who was seated at a table spread with food, "Hand me that battery."

Reaching into his shirt pocket, the third man stood and took a few steps away from the small round table that occupied a place near the rain spattered window. He handed over a small nine volt battery.

A soft click was heard as the battery was clipped in place.

"Try it."

The third man took a small, cell-phone sized device from his pants pocket and touched a button. A corresponding light lit on the surface of a small box in the suitcase.

"Ah, we are in luck, it works. But the battery may be loose. It might rattle."

The third man had returned to the table and had seated himself so as to continue to decimate the pile of fast food. He plucked a greasy paper from a pile of discarded wrappers.

· *Another Redstripe, Please* ·

"Here," he offered, "take this, wind it around the battery and stuff it in." He rose again and strode to the bed, handing over the paper that that had been wrapped around a barbecue sandwich.

The battery was secured. The little battery and box with the light were buried deep under clothing. A jar of peanut butter was placed on top. While the box and battery might alert the baggage scanning equipment at the airport, a hand search would expose the peanut butter first and the threat would be assumed false. Peanut butter was known to set off the alerts on the scanning equipment in airports as it had a similar consistency to the x-ray signature for certain kinds of plastic explosives. The suitcase was closed and left unlocked so as to avoid suspicion. The three men began their wait.

Across the hallway, in room 357, the two small dogs and Cirtron and Sheila slept. The front desk had a wakeup call placed on record in the hotel's automated system for those occupants of room 357 for four o'clock in the morning. A medium sized dog crate rested just inside the hotel room door and two small carry-on suitcases, one with an envelope of tickets and diplomatic papers for Inter-Caribbean flight 4330 to Jamaica inside, kept the crate company.

In room 356 the three men needed no wake up call.

O'Hare waited in the dark for the next morning of flights and the daily commotion of travelers. Cirtron, Sheila, Redstripe and Paris continued to snooze. The dogs dreamed of rabbits and gophers and cats. They twitched and whined in their sleep, imagining chasing little animals in their dog-designed dreams. Sheila had nightmarish visions of bison roaming the hills of Jamaica and snoring Cirtron just slept; his mind blissfully at rest and in its usual state. At four o'clock in the morning the wake up call, a shrill sound from the motel room phone, gave all four of them a start; a

Dachshunds in the Midwest

painful awakening in the morning darkness. Mr. and Mrs. Cirtron groaned and climbed out of bed. The dachshunds had to be mined out from under the blankets. Once the dogs were fed, Sheila and Cirtron showered and the toiletries packed, the four of them, on a total of twelve paws and feet between them all, trundled out of the room, down an elevator, and into the lobby.

The three men from room 356 were already there and waiting for the airport shuttle that would take them all over to O'Hare. Each man had a small carry on. One of them held the suitcase with the small device and battery. The other two also had similar small suitcases packed only with clothes and travel items that would serve to help make them appear as normal travelers. All three had passports and tickets tucked into pockets in their clothes.

Outside the lobby, the October early morning air was chilly. Redstripe and Paris balked at leaving the warmth of the lobby and there was a moment when the dogs stopped, planted their paws and refused to go forward through the door. While Cirtron carried the luggage, Sheila, two strained leashes in hand, gave in and plucked each hound up and carried them out. She took them both out to a convenient strip of lawn and put them down. Neither dachshund was at all pleased having to stand in the dewy grass and let their thoughts be known by snorting and grunting. *This is just too much and way too early! Our paws are all wet! And our tummies aren't much better. What is all this, anyway?* Sheila just let them finish their dachshund business and walked them over to the shuttle van where Cirtron was waiting and the three men were already on board.

Once both dogs and Cirtron and Sheila were on the shuttle, the driver asked which airline all were connecting with so that he would know at which terminal gates to stop. The ride over

• Another Redstripe, Please •

the much-used road to the airport was a rattly, jostling thing and reminded Sheila of Carson's golf cart. The dachshunds were not having a good time.

Cirtron, Sheila, the dachshunds and the three men all left the van at the same terminal. They were ticketed for the same flight. Once inside the airport, eyes trying to adjust to the bright indoor lighting, they headed for the check in counter for Inter Caribbean Airlines. A line of waiting passengers had already formed. All the baggage would be checked, but the three men would not board. Everyone in line waited, shuffled forward, dragging suitcases, and the dogs followed along reluctantly.

A young man and young woman approached the Cirtrons and dogs. They wore blue shirts and dark pants. A label on the sleeve of each of their shirts read "SKY PETS."

The woman spoke first and addressed Sheila. "You must be Sheila Armstead? And these are the dogs? Oh aren't they just so cute? Don't you love them? We're here to arrange their transfer by air to Montego Bay? We'd like to thank you for using the services of Sky Pets?"

Bleary eyed and sleep deprived, Sheila wondered if the woman could talk without a question mark. She wanted to say to her, "*Yes, I'm Sheila, these are the dogs, yes they are cute. Your name wouldn't happen to be Buffy, would it?*" She restrained herself and said, "Yes, I'm Sheila, thanks for meeting us here. We've got the travel crate and the papers here for you."

The young man spoke. "Great. We need to see those papers but really we don't need the crate. We use our own custom designed transports. They are designed especially each for every breed of dog. They will be perfectly safe and secure in the heated and pressurized section of the luggage bay. Gloria here will be flying with you in the cabin should any need at all arise. We just need to see your papers for the dogs, have you sign some things, show us your identification and we'll take the dogs with us up ahead." The man produced a clipboard, Sheila withdrew a set of papers from a pocket on her carry on and handed them over to the woman who began to read them. Cirtron remained quiet and just looked on.

"Oh my, isn't this something? You have diplomatic permits for the dogs? Tim, how often do we see this?" She turned to Sheila. "So, the dogs won't be going into quarantine then?"

Redstripe and Paris were busy wrapping their leads around Sheila's ankles while she gritted her teeth and simply said, "No. Show me where to sign."

With the paperwork completed, Tim and Gloria from Sky Pets collected the two dachshunds, one with Paris and one with Redstripe and carried them off. The departure was sudden and Sheila stood a moment, feeling lost, watching the dogs look back over the shoulders of the two young people. The dachshunds did not look happy. Sheila said, without turning to Cirtron and staring at the receding dogs, "Do you think they'll be okay? I mean, well, they just took them!"

"Ya, mon. Not t'be de one wid de worries, mon. Be it better than traveling in de bag wid no air."

A few minutes later Cirtron and Sheila reached the counter, presented their tickets and passports and received their boarding passes, seat assignments and baggage claim tags. The three men were right behind them and checked in as the two bound for Jamaica left the counter and headed for the boarding gate. But the three men did not follow. Boarding passes in their hands, their baggage checked, they headed back out the front doors of the airport and boarded a little bus back to the Helios Winds hotel. No one noticed.

· *Another Redstripe, Please* ·

Worrying about the dachshunds now in the care of Gloria (Buffy) and Tim from Sky Pets, Sheila made her way to the departure gate for flight 4330. Cirtron walked alongside her, happy to be on his way back to Jamaica. Once at the gate, it was not long before the two boarded, took their seats and settled in for the flight. To Sheila's delight, Gloria was not in a seat near theirs. Redstripe and Paris were down below, not in good moods, but safe and sound and warm. The plane rolled away from the terminal, guided by the guys with the big flashlights, paused at the end of one of the many runways and took off. The vibrations of the take off had the dachshunds up and on their feet inside their little cage thinking, *This is NOT fun. We'd take Carson's golf cart any old day. This is just ridiculous, we're not even hungry. Humph!* The dogs pawed at their ears as the pressure in the hold changed with the plane's rise into the early morning sky.

The three men had returned to their hotel room and were watching out the window; the view included the runway used by flight 4330. They'd planned that.

As the plane rose, the dachshunds pawed their ears, the three men watched and Sheila and Cirtron were listening to the drone of a flight attendant explaining seat belts and safety regulations for the flight, a phone rang in an office at 219 South Dearborn Street in the City of Chicago, the Chicago Divisional Offices of the Federal Bureau of Investigation. Outside calls to that office were not supposed to go through. The caller must have had access to some very special information.

"Ruminiski," answered the occupant of the office.

The caller was brief. "There is a problem on flight 4330 out of Chicago and headed for Montego Bay. I know this. Check room 356 at the Helios." The line went silent.

· *Dachshunds in the Midwest* ·

In the special cargo hold of the flight for Montego Bay, Redstripe and Paris were worrying the clasp that held their little prison shut. The "specially designed transport" cage fell open after just a few moments of pawing and gnawing by persistent dachshunds. The two were quickly loose in the compartment and sniffing around their surroundings.

Ruminiski acted immediately. Taking the call as real because it had come straight to his desk, he gave its legitimacy no thought at all. Besides, he knew that voice. He punched a few buttons on the phone and spoke rapidly. "I need two special forces units to the Helios Hotel and two to the airport. Do it now, do it five minutes ago! I'll have info to radio them on their way." He left his office not waiting for an answer and headed to another room used for communication with the various resources of the FBI.

The three men in room 356 watched the airplane begin its ascent.

Redstripe and Paris, ambling around among cases and crates and packages, found one of the suitcases from the three men. It smelled pretty good. *Ah hah! There must be something good in here. Let's get it!* They began to use teeth and claws on the case. The suitcase latches failed as quickly as the cage latch and the two dogs began to nose around inside, searching for something to eat. There is nothing like the possibility of food to motivate a dachshund. Paws dug and piled clothing out in all directions.

Deep in the bowels of the O'Hare airport, the air traffic control room senior supervisor received a call he did not want. The voice on the other end of the line cited a code phrase, identifying himself as FBI and then his instructions were brusque and clipped. "Get the pilot on flight 4330 to return to his departure point. Hold off all incoming traffic. Hold all aircraft at their gates and stop those out waiting to take off. Shut it down. Shut it all down. Get that 4330 back on the ground. Get it down now! We're on our way."

Paris's nose found the wrapper soaked in grease. Redstripe's nose was right along side. Each hound clamped her teeth on the paper and pulled back, ripping the thing in two. Redstripe's half was still stuck to the battery and she shook it as if she had just clamped down onto some hapless gopher. The force of the shake tore the battery from its connection and the little light on the box went dark.

In the control room, the senior supervisor issued his directions and the air controllers fell to the task of trying to stop an entire airport. They could do it. They were well trained, but many armpits began to darken. No voices were raised, but heartbeats thrummed in the chests of everyone in the room. All along the concourses of the airport, the ceiling hung flight information monitors began to change. Where flights had messages reading "ON TIME" or "ARRV 8:00 AM" or "BOARDING," the displays, one by one changed to "DELAYED," "DELAYED," DELAYED." Groans and curses could be heard all along the concourses as the words changed.

Two large dark trucks arrived at the Helios. Men and women in armor and helmets and carrying automatic weapons swarmed out and into the hotel. Not even stopping to tell the management what was going on, several took up positions to block the elevators. Two separate groups rushed up the stairways. Several ran to the rear and stood to guard the back of the building. Two men in windbreakers with FBI in yellow letters on the back followed in and stayed in the lobby. It was a frightening display made more so because they were all so quiet. Several guests in the lobby dropped half full coffee cups and froze in place before they were rounded up and led outside.

· Dachshunds in the Midwest ·

On board flight 4330, the captain received the message from air traffic control. He was told to turn around, that the airways had been cleared and to descend at his own discretion. He was also told not to spare the passengers. His second in command heard this and began to make preparations while informing the flight attendants they would be returning to their departure point. The descent might be a little rough. He turned to the captain and said, "This is no way to start a day."

"I've had better ones," replied the captain. "Guess we won't need the flight plan book." Both men were shaking but refused to share their fear.

The second in command keyed the intercom to the passenger cabin. His voice was calm and friendly even while his adrenal glands were pumping out anxiety juice. "Good morning, ladies and gentlemen. I want to thank you today for flying with us on Inter Caribbean Flight 4330 with service from Chicago to Montego Bay." He clicked off the mike for a moment to help maintain his calm and then started again. "We've just received a request to return to the Chicago Airport, just a routine double check on our radio equipment. This has nothing to do with the airworthiness of our aircraft today and the delay will add just a few minutes to our trip." He did not feel guilty about lying through his teeth. He continued. "The captain asks that you make certain your seatbelts remain fastened, your trays in the upright position. Please ask the flight attendants if you need any help at all, they will be glad to assist you."

In room 356 at the Helios, the three men could still see the airplane in the distance. The first man just watched, the second one had binoculars and the third held the little cell phone like device. "Now," said the first man. The third pressed a button.

Nothing happened. The third man pressed the button again. And then again. "What's wrong!?" he wailed.

"Wait," said the first. "Just wait, it won't be right away." The second continued to gaze through the binoculars.

The dachshunds were happily chewing and lapping at the greasy wrapper. The captain banked the plane sharply and the passengers could feel the plane vibrate and hear it groan as they were pressed into their seats by the tight turn of the aircraft. Most gripped the arms of their seats tightly and many began to shout. Down below, Redstripe and Paris were thrown over and away from the opened suitcase, bumping and sliding around in the compartment and scrabbling for a solid purchase to stand.

"See?" said the first man at the hotel room window, "Look at the con-trail, its curving, the plane is beginning to turn. Watch now, it worked."

But the plane just continued to turn smoothly and began downward in an even but steep path, arrowing straight back for the runways. "Give me that sender!" shouted the first man. He grabbed the device and stabbed at the button frantically. "It can't be!" He tried slamming the thing down repeatedly on the table and punching the button again. He had no time left to experiment or wonder. The door shattered open with an explosive bang and the helmeted, armored and weapon carrying special forces team filled the room. One man shouldered through the group from the rear and snatched the sending device.

Behind the shield of his helmet, his face was one huge grin. "I hope you won't insult us by asking for a warrant." He held up the little device. "We've go it right here."

As the bad guys (as the FBI called them privately) were taken down, the airplane bearing the hounds and Sheila and Cirtron was coming down too. It dropped steeply from the sky and the heaviness the passengers had felt in the turn now changed to the feeling of being in a descending elevator that was in way too much of a hurry. Unsecured objects began to fly around the cabin and people were screaming. Sheila turned in a panic to Cirtron but there was too much noise to make herself heard. Her heart was in her throat and then seemed to drop back down to her shoes when she thought of the two dogs below. Redstripe and Paris went weightless for just a moment, probably the first dachshunds to really fly, and then plopped back down into a tumble of crates and suitcases as the pilot raised the nose of the plane to a position ready for the landing. They didn't even have a chance to bark. Wheels down at the last moment, the pilot brought the plane down onto the runway hard. The wheels screamed and smoked. But they were down and rolling toward the special forces trucks at the end of the runway. The plane stopped, engines still whining, and was immediately surrounded. The passenger cabin was perfect bedlam.

The Special Forces team had spread themselves around the plane quickly. Two members were up front aiming their weapons at the windows of the cockpit and were relieved when both pilots held up their fists with thumbs extended. That was a good sign. Several more pushed stairways to the two passenger doors and others brought ladders up to the baggage area access hatches. The first hatch was opened wide while more team members aimed weapons at it. Two little dachshund faces appeared and looked down, two little sparrows peering from a birdhouse.

The people on the ground paused, shocked. A couple of them lowered their weapons, others began to chuckle and one was heard to say, "What on God's earth?" Redstripe and Paris just looked. It was a long way to the ground. Two men were directed by a commander to climb up and inspect and secure the baggage compartment.

"Climb in there, but first hand those two dogs down. I don't know what they have to do with this, but get 'em down here." Two men climbed the ladder and the first grabbed Redstripe, then Paris, and handed the dogs in turn down the ladder. They were given over to a big guy who had to stand with the squirming dachshunds held tight against his body armor, one under each arm. He was not pleased. "Why me?" he grumbled.

Why us? thought the hounds.

Inside the plane, the two men looked around. They saw tumbled containers, an open suitcase and a dog crate with its door ajar. A few scraps of paper littered the floor. One man leaned down to look into the suitcase and saw the box with the now darkened lights. Two broken wires protruded from one side. The other man bent down and retrieved the battery where it had landed on the flooring. Two wires from the battery matched those on the box in the suitcase. Both stood and one looked from the suitcase, to the dog crate and then back. He placed his hands on his hips, threw his head back and began to laugh.

Still laughing, he turned to his partner and said, "Marty, I think I know what happened here! Boy, you know I hate these things, but this time, this is an absolute circus! Check around, but I think we're okay here. I've got to see if there are some names on that crate. We'll want to find the dogs' owners but this is unbelievable. The perpetrators here were doomed by dachshunds. I can't stand it!" He looked at Marty who seemed confused and said, "Don't worry about it, just check around. I'll tell 'em outside we're set, just to have the guys get this thing out of here and make sure it's safe." He went over to the crate and scribbled names on a pad from his pocket;

· *Dachshunds in the Midwest* ·

Cirtron/Armstead-Seats 16D 16E. Still laughing softly, he had to wipe his eyes before he climbed out and down to the surface of the runway. He began to explain what he thought to his commander as Agent Ruminiski strode up. Both the commander and Ruminiski listened; they'd heard lots of odd stories and neither one frowned or smiled.

Ruminiski addressed the field commander, "He may be right. I hope he's right. We have the bad guys and it looks like they only had one device. If this is it, we've got it sacked. The manifest has been checked, there are no other accomplices that we can uncover. Let's get these people off the plane, finish securing it, but first let's talk to these dog owners. Have someone go get them off the plane." The commander nodded to the agent that had found the suitcase and device. The man headed off to retrieve Cirtron and Sheila. Off to the side, the big guy holding Redstripe and Paris coughed for attention.

"Hold your horses, fella," said Ruminiski.

"I believe they are dogs, sir," said the hound's temporary handler.

Ruminiski just glared.

Redstripe and Paris just squirmed.

The flight attendants were called to the front of the plane and asked to please have the passengers in seats 16D and 16E come forward. Sheila and Cirtron were led out of the plane and down onto the runway where the big guy with the hounds and the commander and agent waited. The passenger cabin had gone quiet. The men explained what they believed had happened. Sheila and Cirtron listened while Sheila kept looking over at Redstripe and Paris in the arms of the armored gargantuan and then finally asked, "This phone call you received, how did this person know this was a problem? Who is he, can we thank him?"

The commander pointed to a man wearing a White Sox jacket and baseball cap who was leaning against one of the trucks, his hands in his pockets. Dark glasses and the brim of the cap made his face invisible. "That's him. But I don't know his name. I'm not supposed to. No one is."

The man touched a hand to the brim of his cap, waved, and then turned and walked away. Redstripe and Paris were handed back to Sheila and Cirtron.

Ruminiski looked at Paris and Sheila and the hounds. "I really should ask you to come back to the offices with me and ask some questions and check on some things. This is one of more bizarre things I've seen. And I do want to thank you. But I suppose as it seems things are all in hand here, you two can be on your way. The four of you, that is."

Breaking a long silence Cirtron asked, "Ah, ya, mon. But de plane? I would not have de tought she be gonna go someplace soon, mon. It was our trip t'home for me, mon."

Sheila wanted to tell Cirtron to just keep still and that they should just get out of there as soon as possible. But Ruminiski said, "Well, you're right. This plane is not going anywhere. Not today anyway. The airlines will have to find these passengers other flights and that is going to take a while. But I'll tell you what. It'll be the least we can do here. Let me have your passports and I'll take them over and have someone run the numbers through over one of the computers in our trucks. I assume they'll be clear and we'll find a way to get you to, where were you going, oh yeah, Montego Bay. It'll be on us. Fair enough?"

"The dogs too?" asked Sheila.

"The dogs too," answered Ruminiski. "But what do you say we have them ride up top this time?"

· Dachshunds in the Midwest ·

"Ya, mon," said Cirtron.

"Sounds good by me," said Sheila. "What do you ladies think?" she asked the dogs.

"Woof."

ARRANGEMENTS WERE made and a car was brought for Sheila and the dogs and Cirtron to take them from the runway and back to the terminal. Besides the driver, two agents accompanied the group. Each wore a dark windbreaker with the FBI letters on the back, sunglasses, jeans and clean running shoes. They could have served as bookends. The car stopped near an "Authorized Personnel Only" door and everyone got out. As one agent held open the door, his partner said, "Take it easy now. We have to go up through one concourse and then down another to get to the gate we need. There is likely to be some media people around. Things like this have a way of leaking out quickly."

In the door and up a set of stairs, they all went through one more door and out unto the carpet of concourse six. The place was packed with people whose flights had been delayed because of the fate of flight 4330. "C'mon folks, let's go. We'll carry the dogs."

Each agent picked up a dachshund and held it in both arms, a nose sticking out on one side and a tail on the other. "Stay right behind us." Redstripe and Paris tried briefly to wriggle but quickly found they were clamped down tightly. They were safe, but were not too crazy about the travel arrangements.

Word had indeed leaked out. As the group passed through the crowd, people began to point and whisper to each other. "Hey, that must be them!" "Are those the dogs?" "Yes, they must be, aren't those security people with them?" "Sure it is, look at that!" As the crew of the two agents, the New Yorker, the Rasta man and two dachshunds

• *Another Redstripe, Please* •

made their way up the corridor, people began to clap. First it was just a couple of isolated hands slapping together. Then a few more. And more. The sound rose into an ear shattering crescendo of applause. Someone must have recognized the heritage of Redstripe and Paris and began to shout. It turned into a chant as loud as the clapping.

"WAY TO GO WEINERS! WAY TO GO WEINERS! WAY TO GO WEINERS!"

Redstripe and Paris tried to bury their noses deep in the armpits of the agents. Sheila could not walk fast enough and Cirtron was beginning to sweat. They made it, however, to the security checkpoint at the beginning of the concourse, but it was there, not being allowed in with the ticketed passengers, that the media waited. One of the agents motioned everyone to stop. "Slight change of plans," he said calmly. "Mr. Cirtron, sir, here, you take this dog and follow right behind me. Hold it tight with two arms, okay? I need my hands free." He spoke to the other agent. "You're at the end. Mrs. Armstead, ma'am? You're right behind Mr. Cirtron." He waited to see if everyone understood and then said. "Good enough. Here we go boys and girls."

The lead agent was not polite. He just shoved his way through the crowd of reporters and camera people with his charges right behind. No one fell when his hand was planted on the chest of one or two men, even one woman, but cameras and microphones were slapped aside and a few of those hit the carpet. The agent in the rear had only his shoulders to use to push people aside as he had one of the hounds clasped to his chest. The dachshunds held tight and decided this was not a time for brash behavior.

They all got through. The Divisonal Offices of the FBI in Chicago would receive letters from disgruntled editors, but they would be ignored.

· Dachshunds in the Midwest ·

The agents finally delivered their charges to another gate on another concourse. They handed Cirtron and Sheila boarding passes, more papers for the dogs, bid them well and escorted them all the way down the causeway into the plane. The agents stopped at the doorway to the plane. One simply said, "Good luck, you'll be fine from here out. Things will be taken care of for you on the other end."

Sheila leaned over and kissed each agent on the cheek and said, "Thank you. I don't know what to say."

Cirtron raised a fist and said, "Ya, mon. Go wid GA!"

The dachshunds, released and down on the flooring, looked up and barked.

The agents looked at each other, shrugged, turned to the travelers and said, "No problem, ma'am, sir." They turned and left but not before one of them bent down and scratched the ears of both hounds.

Four leather clad seats in the first class cabin of the aircraft had been reserved for the two humans and the two hounds. Later, there would be dinner and wine on china with real knives and forks, the main course and other tidbits shared with Redstripe and Paris. Sheila and Cirtron sank into their own seats and the flight attendants fussed over the two dachshunds, petting them and using blankets to make them little nests, each in their own first class seat. The two humans were asleep before the plane reached its cruising altitude and Paris and Redstripe had already left their own nests, opting to crawl up with Cirtron, both sinking into a deep snooze. It was unbelievable, maybe, but they'd had enough fun for one day.

The landing at Montego Bay lay ahead of them all and there would plenty of new adventures to be had after everybody was rested.

Epilogue

Redstripe's Inn—Negril

WE'D BEEN SITTING around a rickety table with Red Stripe beers in hand while we listened to the new stories. After I'd met Cirtron on the beach and returned to Jill to tell her about it we'd both gone over in the late afternoon to the Redstripe's Inn to hear the latest. Cirtron had finally wound down. We'd all missed the sunset so famous in Negril. But after the tales, Jill and I still were left wondering how the dogs and Sheila and Cirtron had come to be at the Redstripe's Inn. He'd ended his tale at the Chicago Airport and the transition from bison ranchers to rooming house hosts was a mystery. "Cirtron," asked Jill, "um, how did you all end up here, at the Redstripe's Inn, I mean."

I went on wondering in silence, still trying to digest the stories, about the wisdom of taking on the place. Looking around, I had lots of questions like: would the roof fall in on my head right away or would that be later?

It was Sheila who replied and answered, "We sold the farm, the ranch, deposited the bucks in the Nova Scotia Bank here in Negril and then just bought this place. Cirtron knew about it; it was for sale, so we just went ahead and did it. We haven't had much business, there is some, not a lot, but we have plenty of money left over to see us through. We do get guests but we hope for more later on."

I was still wondering. *Plenty of money to see them through?* The place was a mess. The electrical wiring looked pretty scary and the paint on the walls was peeling like the aftermath of a bad sunburn. Where the concrete blocks used to build the walls were bare, portions could be seen to be crumbling. During the day I was sure I would be able to see light seeping through the mortar joints. It would take a lot of money and effort to put the place back together. Compared to this project, Humpty Dumpty would have been a snap. And that wasn't even considering the jungle foliage outside the building that was making a concerted effort to reclaim the entire place. In a real estate ad it would not have been listed as a 'handyman's special.' It would have to be described as a 'handyman's horrendous nightmare.' I had to ask.

"But this place, you've got a great name for it, I love it, but it really needs some work. I don't mean to be rude, but are you two sure you can make this go? From what I've seen, I wouldn't even know where to start."

Redstripe and Paris had wandered in from somewhere or other and began to circle and snuffle around Sheila's ankles. She did not answer right away and just reached down to scratch two pairs of dachshund ears. The hounds rotated their heads back and forth in order to present the exact itchy parts for Sheila's fingers. Paris yawned widely with a little squeak for emphasis.

"Well," said Sheila straightening up from her hound scratching, "You're right." She looked over at Cirtron. "And I'm afraid Cirtron's talents don't fall into the fix it up category. As for me, a paintbrush in my hand is a dangerous weapon. We know we are going to need some major help."

Jill, I suppose, spoke without thinking. She certainly did not conference with me before she said, "Jack could help. He's pretty good at almost everything. I always tell him that he's a Jack of all Trades." She laughed and I cringed. Yes, I'd spent some of my former lives as an electrician, carpenter, bartender, janitor and other things that were more academic, but I had the sudden sinking feeling that I'd just been contracted out to a sure fail project.

"Really?" asked Sheila with a grin on her face.

"Yes, mon?" responded Cirtron. "You could bring y'selves here and we do it all in de family way, all t'gether? Fix up de Redstripe's Inn?"

I stared at Jill, who was still laughing, and took a look around the place once more; seeing the peeling paint, crumbling concrete and sagging roof and said, "Oh boy. I don't know about that. To move us down here for a long time? It will take a while to get this place in shape, the money to do it not withstanding and, man, I just don't know."

The dogs, Redstripe and Paris, had seated themselves on their backsides on the floor and were looking up at me. The three humans looked at me too. The idea was intriguing, I had to admit, but the problems were severe. Just moving us, even for a period of six months, to Negril would be complex. Interesting or not, I had to underscore my misgivings and said, "What would we do with Belle, our dachshund?"

Sheila had the answer all ready. "No problem, I can call Carson. She can fix it so Belle can come here, then we'd have a regular herd of hounds." Redstripe and Paris tuned into this and began to bark. *Yeah, Yeah, the more the merrier!*

I looked at the expectant faces, two canine and three human. I tried to wiggle just a bit out of a commitment and said, "Let me think about this. I believe it needs some thought. For now, though, while I am considering, you understand, I would really like another Red Stripe, please."

Redstripe's Inn

Dachshunds in Jamaica

Redstripe's Inn

Dachshunds in Jamaica

By Jack Magestro

Unlimited Publishing LLC
Bloomington, Indiana

© 2005 by Jack Magestro

All rights reserved under Title 17, U.S. Code, International and Pan-American Copyright Conventions. No part of this work, whether in printed or digital form, may be reproduced or transmitted in any form or by any means, electronic or mechanical, including (but not limited to) photocopying, scanning, recording, live performance or broadcast, or duplication by any information storage or retrieval system without prior written permission from the author and publisher.

Unlimited Publishing LLC ("UP") works with professional authors and publishers, serving as distributing publisher. Sole responsibility for the content of each work rests with the author and/or co-publisher. Information or opinions expressed herein may not be interpreted as originating from, or endorsed by UP, nor any of its officers, members, contractors, agents or assigns.

This is a work of fiction. All characters, products, corporations, institutions, and/or entities of any kind in this book are either the product of the author's imagination or, if real, used fictitiously without any intent to describe their actual characteristics. CASTAWAYS TRAVEL™ is used with permission.

ISBN 1-58832-139-8

Contributing Publisher:
Belle Ink LLC

Distributing Publisher:

Unlimited Publishing LLC
Bloomington, Indiana
http://www.unlimitedpublishing.com

Contents

New Plans — 1 —
Road to Negril — 7 —
Break Down — 13 —
The Inn — 19 —
Alfred's — 23 —
Building Inspection — 29 —
On the Beach — 35 —
The New Truck — 37 —
Builder's Supply-Jamaican Style — 41 —
Red Sox Jacket — 45 —
Rehab and a Night Parade — 51 —
Kingston and England — 61 —
The Dachshund's Photo Op — 65 —
Arriving on a Jet Plane — 71 —
Resort of the Lost Beach — 75 —
Glamour Photography — 85 —
Nothing Ever Stays the Same — 89 —
A Jamaican Celebration — 97 —
Home Again — 107 —
Epilogue — 111 —

For my grandmother,

Rose Svanda-McCall, 1906-1983

She taught me tolerance, to cook, and was too polite to tell me she suspected I would never grow up.

Author's Note:

I should probably take a moment to explain something. I don't usually talk about this outside our house. But one needs to understand that I can hear dogs and cats talk. This may sound crazy, but it is not. It is just sort of a thing that my wife and I have come to accept over time. In our home, I always "hear" what Belle has to say. Sometimes it gets me in trouble. A good example might be from some cold evening when Jill is watching television, wrapped in a blanket by the fire, and Belle wanders into the room. Belle would be prone to give a little snort and I would hear her say, *Hey, Mom! Move over on that couch! I need a place to lay and get warm too. Move it.* In all likelihood, I would repeat to Jill what Belle had expressed and, also in all likelihood, Jill would say, "Shut up Belle, go lay on the rug by the fire and leave me alone. Be a dog. Get your own space." And then, "Jack, would you do something with her? She's being ugly." Jill would just assume the transfer of thought between me and the hound without question.

Do you see? At our house, it is just a way of doing business. It's nothing unusual for us.

The whole dog brain to human mind thing is just something we accept. We don't even give it a second thought. And this ability of mine, unfortunately, extends to nearly all of the breeds of canines and felines. I've come to understand that dachshunds, when they begin to bark and howl and snort and such are not so much annoyed as they are exuberant and opinionated. This is not true of the other breeds. German Shepherds, Rottweilers and other breeds really do get annoyed. Of course in the case of Golden Retrievers, they would not even understand the word annoyed. Cats are annoyed all the time and let everyone that can hear know this. The trouble with cats is they mumble. When a cat comes along to meet me, I often hear something like, *Hey!? Who are you, you sorry looking mrmphes. Do you think you even are going to have the opportunity to pet my srzesmph? Ha! Don't you lay any mnstez on it.* Mumbles or not, cats are just rude.

This ability to hear the animals talk is not really a gift. It is more of an irritation. It can really be an actual pain in the back pockets. Too much information is not always a good thing. I only mention this here so that when you read what the dogs have to say later in the story, you understand that this is really what the dogs are thinking about, and that it is not a figment of my imagination. The dog's opinions do not necessarily reflect my own. In fact, a good bet is always that they are opposite.

Dachshunds in Jamaica

New Plans

My wife, Jill, and I had just returned from Jamaica. The night before we'd landed in Milwaukee, driven out to pick up our dachshund, Belle, from the dog sitter and finally returned to our home in Hartland late at night. Now, the next morning, we had finally risen from bed to slurp at micro waved instant coffee at about eleven AM. Still grumpy from traveling back from the Caribbean, short on patience caused by the psychological let down so common at the end of our trips to the beautiful islands to the south, neither of us was fit for company, let alone each other's. Unpacking suitcases filled with damp and sandy clothing was not high on our list of tasks for the day. Belle, excited to be back in her familiar surroundings and back with her "mom and dad," trotted into the kitchen where we were seated at the table with our coffee and went over to bang on her food dish.

And would one of you two care to get out of your chair and feed me? And then, if you could possibly tear yourselves away from the table, I would like to go out. There are things to do and squirrels to watch

"You want to get it?" Jill asked me.

After more than a decade of marriage, I knew this was not a question. It was a directive. I got up to feed and water the little hound. While Belle was crunching on dry dog food and then lapping at her water bowl, I sat back down and tried to decide whether to take a shower or go back to bed. I was thinking maybe I would sleep a while yet, like perhaps for about three days. I delayed my decision too long and the caffeine kicked in to make the shower option more acceptable.

"Honey," I said to Jill, "I'm going to go and get cleaned up and then put Belle out. Then I suppose I should check on the mail and my e-mail and all that. What are you going to do?"

"Ummph," said Jill.

Redstripe's Inn

"That's fine," I said, and headed for the bath wondering if I'd remembered to restart the water heater after our absence. Belle was busy finishing her breakfast. It turned out the water was hot and I was able to clean the grunge of travel off of my body. After being in Jamaica, the warm and steady water that flowed out of the shower head seemed like a new experience. It was very nice. I dried, dressed in old clothes, and returned to deal with Belle. She was waiting.

Ah, so you finally got back? Well, I need to go out and deal with business and look for squirrels. Hurry up about it, would you?

"Yes, Belle." I picked her up and took her out to the back yard. With the mission accomplished and squirrels having been given the evil dachshund eye with a few barks for emphasis, the two of us returned to the house and commandeered a couch for a nap.

It was much later in the day, evening, I suppose, when we found ourselves seated back at the kitchen table with a dinner of baked up frozen pizza and canned soda in front of us. Belle was on the floor nearby harboring hopeful dreams of scraps.

"Jack?" Jill started, "I think we should do it."

I groaned and replied, "That sounds great, but, listen, I'm sorry. I am just too worn out. Can I take a rain check?"

Jill, as always, had an answer. "No, stupid, I don't mean that. I mean we should go back to Jamaica and help Cirtron and Sheila repair that inn. You could do it. I know you could. And don't compliment yourself. I didn't mean "do it." Besides, my dear, you could use a shave."

Belle's nose was twitching. *Hmm, any pizza crusts left up there? I'm waiting down here. It says in the mortgage agreement that anything on the floor is legally mine.*

I admonished the dog, "Shut up, Belle. Wait a minute. Besides, so far as I know, you can't read a mortgage. You can have a couple of crusts in your dish when we finish."

"WOOF!"

"Jill," I said, "We can't just pull up and go to Jamaica for any length of time. Do you know what it would take to repair that place and get it ready for business? It's a mess! We've

Dachshunds in Jamaica

got our house here; I've got my writing and remember now I am working on promoting other authors. We can't just leave on a jaunt like that. And what about Belle? We can't take her to another country. The red tape would be terrible if we could get through it at all."

Jill had her answers. "Look, you always say you can work from anywhere as long as you have a computer connection, although god only knows what it is you do with all of that. I'm sure they have something in Jamaica. And Belle? Didn't Sheila and Cirtron say that this Mrs. Carson, or whatever her name was, could fix it so Belle could get there with no fuss? C'mon. Redstripe and Paris are there. Why not Belle? We can do it. All we need is to make some arrangements and have someone look after the house. Jonathan can watch the house. That kid of ours owes us a favor."

"You are crazy," I said.

"No, I'm not. Think about it. We've always said we wanted to live there."

"This isn't possible. It's a pipe dream."

Jill insisted. "You know what? I think I have that Mrs. Carson's number on a scrap of paper in my suitcase. I'm gonna call her."

I was able to hear Jill's side of the phone conversation with Mrs. Carson.

"Hello? Mrs. Carson? Rose Carson? Yes, my name is Jill. My husband and I are friends of Cirtron and Sheila. You know them, I'm sure…"

"Oh yes, uh huh, they're lovely…" Jill laughed, "Yes, I know Cirtron can be a little strange at times. That's just him, I suppose…"

"Listen, I hope I am not being a bother, but Sheila said to call you. She thinks you might be able to help us. To fix something…"

"What? No, we don't need any trade…"

"Well, thanks, but ah, no, we don't really need any bison meat, either…"

"Yes, I am sure you have plenty of both, but what we need is a few strings pulled here. We want to take our dachshund

 Redstripe's Inn

down to Jamaica and help Sheila and Cirtron fix their place. We were just there visiting and want to back but we'd have to take Belle. It would be long stay. We understand you might have some contacts that could help us get our Belle into the country without a fuss. Can you do that?"

"Yes, I know. They told us all about the wedding and that it was you that set it all up. We know they appreciated everything you did for them. That's why they must have felt comfortable suggesting we call…"

"The dog? Our dog? Well yes, of course she's a dachshund. And yes, she is just like Redstripe and Paris…"

"You can then? That is so great!"

"You know Senator Kohl? Really? He didn't, you know, um, trade with you, did he?"

"Oh, sure, I am certain you wouldn't talk about that. I'm sorry. I just don't know many people that actually know a Senator they can just call for a favor…"

"I see. Ok.. So we call you back in a couple of weeks if we don't hear?"

"Mrs. Carson, thank you so much! And no, I had no idea there would be an ambassador from Jamaica here. I never thought of it."

I heard Jill repeat her thank you and promise to call in two weeks. I was stunned. And I was little worried. Things seemed a little out of control. But, I thought, what real chance does this lady have of making these arrangements anyway? Nah! It can't happen. But as Jill hung up the phone she was grinning and turned immediately to Belle. "Hey Belle! Wanna go to Jamaica? Mon?"

I did not realize how much trouble we really were in until a letter arrived with a gold seal on the envelope by certified mail two weeks later. It looked pretty official and my first thought was the IRS was sending us some sort of nasty-gram. Thinking back, that might have been better.

Dachshunds in Jamaica

 Redstripe's Inn

Jamaican Consulate
The Honorable J Peterson Powen

To whom it may concern:

I, J Peterson Powen, representative to the United States of the Americas, from the free government of the Island of Jamaica, do affix my signature below and bestow upon the named persons below the right to free and uninterrupted travel by any means to and entry through any port of call, common carrier or other contrivance, without delay, interruption or question to the Island of Jamaica. I do this by the authority of the Jamaican government vested to me as ambassador to the United States of the Americas and may all be pleased to comply.

The persons traveling under the protection and recognition of the free government of the Island of Jamaica are named as:

Jack Magestro
Jill Magestro
Belle Magestro

J Peterson Powen
nmc

Jamaican Consulate *510 President Avenue* Washington, DC, USA 05007

Dachshunds in Jamaica

Road to Negril

We'd never taken the road from Montego Bay to Negril along the western Jamaican coast. We'd been told that in earlier times, it was a frightening trip. On this trip of ours, on our way to Redstripe's Inn, we were forced to hire a van and not a small plane to get us to our destination. We had too much luggage for a chartered air flight as we were planning a long stay. If the trip in earlier times was frightening, it must have been understated. Our trip was horrifying. In earlier times, it must have been debilitating.

After landing at Sangster International Airport in Mo' Bay, we collected our luggage, hauled it all and our dachshund in arms out past the hawkers in the lobby and out onto the concrete shaded by a large overhang. Out past the shade on superheated asphalt were all of the taxis and vans and tour busses waiting for passengers. The Jamaican men and women trying to solicit business were like so many flying bugs with attitudes, all wanting to bite us and suck whatever they could from our wallets. But we were veterans of travel in Jamaica and knew enough not to let anyone touch or take our bags until we had negotiated a fare. We made a deal with one man who told us honestly that at the price he mentioned, we would have to share a ride with two other couples. That was fine, we told him we would pay when we were delivered and followed him out to an older van in the back of the lot. Belle was already panting in the Jamaican heat and we plopped down onto a curb while a young man dragged our luggage out and lifted it into the back of the van. We gave the fellow a dollar. He seemed pleased.

We'd been waiting about twenty minutes when Jill declared, "Hold the dog, I'm going over to buy a couple of Red Stripes. You want a lemon?"

 Redstripe's Inn

I took the panting Belle into my already sweaty lap and said, "No, just cold will be fine. Besides, you don't put lemon in a Red Stripe, you put it in a Corona."

Jill frowned at me. "This is the wrong country for that, Jack."

I just looked off somewhere and said. "Whatever." Neither of us was long on patience. I reached up under my glasses with one finger and wiped some sweat out from the corner of my eye. I wanted to wipe the second eye, but that hand was busy restraining Belle. I did not feel, in the heat, that I was coordinated enough to reach with my one free hand and cross over to my other eye for a second wipe. Belle's hot breath was cooking my lap. As I sat with Belle, the driver was directing two more couples to the van. Jill returned with the beers and we all climbed in.

As the driver started the engine put the vehicle in gear and the van began to roll away, we all introduced each other, leaning and shaking hands over the seats. It was difficult as we each had a beer in one hand and we had Belle to keep safe and still. One couple was on a honeymoon and the other was boy friend and girl friend. The man of that second couple stated he was a counselor for abused children. Once the hellos were over, the honeymooners kept to themselves, lots of whispers and touchy stuff, and we had little further conversation with them. But the second man just had to explain what he did for a living. It was depressing. Sometimes there is such a thing as too much information.

Belle panted and the van made its way out of the airport and through the always under construction streets of Montego Bay. The trip, while slow and hot, seemed that it was going to be fine. The air conditioning was only a rumor and the beers were dripping condensation all over our laps, but I figured we could stand it. The whole road trip was only to be about eighty kilometers. We left the city and hit the highway of Norman Manley Boulevard. And the fun began. Patrons at an amusement park in love with roller coasters may have liked the ride. We did not.

Dachshunds in Jamaica

The driver, on this twisting and narrow road to Negril, seemed to view any vehicle of any kind that was even remotely slower than the van in which we cringed, as a challenge and a reason to pass. He did so. The van's little engine would begin to whine louder as it approached anything in front of it and a quick right dip into the other lane, a surge of acceleration, would take us around and about. That was not so bad even though I banged my head twice on the window glass as I was tossed about during the darting maneuvers. The bad part was there was little planning by the driver for oncoming traffic. The idea is to pass no matter what and honk one's horn like crazy at any other vehicle that looks as though it might hit you head on. For eighty kilometers, we played "chicken" with oncoming traffic. Gripping Belle, gritting my teeth and hanging onto the back of the seat in front of me left me weak after only a few clicks. The beer bottles lost their contents to soak into the already sticky floor carpet of the van. All six passengers became very quiet, the women were pale, the men stoic, and Belle began to tremble like a rabbit in the gaze of a coyote.

Gratefully, we slowed down in a few places and we had a chance to look about and not just forward to gauge the chances of a collision. We first slowed down through a little town called Lucy where we noticed the Love Circle Bar on the side of the road. Maybe it was a nice place.. But only the bottom story of two seemed intact. The roof of the second had caved in. Next, around a curve, was the Uprising Bar. There was nothing uprising about that one. It looked as though one might contract a major disease just by grabbing the handle on the entrance door. We passed Edy's Highway Pub, the Cold Beer Joint, (A. Shacker-Operator) and the Craven-A Overproof Rum Bar. The places were all in various states of repair or disrepair and some buildings nearby could not be determined to be under construction or in the process of being torn down. You just could not tell. While the tropical scenery was of interest, we were most amused when we passed a factory the sign of which announced that Jockey underwear

Redstripe's Inn

was produced there. We laughed and promised to check each other for a "Made In Jamaica Label" later on.

Finally, we stopped, forty kilometers into the trip, at the Midway Tavern and Jerk Center. As the driver stopped the van, he told us we could go in, get a drink and take a rest. I was thinking seriously about walking the rest of the way to Negril.

The Midway Tavern and Jerk Center was not a bad place. I assumed anything we spent there would result in a minor kick back to the van driver, but that was okay and to be assumed. The place was mostly open to the air and breezes and was painted with pale greens, pinks and yellows. A bar occupied the back of the place and tables were distributed toward the front. Large reddish tiles formed the floor. Two girls with braided hair stood expectantly behind the bar. Jill took a seat at one of the tables; I steadied myself and approached the girls. "Hi. Do you have a couple of bottles of Ting back there?"

"Ya, sur," one girl replied. "No problem." She produced two bottles of the grapefruit flavored soda, popped off the tops with an opener and handed them over. As I paid for them, the girl asked, "Sur, y'lady dare? What kind of dog does she have? A pretty ting." The young lady was intrigued, or at least pretended to be.

I turned to look at who was Jill seated at a table with Belle in her lap and answered, "That, my friend, would be a dachshund. She is very important to us and travels with us everywhere. She might be a little overheated just now."

"Ya sur, a little water for de dog?"

"Uh, yeah. Thanks. That would be great."

My tip over the bar for the sodas was probably enough or more to pay for a plastic dish of water the girl produced and carried out from behind the bar to give to Belle and Jill. I saw the water come straight from a tap behind the bar. I figured any nastiness in the unfiltered water would not affect Belle's doggy lower track and was happy to have Belle get a drink. And as a bonus, we did not have to burrow through Jill's purse for the little water dish we always carried for Belle

Dachshunds in Jamaica

during our travels. All was well. Jill let Belle down onto the red tiles to lap at the offered water dish and we sipped our Tings. Our other travel mates from the van made their way to the bar, ordered and then wandered off to one side of the place where silk screened t-shirts were clipped to a cord strung between two palms. The driver stepped over to our table. We were not surprised when he began to make a pitch.

"Hello, my friends. Do you smoke? I have something for you and you do not have to worry here." He pulled the corner of plastic bag from his front pants pocket and showed us the green and brown shredded leaves he had to sell. Belle sniffed at one of his shoes.

I was polite as I could be and told him, "No, we don't. But I'll tell you what. Those two passengers of yours that can't seem to keep their hands off of each other might be interested. Ask them." I pointed to the honeymoon couple who were busy looking at the t-shirts outside the bar. I didn't think it was necessary to tell them any purchases they made likely were manufactured in Taiwan. Ignorance, while sometimes dangerous, is always blissful. In Jamaican tourist areas, fools and silly t-shirts are soon joined.

The driver smiled and nodded. "Okay, thank you, I will ask them, but if you change your mind…"

"No offense, but no. Irie."

"Respect."

"Yes. Respect."

The driver walked away and we watched him approach the honeymooners. While we could not hear over the distance, we could see by action what was happening. The man of the couple listened intently to the driver and his companion began to hold a hand to her mouth and appeared to be giggling. A quick exchange, able to be noticed only by the informed, was transacted and we knew that the couple would have an interesting time later in the day. I was hopeful they would wait until we were quit of them to enjoy their clandestine purchases. Few observers would have noticed or understood what had occurred. I looked at Jill with a raised eyebrow and she looked back at me and just shrugged. It was Jamaica.

 Redstripe's Inn

Belle was lying beneath our table on the somewhat cool tiles. *You two aren't going to be putting me in that blasted van again, are you? The thing doesn't even have seatbelts. A dachshund should not have to put up with all this. No, no, no.*

Dachshunds in Jamaica

Break Down

At times, I really am embarrassed by my fellow Americans when we travel. Some of them just have no sense of the need to treat anyone in a country outside the United States with any dignity at all. It is terribly annoying to me. Just after leaving the MIDWAY TAVERN and JERK CENTER, I was presented another example of this ego-laden attitude. Susan, the new bride of the honeymooning pair, just married to Jerry, leaned forward to ask the driver what was in a white paper bag near his seat. The man answered with all respect.

"Ah, miss. Dat would be my lunch. Got it in Mo-Bay."

"What's in it?" Susan asked.

"Ah, I have a hamburger and a chicken sandwich. I will eat when we get to your places and I turn around. Then I will have my lunch an y'enjoy your trip, irie?"

Susan asked, "Well, I'm hungry. Could I have one of the sandwiches?"

The driver looked up into his back view mirror to meet Susan's eyes and said, "No, really? You want my lunch, miss? I was gonna wait 'till d'drive back when I get hungry."

"Yes, I'd like the chicken, please."

I looked at Jill. Jill looked at me with a blank stare and new hubby Jerry stared out the window. The driver told Susan, "Well, if you want my lunch, you are welcome." He then tried to lighten the situation, "But, you n'spill on my back seats, Irie?"

Susan had an answer. "I won't. Thanks." She reached into the white bag and took a sandwich and said, "I'll just save it for later."

Even the dachshund was cringing on that little deal. But we drove on. I thought seriously of getting a passport from somewhere other than the United States just to dissociate myself from people like Susan.

Redstripe's Inn

I do not think we had been back in the van after we left the Midway Tavern and Jerk Center for more than fifteen minutes when we began to lose speed. We were on a stretch of open road, a field with a few bored goats on the left and the shallow ocean with the coral growths visible on the right. The van, as it slowed, was shuddering and heaving. Noises, more felt than heard, rumbled through the cabin of the van and sounded as though something had gone wrong that would be expensive to repair. The driver tapped at the dials on the dashboard and mumbled something I assumed was a curse. The curse was on us. The engine stopped its whine and the only sound was the wheels plowing through gravel as the driver made his landing onto the side of the road. He picked up a cell phone from somewhere, punched at it, listened with it plastered to an ear, and shook it. He put it down on the sun punished dash. He turned back to face us. He smiled. "We seem to have just a bit of a little problem, nothing to worry 'bout. The phone does not seem to work, so I will have to walk up a bit and find a phone and call for another van. You nice people, please, just wait a bit. I will be back in just a while." He climbed out and we saw him begin to walk off towards the south with no more ado. This was not a good thing and not part of our itinerary.

The six of us, seven with Belle, were suddenly stuck. The honeymooners had stopped their incessant petting and the counselor and his girl friend both turned to me as the man said, "Gee, now what?"

Belle was wriggling in my lap. *I thought we were not going to be walking. What is this now? I am really tired of the whole thing, you know.*

I admonished the hound. "Shut up a minute, would you?"

The counselor, head pulled back and with wide eyes looked at me at said, "Excuse me?" The poor fellow looked as though he just might be winding up for a full snit.

"Oh, sorry about that. I didn't mean you; I was talking to the dog."

"The dog?"

"Yeah, never mind." Jill was laughing at my expense but reached over and patted Belle's head.

Dachshunds in Jamaica

I had a temporary suggestion. "Well, folks, this isn't good. But I think we should get out of this van. We'll cook in here. At least outside we should get some breezes off the ocean and maybe the driver will find someone to get us out of here and the rest of the way to Negril. We all piled out. Jill took Belle a few paces off the side of the road and away from the van so that the little dachshund could leave a couple of little doggy deposits near the Jamaican roadside. The female partner of the honeymooner couple, after stepping down and out the side door of the van, took a position with her feet planted and hands on hips.

"Jerry! I told you we should have taken one of those vans with the nice signs on the side! Now what are we going to do?"

Jerry tried to calm his new bride. "Hey, don't worry about it. I'm sure someone will be along soon. Didn't the driver say he was going for help? Settle down, huh? Think of it as an adventure, Susan."

"I don't like adventures," Susan sniffed, "and I need a shower." She took her hands off of her hips, crossed them over her chest and turned to gaze out over the ocean. Jerry rubbed his forehead. I wondered where this marriage was going to go.

The counselor approached me and asked, "I don't think I gave you my name, it's Harold and this," he nodded at his companion, "is Cidco. This is our first time visiting Jamaica, have you been here before?"

I reached out to shake his hand a second time and told him, "Yeah, actually, we have been coming here for quite a few years. I've lost count of the times."

"So," Harold asked, "What do you think we should do? Do we just wait?"

"Yup, that would pretty much sum up the situation, I guess. We wait. Jill? Do we still have some bottles of water in the carry-ons? Hand me Belle and why don't you get those out and hand 'em around. I don't want to see anyone get dehydrated in this heat."

Redstripe's Inn

Susan spoke up. "I can't drink too much water; I'll have to use the bathroom."

I told Susan, "Well, don't worry; you do need to drink, especially if we are here for a bit in the sun, and you can always do what Belle did."

The young woman looked at me as though she really could have used a club right then and there. "You are disgusting."

I smiled my best smile, "Yeah, I've been told that before. Suit your self. But drink the water and, by the way, those beers you drank back at the last stop will be mentioning their name to you pretty soon, I would think."

Harold pressed me. "Really, if you two have been here a lot, don't you know what we should do? I don't want to just sit here and hope someone comes. What do we do?"

I couldn't help it. My mouth always gets me in trouble. I gave Harold an answer in Patois, the Jamaican language, "Wait, nuh t'other robot naw run tiday" I thought it was funny but Harold did not.

Harold's mouth opened and he looked at me as though I'd just landed from another planet. He shut his mouth after a long moment. Susan looked over at me, after hearing my answer, and rolled her eyes. Belle was in Jill's arms, *Uh, Dad? I think this might be a really good time for you to shut up yourself.* Jill spoke out loud for Belle. "Jack! Stop being such a jerk. Nobody needs the Jamaican stuff from you. Tell the poor man what you said."

"Sorry, Harold. That was Patois. It means…"

"A Patio? You mean like concrete? What are you talking about?" Harold was confused. I did not have high hopes for this man.

"No." I tried to explain, the language is, is a mix of, well never mind, you will get used to it if you hang around here on the island long enough. I just said that it was not likely a taxi would be going to show up any time soon."

"I see," said Harold.

He did not see at all.

We all turned to the sound of a car approaching and we watched it slow, pull to the side and stop in a cloud of dust

Dachshunds in Jamaica

and gravel spatters. We could smell burning oil from the overheated engine and a man with short cropped grey hair, a full beard, and dressed in a button down shirt and blue cotton slacks, stepped out of what might have once been a tan Chevrolet. His feet, dusty and callused, were adorned with sandals. He raised a hand. "Jahk and Jeel? I see de dog dere. Must be you! I was looking for you both back by de airport. I am Basi. Cirtron, he sent me. Ya, mon?"

We were saved.

Our traveling companions, not used to things on the island, stood back, reluctant to come near this man from the old chevy. I shook hands and tapped knuckles with Basi and said, "Uncle Basi? Respect."

"Ya, mon. Respect. I see de troubles witt de truck here. Irie. Nah, t'frown, mon. I will take you to Negril an Cirtron an Lady Sheila. Have de'bags?"

"Um, yes we do. They're in the van. Can we put them in your trunk?"

"Yes, mon. You d'carry. I will open d'bonnet, mon. Extras go inna back." Hah d'lady and de little dog get in and we can go."

Susan must have summoned some courage or perhaps put her attitudes aside for a bit and called out, "What about the rest of us?"

Uncle Basi was the one to give her an answer. "Ah. No. I have come just for Jahk and Jeel. It will be sure that someone comes for you. Come soon." I noticed Basi was trying to speak a little better English during this explanation. Apparently, he was not interested in additional passengers. He turned to me and whispered. "She did a expect d' flood an sure she did take de measurement inna wata." Basis was commenting on the woman's Capri pants that ended mid calf and seemed too short to him.

Susan tilted her head at us and asked me, "What did he say?"

"He said he thought your slacks were very cool."

"Oh! Well thank you very much, how nice."

 Redstripe's Inn

Jill and Belle and I climbed into the old tan Chevy with Basi at the wheel and left our fellow travelers behind. I felt a little bad about it, but we'd left them water and maybe the driver might even return. Maybe Susan would share her sandwich. I looked down at Belle, scratched an ear, hers, not mine, and figured Susan might just have that adventure she did not want. Jill looked at me and said, "Nice to have friends in Jamaica, isn't it? I doubt we could have gotten any help from American Express on that one. This is great."

I don't' care about anything as long as I don't have to walk. When's dinner?

Jill was right and Belle, of course, was being obnoxious. "Jill, you are absolutely right; we got lucky on this one. I'm glad I could get it worked out. Belle, just be still, okay?"

Okay.

"Don't compliment yourself just yet, buddy. We've got a ways to go and it was our Uncle Basi here, whoever he is, that came looking for us. I don't seem to remember you doing much of anything but ordering people around like usual."

I didn't answer Jill and shrugged off her comment as part of the testiness brought on by travel.

Basi was a more careful driver than the pilot of the van, but the difference was not very much. We made our way along the next sections of highway, passing cars with alarming intimacy, and I kept one hand for balance, seated up front, on the dashboard while Jill and Belle careened around at times in the back seat. We nearly gave a free ticket to the butcher to a lone goat. The animal had found a special spot in the road that it was not going to give up and Basi did a quick swerve back and forth and around while we held our breath. We survived that one. So did the goat who appeared to remain stoic, guarding his chunk of asphalt, and waiting for the next four wheeled challenge as we left him behind.

Dachshunds in Jamaica

The Inn

Thankfully, we saw a sign for Negril along one side of the road and Basi slowed to a speed that was concerning but not particularly life threatening. As the road narrowed and we continued at a slower pace, the backsides of resorts, high class, not so high class and just plain old places to stay, lined up outside the open car windows and fell back behind.. Basi stopped the Chevy in the road for a moment and then turned right out of the left lane onto a dirt and gravel path that had no sign, mark or indication of the location at the end. We knew it could not be long. We could see the ocean between the building and trees. The ocean was far the nicer view.

I swiveled in my seat and said to Jill. "This must be it." My wife was a little pale and Belle was standing on the back seat with all four legs straight and rigid while she panted and vibrated. Her tail was tucked down. I suspected Jill's would be tucked also if she had one and I knew both were not excited by the arrival but shaken and anxious after the trip. I spoke to Basi. "Is this it? Is this the inn?"

"Ya' mon."

"Great! It looks nice." But it didn't. I was just being polite. The view through the windshield was that of a single story block building with a thatched roof. The roof sagged and the once white walls were stained with brownish streaks. Around the structure were piles of undefined rubbish, burned out barrels, spilled plastic bags that were trying to hold trash and an old rowing boat rested upside down to one side. The only water it would ever see again would likely be rain. When we'd visited before, we'd not been out back. I remembered the front and inside well enough, not with kind thoughts, but the back looked like an unlicensed landfill. Jill was taking it all in and was silent. "Well," I said, "I doubt there's a doorbell, but let's go knock.."

Redstripe's Inn

Basi took the lead and we followed him around the side of the structure to the ocean side front. Belle, once out of the car, made a quick inspection, filing smells for later review in her dachshund brain olfactory lobes from the plastic garbage bags and then trotted along with us. Overgrown jungle plants crowded us as we walked along the little path leading to the entrance.

Basi stepped up to the front door, opened it and shouted, "Ya' mon. Day be here! Jahk and Jeel and d'little dog! Found 'em side d'road wid de sleepy robot!" Basi entered and we trailed in. The first room was pretty much as we'd seen it before. The décor was stained walls, worrisome fixtures and walls that looked to be standing by balance alone. A short elderly white woman in a printed housedress greeted us.

"Ah! Okay! You must be Jack!" she smiled.

"Yup, that's me. You must be Mrs. Carson? We didn't know you'd be here. But we know about you, pleased to meet you. And we owe you a big thanks on helping out with our canine travel concerns. It all went slick." I turned to introduce Jill but was too slow.

The now identified Carson turned to Jill, "And you, honey, you must be Jill. Right?"

I believe Jill was still thinking about the back yard, she just said, "Yes, that's right, hi! I'm Jill."

"Hi indeed," said Mrs. Carson. "Did this old codger of a cab driver get you here without scaring you into messing your underwear? Basi? Did you give 'em a decent ride or did you drive as usual? Don't lie to me. Jack? Jill? How'd he do?" She looked Basi in the eye and waited for an answer.

I reached over and clapped Basi on the shoulder, decided not to mention the goat and replied, "Oh. No problem. Smooth as silk. In fact, Basi rescued us when our van broke down. I don't quite know what we would have done if he hadn't showed. It's a long walk." Jill looked at me with her eyes wide open as if to say, *"Hey! Were you in the same car as me?"* I ignored her as the safest of several options. Basi smiled and nodded. I think he actually believed in my assessment of his driving.

Dachshunds in Jamaica

With the *'you must be's'* over we all heard a soft *woof* from down below. Carson looked down and then made a creaky descent on old legs to kneel in front of Belle. She reached out, scratched the side of Belle's neck and said, "And this, I know, is Belle. Hi there little sweetie! Welcome to Jamaica."

Carson was still scratching Belle when Sheila, Cirtron and Redstripe and Paris came in with hugs, sniffs and handshakes and a back and forth stream of: *'I can't believe it, this is great, Ya' mon, Irie, how was the trip? It was fine, Carson helped us with the doggy paperwork. Were so glad you're back! Glad to be here. Gonna fix d'place? We'll try. We'll see what we can do. Outstanding! Ya'mon.'*

Redstripe, Paris and Belle exchanged their own dachshund style greetings, most of which would be frowned on in polite human circles. There was way too much sniffing of inappropriate areas. All greetings accomplished, Cirtron and Basi helped haul our bags to a bedroom in the back and I marked the trip complete. After some discussion, we all decided we'd dine later at Alfred's Restaurant and Beach Resort, dogs and all, which was a fifteen minute walk down the beach. Jill and I looked forward to it. It was a favorite place.

 Redstripe's Inn

Dachshunds in Jamaica

Alfred's

At Alfred's, nobody cares if you are a dog. They don't care who you are, what you look like, what state of mind you are in or from where you come. They are a little picky about having the bill paid, but after that, everything is tolerated if you do not cause a major fuss. This includes those that are a little disabled from the use of certain things inhaled or swallowed, small children and, of course, dachshunds and any other breed of canine. As long as nobody bites anybody and does no damage, every thing is all right, irie. We'd made our trek down the beach on the first evening of our arrival, along with the three dogs. Basi was invited and that made six adults with the compliment of three four footers. The reggae band for the night was setting up on a wooden platform to one side and a triangular tower of piled driftwood was ready nearby for a late night bonfire.

    We chose a large picnic table among others that had been placed out on the sand. We knew, if we stayed long enough, the tide would come in over the barely slanting beach and cover our feet later on. That was part of the fun. But I also knew we might have to find higher ground for the dachshunds, most likely in our laps. The table at which we all sat to ready ourselves to order held two candles stuck into the tops of old Red Stripe beer bottles filled with sand. Each candle had been stuck through the bottom of a paper cup which was positioned upwards so as to keep the ocean breezes from blowing out the flame. The dachshunds assembled beneath the picnic table.

    A girl came out with a tiny notepad and took an order for drinks. We ordered Red Stripes all around save for Basi and Cirtron who asked for Heineken. I've never understood the Jamaican predisposition towards that brew. To me, it smells like skunks. The beers were brought out while the sky was

 Redstripe's Inn

beginning to darken as the sun was putting itself to sleep out over the ocean. Every thing was perfect and I reached over to pat Jill's wrist. We locked eyes and she said, "Can you believe it? We're back. And Belle's here too."

"Seems that way, doesn't it?" I withdrew my hand and placed my elbows on the table to brace for lifting my bottle. The girl with the tiny notepad returned and took orders for plates of lobster, fried potatoes and rice with peas. I could feel my salivary glands pull adrenalin from my bloodstream and the muscles in my jaw were beginning to twitch. The dachshunds under the table were also twitching; their noses were flaring and taking in the breeze driven scents of jerked meat sizzling over open coals in the back of Alfred's. I thought once more that everything was perfect. The dachshunds were going to convince me otherwise.

By the time our plates arrived and we'd been through one more round of beverages, the sun had gone down and the candle stuffed beer bottles were our only light on the table. That was fine as our eyes had adjusted. Carson was the first to attack her lobster.

"I can't figure this out, the way they cut up these big bugs is like they do the chicken here. It's fine. The stomach doesn't know, but it is a little screwy." Carson was referring to the culinary habit of hacking through a chicken at odd angles before grilling and also that the lobsters on our plates had been split down the middle. Each was laid out sideways, meat up. They were not lobster *tails,* they were complete lobsters cut in half and grilled with tails, torsos, heads and claws all intact. Main lobsters they were not. They had been trapped and brought up out of the warm waters of the carrib likely just off shore of Alfred's along the reef. "Can't say they aren't good, though. Right up there with good old American beef."

Cirtron's mouth was full and he said nothing but Sheila commented, "I don't care how they cook these things, they're great." She busied herself, as did Jill and I, selecting a few morsels to hand down to the hounds. Teeth snapped and jaws clamped just missing fingers below the table.

That's it? Is there more? Huh? Is there?

Dachshunds in Jamaica

We were continuing to clear our plates, feeding the dachshunds below, when the band came out to begin their set up on the wooden platform. The group appeared to consist of a drummer, two guys with guitars and a lead female singer. A tape with music from Bob Marley played from some piece of electronics as they hauled their equipment and plugged things together. The lead gal was dressed with more skin showing than cloth and Carson made a comment. "Ha! Can't you wonder what that little honey is trolling for?"

Sheila said, "Rose, be nice. It's just a band. Behave."

Carson was not to be put down, "Hey, at my age, I'm privileged to be able to comment on anything I want. I've earned it." She cackled and said, "Besides, you have to wonder about that set of bottoms she's got on, looks like she is gonna floss her behind! In my day, we kept that stuff in the bedroom, not that Mr. Carson ever had much interest in all that but..."

I was more than amused but thought I should diffuse.

Yeah, things are different here, but how about this food, I love it. Jill?"

Carson was bent on her observations. "Food's great. I could do better. But I guess we're not in Wautoma anymore, hey?"

Jill tried to help and added, "We've come to Alfred's every time we've been here. It's always great and it's one of the places we always remember." She scooped some veggies onto a spoon to hand down to the hounds, reached under the table, and looked up at the rest of us. No hounds had attacked the utensil. "Oh! Where did the dogs go? They're gone! We've got to find them before something happens!"

Sheila stood, her mouth opened and her eyes widened in alarm. She called out. "Paris! Redstripe! Belle!"

I was not surprised that we heard no answering barks. I looked around into the darkness and only saw some one from Alfred's kitchen bringing out paper plates with what looked like jerked pork sandwiches for the band. Jill stood. She was looking about with a hand clamped over her mouth. In the darkness, it would be near impossible to see the three dogs

 Redstripe's Inn

against the dark sand, but my hackles rose as a suspicion took form in my mind. Pork sandwiches and dachshunds seemed like a perfect match. I got up from the picnic table and made my way over the wooden platform where the band was preparing for the night music. I was right. But I was too late.

Sheila, Jill and Cirtron had made their way into the open structure for the bar that was Alfred's to look around for the hounds. I was by the band. I saw that one paper plate of food had been placed on top of one of the big amplifiers to be used to blast the music out over the sand and water. I didn't see any hounds, but I could sense them. I waited. It only took a moment.

One by one, Redstripe, Paris and Belle came out of the darkness and clambered up onto the platform. Their goal was the amplifier with the plate bearing sandwich. A couple of sniffs and a paw push was the foray and then all three jumped up against the amp. Under the weight of the three little hounds, the thing toppled, spilling the food onto the planks. The three dachasteers were happy to start lapping but were interrupted by a loud and ear piercing screech, even for human ears, as the amplifier lay on its back, pulling on the cords for power and input. The hounds froze, looked about, saw me and pedaled across the planks to me hoping I would save them. I did bend down to grab two, grasped the third, but there was at least one dachshund bottom hanging down precariously. The rest of our party heard the noise and ran up to the edge of the platform. Sheila grabbed the dangling hound and Jill took one more. Cirtron stood behind. The lead lady singer began to shout at us.

"Dese be your dogs? Geetem outa here. Geetem out! No way we gonna take de damage without you pay, understand me?"

I understood clearly. This was not good. But I really doubted if the amplifier was really damaged by a spill over. I was composing a careful and polite reply when the manager, I supposed he was, came over. "These are you dogs?"

What else was I to say but, "Uh, Yeah, they're ours. I'm really sorry about this, I…"

Dachshunds in Jamaica

The man leaned towards me and whispered, "Irie, No doubt de trouble not be so bad. De, lady, she can be a bit of d'problem. Big head more than she has. No matter, she sings well and we have lotsa people come. So. Gonna take de dogs and go on? Leave be, irie."

I felt a little relief. "Sure, we were done anyway. But we need to settle the bill first."

The man whispered to me once more. "I will take care a'dat. Best you go. Take d'little ones and let be. No problem, mon. You make it up later, okay?"

"Thanks, okay." As I said that Carson came up to our group of folks, band members and dangling dogs.

"Well, I see you have the dachshunds. That's good. Wouldn't want any harm to come the little sand sharks, would we? But we should probably go, though, and pay up. Whose treat tonight?"

I answered, "It's taken care of but you're right. Let's go."

Carson looked at me. "Well, now, there is a gentleman. Thank you. But the least I could do is leave a tip."

"No, Mrs. Carson. We need to go. Now."

We left Alfred's and I was wondering if we would ever risk going back. And worse still, we missed the bonfire.

 Redstripe's Inn

Dachshunds in Jamaica

Building Inspection

Even though exhausted from traveling and Alfred's from the previous evening, Belle, Jill and I rose just as the sun was doing the same the next morning. As I threw one leg out of the bed and planted a foot onto the damp floor of our quarters, Belle shook off her cover and stood on the mattress, ready to go outside. *And you'll be taking me out now? I would hope so. No time to wait, y'know.*

Jill just looked at me. There was not a question that I would be the one to supervise Belle's morning routine.

Belle's business concluded, not mine, the two of us entered the inn and found our way to the kitchen where Carson was stirring some oddly colored eggs in an iron skillet. Slices of bread, simmering in another pan in a little of what I hoped was butter, were making their pilgrimage to reach the state of toast. All in all, it did not smell bad at all and my stomach made a little gurgle in agreement. I could smell coffee and Belle's ears were perking and she was paying very close attention to the cooking. Paris and Redstripe galloped in followed by Jill, Sheila and Cirtron. Every one looked hungry, moistening lips and swallowing. Sheila grabbed some plates and cups from a shelf to place on the table. Carson picked up the pan of eggs and I was ready to have a few bites. I was disappointed.

"This is the first batch, you folks, they're for the dogs," Carson announced. And she bent down to scrape the cooked eggs, three equal portions, into bowls set out on the floor for the hounds. Three long furry snouts attacked the egg filled bowls and the only sound in the room was the slurping of dachshund tongues and the sizzling of toasting bread. Carson broke some more eggs into the iron skillet after replacing it on the stove. She was kind enough to use a set of tongs and deliver a piece of toast to each of our plates and then directed, "Cirtron, pour that coffee. It should be ready."

"Irie, Ya' mon." Cirtron did not jump up right away.

Carson looked at Cirtron and stared a second.

"Yes, ma'm. I will pour d'coffee."

It was just coffee and toast. I was feeling like I was at home already.

Eventually, we got some eggs to compliment our coffee and pan fried toast. What bird had produced the eggs was unknown. I figured it would not be appropriate to ask. While eating, I thought that I was pretty sure goats did not lay eggs but the cheesy and greasy flavor made me wonder just a bit. The taste had not seemed to interfere with the hound's enjoyment so I put my concerns to rest and just ate.

Jill spoke around a mouthful of toast. "So, what do we do today? Just hit the beach or..?"

Carson answered. "With all of you here, and I am so glad you are, don't forget that, we're going have to get some more groceries."

Sheila said, "Yeah, I suppose so," and turned to Cirtron. "Can you find one of your friends to take us into town?"

"Ya' mon. No problem."

"Good enough," said Carson. "Let's all go and get what we need in town for the next few days. I can't cook with just air, you know. Maybe we can take the dogs, just for fun."

I spoke up. "Would you mind if I just stayed here? I need to start to look around at this place and figure what needs to be fixed. That's why we came back, after all, and I would not mind a little time to just look around alone. The dogs can stay with me. You guys go. We'll be just fine."

Sheila said, "That works. But we need to at least take Redstripe with us. We always cut better deals with her along. She's good at harassing ankles while we negotiate and the vendors get confused and distracted so we get better prices."

"Really?" I asked.

"Does that work?" asked Jill.

"Yup, that's our way to do it, yup." Sheila affirmed.

Dachshunds in Jamaica

Darn it if I did not hear a little of a dachshund accent in what Sheila had said. She must have been around Redstripe and Paris too long and I wondered how sensitive she may have become to the dogs' mental messaging system. I did not think it would be very helpful for me to ask at that point. Discretion is always the better part of valor. It also is part of common sense.

Redstripe's Inn was a mess. Between the effects of bad construction to begin with and neglect afterwards, the place was in need of a great deal of work and repair. The electric wiring was all surface mounted, in some cases it was just bare wire wrapped around nails pounded into the walls, and major portions of the cement walls had lost the material from the mortar joints between the blocks. The entire structure was standing only by the force of gravity, a pile of school house blocks, and the roof was a disaster. That was easy to see. There were no ceilings and the thatch covering the pole joists forming the roof could be seen to be rotting, damp and critter infested. The birds must have loved the roof. Their idea of plumbing was to use the floors below as a drop zone and this made me wonder about the human water and sewer lines as an aside. Paris was with me on my inspections and a bird eliminated a package of the last night's avarian dinner straight down to land expertly on the little dog's head. There was the sound of a definite splat.

Paris was not pleased. *What was that? If I wanted to deal with pigeon droppings, I'd stayed in New York with Sheila! This is disgusting! A dachshund should not have to put up with this!* The little dog shook her head, ears flapping loudly against the sides of her small skull, and most of the offending offal flew off to land on my lower legs and the floor. I figured she would survive for the moment and continued my look around. I was dismayed.

The inn consisted of a large kitchen with an eating area, a room that could be used to house a table for nicer dining and a row of eight bedrooms in line towards the back all opening along a narrow hallway. The cement block walls rested on a concrete slab, chert, by name in the local dialect, and the roof was thatched with palm leaves covered by netting that was supposed to keep out the birds but was not doing the job as Paris had realized. Every other one of the "guest rooms" held a toilet and a shower and the water supply sort of worked and the toilets sort of flushed. The plumbing was probably just a matter of cleaning pipes but the structure of the walls and roof were troublesome. Light broke through in places between the cement block. I began to make a mental list of the work to do.

We'd have to clean the water and sewer lines, replace some plumbing fixtures and perhaps give up one of the bedrooms for a shared bathroom for the guests rooms without. The roof had to be renewed, but before that, the walls had to be reinforced and the old mortar chiseled out and replaced. I was thinking that running some re-enforcing iron rods placed down through the outside support walls might be a good idea. Outside, the electric service box would need to be examined and inside, the wires for lights and outlets needed to be torn out and substituted with new copper, probably incased is some sort of surface mounted channeling. Other than all that, things would be okay if there was not some sort of strong wind in the weather forecast.

While I was thinking, looking and poking around, Belle joined me and Paris. She sniffed at the floor, my legs and at the top of Paris' head. *And you too have been doing what? I can't say I really like that smell much. It makes my nose itch on the inside.* Belle snorted and sneezed. I didn't blame her at all. Paris gave her a look. *Oh yeah? Wanna chase some birds and make yourself useful?*

I returned to the kitchen after the review of the guest rooms and took a look at the stove. The two dachshunds were happy to crawl underneath the combination stove and oven appliance and could be heard scratching and sniffing at things better not seen until later.

Something must have died under here! Wmff! We really need to roll around for a bit, just to absorb the smells. Yup, yup.

The stove and oven appeared to be fueled by gas. That was a surprise but I did not know what to expect anyway. I was

Dachshunds in Jamaica

thinking wood or oil or something worse. The dachshunds were still underneath and I peered behind the thing. I saw copper lines leading to the stove. That did not seem right. I expected iron pipe if the stove was gas but this was Jamaica and I held my opinion. "Belle, Paris! Come out of there! We need to go outside and check on these gas lines."

The two hounds scrambled out and looked up at me. *You're making us miss some really great smells. But okay, outside. Yup,. yup.*

Outside of the kitchen, supported in a wooden cradle and leaning at a dangerous angle, was a large propane tank. That was the fuel for the stove. I wrapped on the side of the thing and the hounds began to bark at the sound. The tank rang near empty and that was the most dangerous of all situations; it was a tank with flammable gasses in the heat of the Jamaican climate and a bomb primed to go off. I looked at a gauge at one end and tapped at it. But the insects that had crawled in and lost their lives behind the glass of the gauge had glued the needle into place with their tiny rotted carcasses. The tank would have to be purged and checked for tightness and I added that to my list. The dogs were not interested. *Hey! Can we go back now and play under the stove? Let's go in. This is really boring.*

 Redstripe's Inn

Dachshunds in Jamaica

On the Beach

The sun, an orange ball of mystical proportions, was falling, a leaking balloon that quizzically swelled instead of shrinking as gravity pulled it down towards the surface of the ocean in the west. Cirtron and I sat on the beach with a pair of sand covered dogs, one each reclined at my left and Cirtron's right, us in the middle. The hounds were the bookends for the two of us. I pulled a lighter out of a pocket to reintroduce flame to the tobacco in my pipe and Cirtron held his own vice between the tips of two fingers. I looked down at the little sand rat beside me and scratched her ear. Belle only yawned. Cirtron spoke.

"So mon, how d'you tink de work for de inn, mon? Good?"

Belle kept yawning while I kept scratching. "Cirtron, I don't know. Maybe it isn't so good. I mean we just got started, and man, the work to do and the materials we are going to need are both staggering. It's a lot."

"Yes, mon. De work not be much fun alone, but together, ah, we have de smiles 'pon us!

I sighed and answered. "Cirtron, it isn't the work that gets me. That's just time. But the money for materials is going to be a lot. I know you and Sheila have money in the bank, but I haven't seen the accounts and everywhere I look in the place, I see dollar signs."

"Jays, mon. You call de money here jays. Don't have de worries mon, de money she come."

I wanted to say, *"Oh, yeah, right. Like the stuff is growing on the trees around here. All I can see is coconuts."* But I stayed quiet and looked out at the sun balloon over the water.

Cirtron must have sensed my concern and he stood up. "Yes, mon. She come. Lemme show some ting for you. Wait, mon." He took a few steps away from where he'd been seated

and peered down at the darkening sand. After a moment, he reached down and plucked a bit of some sort of trash and came back to me, held it out for me to take and said, "Look, mon. Tell what you see dere."

I was getting annoyed. I looked at the piece of beach refuse and then said, "Cirtron, it's a cigarette butt. So what?"

"No, mon. You look not so close. In Weescoonseen and in New Yark, d'mon finds such on de street. But day be very different. Y'see, dis one, she be smoked all de way. In your country, de cigarettes on de ground have not been smoked down smoked so low."

I looked at the butt once more. Sure enough, not only was there no paper left with tobacco at the end of the filter, the end of the filter which would have been opposite the absent and littering smoker's lips was burned.

"See mon, de Jamaican people do not waste any ting," Cirtron said, "We be find de tings and money, mon." Cirtron turned away and headed back to the tottering inn leaving me with his island wisdom, the two sand covered dachshunds and the sun balloon which was still sinking, and likely nearly out of air.

The sun and conversation left little impression on the hounds. Their only concern, as always, was food. *Shouldn't we be going back in about now while Carson is cleaning up? We don't want Paris to hog all the floor snacks! No, no no!*

I rose, turned away from the water and sinking sun and motioned to the dogs to follow me.

About time, yes it is don't you know! Time for snacks,. yup, yup, yup.

Dachshunds in Jamaica

The New Truck

On another morning, the sun rose once more out from under its blanket of darkness and cast clean early light through the windows of the inn. The air was still cool and snuck through openings to touch us with invisible feathers. It was quiet and peaceful as we sat at the table while Carson prepared breakfast; the first portions would go as usual to the dachshund bowls. A cup of Blue Mountain Coffee sat before each of us. The dachshunds stood guard near Carson just in case something was missed.

And how about those eggs? They ready yet? We aren't going to wait here too long without creating a fuss, you know. Nope, nope, nope. Long little bodies trembled.

Cirtron's nose was in his raised coffee cup when he said, with a ceramic echo, "I tink maybe we should geta truck or some. To move da tings."

"What tings?" Jill asked and I chose not to correct her accent. Next thing I knew, she would be on the beach and making money braiding hair. That would have been fine; we could use a few more jays.

"Tings," said Cirtron, this time more clearly, having put down his cup.

I followed on Jill's question. "You mean materials to fix this place? Lumber and paint and all that? Not bad. If we had a truck, even a small one, we wouldn't have to pay folks to deliver, but where do we get it?"

"Yeah," said Sheila, "I haven't seen any used car lots around here. anywhere."

Carson looked over her shoulder. "Hmm. Maybe we could just hijack a truck from the pizza delivery guy."

"Piece of what?" asked Cirtron.

 Redstripe's Inn

"Never mind." I was curious. "Where do you propose to get a truck?" I glared at Carson. She was a dear but sometimes less than a great help.

"Ah. Irie. Gonna go t'day and talk 'round. I will find one. Maybe take de dogs."

Go for a ride! Yup, yup, yup. Go for a ride! The dachshund's ears were perked and they were interested even though food delivery was imminent. *And what's this about pizza? Remember, we get the crusts. Yup.*

After breakfast, Cirtron took off on foot with the three hounds. I was worried whether all four would return and that the three four footers would not be eaten by goats. Jamaican goats are not to be trifled with. It became a long day and my finger nails got a little shorter. Goats were not the only problem. Cirtron had taken off for Norman Manley Boulevard and the drivers on that road had no compunction for safe driving. This I knew from experience. Most of it was bad. Thinking more clearly, I had to tell myself that all of it was bad. In Jamaica, the convention is to drive on the left side of the road. Jamicans are not much for convention. They drive on both sides of the road depending on the whim of the moment.

During the day, in the houndless inn, the rest of us spent some time cleaning things and I took some time to poke around some more to determine what needed to be repaired. The more I looked, the more I thought about a big fire and starting over. The place was not a handy man's "fixer upper," it was a builder's "put you under." My miserable musings were interrupted late in the day by the auditory warning of Cirtron's return. He was coming down the drive from the main road to the inn in a small pickup. One dachshund was in his lap, another had back legs on the passenger seat, front legs out the side window and the third was perched with front legs on the dash with hindquarters on the seat. The noise was ear pounding. By contrast, a Harley motorcycle at full throttle would be considered a lullaby. It was not that the truck had a muffler in need of repair, it just didn't seem to have one at all.

Dachshunds in Jamaica

Cirtron's grin pierced the windshield as he rumbled to a stop. I took my first look at Cirtron's acquisition.

There was not much rust on it, not enough to worry it was going to collapse into a pile of red dust in the next day or two. The tires masqueraded as inner tubes; there was little or no tread. The bed had been reinforced with a layer of plywood and there was no tailgate. It was just an old truck. But the color was fascinating. The best body shop in the United States would have drooled and not been able to duplicate the appearance. The Jamaican sun had done a number on the paint.

In another life, the truck might have been fire engine red. But the sun had faded it. Yet it had not faded it evenly. The top three quarters of the vehicle looked pink; a natural fade from red. But down below, near the rocker panels, the sun had not been quite as cruel and the paint had faded only to a deep coral. The gentle blend between the two colors was striking. The thing would have been chick bait on a California beach. Whether it would keep running and whether the tires would hold air was another matter.

"Cirtron, where'd you get this thing?" I asked.

"Basi." He had d'truck and said we could keep her if you write a letter."

"Me?"

"Irie. You write, ya'mon?"

"I write for the truck? What's this letter?"

"Basi paid someone for d'parts. He didna get 'em. Ordered from, ah, Venezula. Maybe you write t'dem and make it irie. Den we keepa truck. 'Kay?"

I started to laugh. Cirtron frowned. "No?"

"Yes," I chuckled. "I guess we have a truck."

 Redstripe's Inn

Dachshunds in Jamaica

Builder's Supply-Jamaican Style

I was sitting at the kitchen table, blue mountain coffee in a cup in front of me, wondering about the day, when Cirtron came in. "Ya, mon. De day, she look to be nice, ah?" Cirtron took a cup from a shelf and poured coffee for himself from the pot that was heating on the stove. He sat down across from me, slurped his coffee and then asked,

"You remember, I say dat all tings, day come, yes?"

"Yeah, Cirtron, I remember, but I'll feel better when I see things arrive and I can actually get my hands on them, the materials we need, and begin to really work on fixing this place." I was responding with less than my usual enthusiasm and with my always there, just below the surface, doubts. "So, what do we do? Wait for United Parcel Service?"

"Ya, mon! Tom Hanks! Like him, mon."

I did not realize that Cirtron was trying to make a fool of me and retorted, "Tom Hanks was stuck on a desert island in that Castaway movie. Maybe just like us. Besides, that was Fed Ex, not UPS."

"You pee what?" asked Cirtron. "Whad is dat?"

I was already working on my annoyance. "Never mind. Forget it."

"Not to mind," Cirtron's undiminished positive attitude would not be dampened. "Today we go anna get de tings, some tings we need. Together we can do dis ting and have our smiles 'pon de face!" He spread his arms, pink palmed hands opened and he grinned with yellow teeth."

I looked him straight in the eyes, above the beard and yellow teeth. "You got money? From the bank? Or did you just rob it?"

Cirtron lost just a little of his grin. "Have de respect, mon. Dis be some ting 'pon which y'need d'work, ah? No money

- 41 -

Redstripe's Inn

today. Today, we see d'cousins. Let us go, uh? And we gone t'take d'truck."

I had no idea what he was talking about or planning and just said, "Ok fine. Let's go. Would now be good?"

"Ya, mon. Now be good. Early in the mornun', and de people, day be ready to help 'bout now. We gonna get wad we need, fix d'inn now. Irie."

We rose from the table, left the coffee cups and headed for the back door. Redstripe, Paris and Belle had just unburrowed themselves and passed us on the way to the kitchen.

Ah, breakfast! Yup. Hey, where do you two think you're going? The least you could do is fill our bowls. And do the water dishes too, would you?

"Ask the girls, you three little rats. We're in a hurry." I heard several indignant snorts when I said that, but we made our way out to the truck just the same.

We made our first stop at a construction site a mile south of Redstripe's Inn. The sign at the end of the gravel entrance said "SANDER'S RESORT-COMING SOON." A couple of rusty trucks, a small bulldozer and back hoe slept to one side in the sun appearing as though they would never move and had not for some years. Half a dozen Jamaicans wandered about with out any observable purpose. Sander's resort was, at that time, a partial shell of concrete cubicles with no discernable shape. Like most island construction, one could not tell if it was going up or coming down. Cirtron left the truck, craned his neck and head a bit to look about and then headed over and began to talk with one of the men ambling around in the dust. A conversation ensued, but the Patois was so heavy, I could not understand it. Cirtron laughed, his conversation partner banged knuckles with him and then shouted to two other men. "D'extras, mon. D' wire. Pudem on de truck!"

As I watched, two men walked over to a pair of wire spools. They were the large kind you see on the side of the road for electric company workers but the gauge of the wire looked to be about twelve or fourteen. It would be the stuff used to wire outlets, switches and ceiling fixtures. The

Dachshunds in Jamaica

Jamaicans tipped the spools onto their edges and rolled them over to the truck, muscled them up and over into the bed. I guessed we had just taken on one thousand feet of copper wire. I wondered how this would be paid.

Cirtron turned back, waved and shouted, "Respect! Go wid Ga, mon!" He motioned for me to get in the truck. "Go, mon. We have more t'do yet."

I was confused and wary. "Cirtron, who pays for this stuff? Do they like send us a bill or something? Can we just take this?"

Cirtron smiled as he seated himself behind the wheel. "No, mon. Yes, mon. Y'see, these be de extras not to be used. My cousin say we can take d'stuff and it will not be missed by d'man."

"Cirtron, for pete's sake! Are you telling me we just stole this wire?"

"No mon, here in Jamaica, de people all share. No need to keep something not to be used. Do you see dis?"

I saw it alright. We'd just stolen a bunch of wire worth a ton of money through some supervisor that Cirtron knew by acquaintance or family. Back in the United States, the people who kept track of supplies at construction sites or retail stores would call this "shrinkage." I called it stealing and said so. But Cirtron would not listen. "Not t'worry, mon. Irie."

I did indeed feel that the developers of SANDER'S RESORT-COMIING SOON would not miss a couple of spools of wire. But the only Jamaican sharing I was concerned about was that of sharing a jail cell with Cirtron. We left the site and went on to the next and then the next. Each time Cirtron knew someone, supplies were loaded, and we made our way back to Redstripe's Inn with wire, miscellaneous lumber, bags of cement, paint and plaster. The truck was full and while I knew we could use the stuff, I felt I just might like to get back, grab a dachshund for my lap and perhaps put some of Carson's trade in my pipe just to try and get calm. I told myself I did not mean the latter. But the whole experience left me a little weak. Cirtron's reaction was to

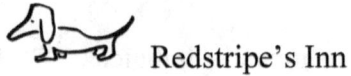 Redstripe's Inn

simply hum Bob Marley tunes while we drove back to Redstripe's Inn.

Dachshunds in Jamaica

Red Sox Jacket

Anyone who advises that a German Shepherd, a Rottweiler or any other breed of dog make the best watch dog is wrong. Dachshunds are the best ones, paws down. Dachshunds are bred for noise. The point, in days past, was that the ability to bark at levels to damage human hearing was a good thing so as to be heard when the little hounds were down in the dirt tunnels hunting badgers. Dachshunds bark. And they bark with absolutely no discretion. Belle is no exception to this rule. At home, we let the doorbells rust away into disrepair. We had our own furry dog bell. Any one or thing approaching the door initiated a symphony of barking, growling, scrambling, raised hackles and barred teeth. The United Parcel Service fellow would drop packages as fast as possible and run. The mailman seldom dared approach the door; he tried to stick with the mailbox at the end of our driveway unless some package would fail the cram test and not fit in the box. Trying to restrain the dachshund and avoid sharp and snapping teeth was a family project, carefully orchestrated, just to be able receive and pay for a simple pizza delivery without a trip to the emergency room for us or the poor person with the card board packed snack. Woe to the squirrel cracking an acorn too loudly from a hundred yards away. Dachshund's ears work better than weather radars. The whole thing can be exhausting.

In Negril, the problem was multiplied by the power of three. We had the Belle bell, the Redstripe warning and the Paris alarm. All would go off simultaneously, sometimes at just the sound of night wind in the palms. I never heard the knuckles rapping on the door just warming with one morning's sunlight. The triplicate dachshund warning system let me know someone was out there. I had to make my way through the scrambling hounds to the door and opened it. A man in a red sox jacket and baseball cap, wearing sunglasses, stood there on the porch. He touched a hand to his cap brim. The dogs shot out to circle around his ankles. He did not look down and did not move. I thought he was a little overdressed for the weather.

Sheila had heard the dog alarms go off and came up behind me to look over my shoulder at the visitor. She looked. "Oh my god! It's, you!"

I turned, "Who?"

"This is the FBI guy. Remember? We told you about our trip out of Chicago and there was a bomb on the plane. This guy found out about it all." She addressed the man, "You're the guy, right?"

"Yes, ma'am."

My brain was storming. The first thunderbolts in that mental weather echoed with, *"FBI. I knew it! They found out about the stuff Cirtron and I borrowed. Oh man, this is going to be really bad"* I did not occur to me that Jamaica probably did not even have a FBI and that no one from the states would be bothering. It was just a panic thing on my part.

Sheila went on while the hounds kept circling. "What are you doing here? Are you, like, ah, looking for terrorists or something?"

The man smiled and finally looked down to regard the three dachseteers. "No." He waved one hand, palm down at waist level as if jerkily sweeping off invisible dust from an invisible table. "But if I wanted to find some, these three would certainly do just fine. I just came to visit. 'Hope I'm not intruding."

"Of course not," Sheila answered. "Come on in here. We have a ton of questions. How did you find us? We always wanted to be able to thank you."

The man still did not move. "Well, that's what I do. But I got a little tired so I thought I would come down here and look around for awhile. I'm Mike."

"Good to finally meet you, Mike, I'm Sheila."

The hounds, hearing the calm in Sheila's voice had gone quiet.

Dachshunds in Jamaica

I wondered if the guy had a warrant or something.

"Well, Mike, come on in here, you're gonna have to tell us some things."

Mike nodded, walked through the door and around me, leaving me feeling a little transparent like that invisible dust on that invisible table of his. The three dachshunds were bringing up the rear guard behind Sheila and Mike.

Once in the kitchen we all saw Carson puttering with something on the side counter. She turned and greeted Mike and then asked Sheila, "New guest?"

"I don't know, really. Mike? Are you here to stay with us?"

"Thank you, but no. I rented a place up in the rocks near town. I'm all set. But thank you."

Carson wasn't done. "Good enough. Want coffee? And if you're going to sit at that table, I expect you will do us the kind favor of getting rid of that hat and those glasses here. Respect."

"Yes, ma'am." And Mike pulled the cap from his head and used two fingers to grasp and remove his sun glasses. He revealed cobalt blue eyes surrounded by deep creases at the outside edges and a head covered with inch long grey hair. His sideburns looked clean and even as if trimmed off with a straight razor. "I would very much like a little coffee, if that's alright. I'm told it is pretty good here."

Sheila started in right away. "So, Mike, we never had the chance to really thank you for what you did for everyone in Chicago. Really, we were told you were the one that sort of blew the whistle on the bad guys who planted a bomb on our plane. You saved everybody! How did you know about it?"

"That's what I do. But I think the dachshunds really were the ones who took care of it. They were the one's that got loose and chewed through the wiring to the device."

"So," I cut in, "you work for the FBI?"

"No, not really. I'm what you would call an independent contractor."

Carson came to the table and put a cup of coffee in front of Mike. "You're one of those spy guys?"

Redstripe's Inn

"No, I just listen around and tell the government what I think. Sometimes I get lucky and sometimes I don't. That's what's made me a little tired. I don't always win and when I don't, things happen that are not very nice. People sometimes get hurt or worse. I've been having trouble sleeping lately when I think about it all. That's why I came here."

Sheila pressed on, "But how did you find us? Does the FBI have, like a file on us or something?"

Mike explained. "No. Yes. But that doesn't have much to do with it. Your names and destination were on the roster for the flight out of Chicago. I read it. Then I called the local bank here and asked for the balance of any account you may have had under those names. They wouldn't give it to me, privacy and all that, but I complained that I did not have the latest report and that it must have been sent to the wrong address. They were very polite and confirmed the address on file, this one, and that's how I found this place. Simple. You don't need to be a spy to do that sort of thing. You would be surprised what you can find out just by asking the right questions. In my job, I tend to ask a lot of questions."

"Why us? Why here?" I asked.

"I just have been feeling a little tired lately. And I wanted to see the dogs. I didn't know there would be three. Can I pet them?"

I realized that while the man was minimizing his role, he was a major player in the unseen world of international intelligence gathering. It made me cold. The scariest part was that he looked so normal. I made a note that I did not want him mad at me. "Pet away, Mike. They love it."

Mike leaned down towards the dachshunds who were hanging out and sniffing around his chair. He picked up Redstripe, then Belle and finally Paris and placed them all in his lap. He was not a big man. He had to circle his arms around the hounds in order to keep them in place on his thighs. He had no free hands to drink his coffee. Carson looked at the three little lap dancers and reached to help Mike scratch an ear. She asked, "Where did you say you were staying?"

Dachshunds in Jamaica

"I didn't. But the place is called the Rock Cliff Cabins. It's nice. I like it. It really is quiet and the folks there are nice."

"Look, the dogs like you so you'll stay here. That's it. No one argues with me around this place and you are not going to be the one to start. Jack, go find Cirtron and tell him to go up to Rock Cliff and get this man's luggage. Tell him to go straight up there and back and not to stop and loiter around with his friends."

Mike was not used to Carson and he quietly objected. "You don't need to do that. Besides, I don't have any luggage. I guess I travel light."

"Easier even so," replied Carson. "JILL!" she shouted.

Jill called out from one of the back rooms. "What do you want?"

"I want the last room fixed up. We have a guest."

The dogs were still crammed in Mike's lap.

 Redstripe's Inn

Dachshunds in Jamaica

Rehab and a Night Parade

The rehabilitation of Redstripe's Inn was not so much a nightmare, but rather a recurring bad dream. Every problem noticed and uncovered presented at least two more. Mike extended his stay in Negril and stepped up to help. He was good at taking directions, but Sheila, Cirtron and Jill had lots of plans of their own that did not match mine. Trying to keep everyone coordinated without bringing the whole tottery structure down in one sad heap was maddening. And of course the dachshunds had their opinions too. The habit of dachshunds, being close to the ground, is they tend to sneak up behind you and trip you. Then they give you a look, as you are lying on the ground, dust embedded in your backside as if to say, "What is YOUR problem, you clutz! Watch where you step. And please exercise your clairvoyance so you know where we are going to be, exactly."

Sheila had once told us a paintbrush was a dangerous weapon in her hands. She was right. I found that my wife Jill had absolutely no eye to hand coordination when it came to tools. I gave them both hammers and told them to have at the failing plaster on the walls. They apparently quickly found their calling in destruction. They each had a wicked wield with a swinging hammer. I suspected they were transferring thoughts about old boyfriends. Damage and demolition were the goals, not accuracy. They did fine.

Cirtron was a supervision disaster in and of himself. I asked him to move the stove. I didn't tell him to close off the gas line and disconnect it. We came close to having a real wiener roast on that one.

Carson did her own thing, pitching in where she could but mostly advising. I watched her show Mike how to soap screws to make them easier to drive while he was repairing a porch rail. I heard her tell the girls, "Give me that! Let me show you," and then explain one should hold a hammer at the end, not the middle, to save the strain on the wrist. She did the best she could to keep the hounds out of harm's way and little by little, chopped away at the outside foliage making things look as if one day they would really appear to have been landscaped. She still managed to cook for us all. For a while, all she had was an outside fire while the stove was displaced.

Dachshunds were problems.

We learned quickly that it made sense to always use latex paint when there are dachshunds around.

I hadn't remembered we had a piebald in the dachshund herd and we didn't. It was just Redstripe's reddish brown coat splattered with white paint splotches. Darker areas were just dirt.

I looked down at the spotted and speckled hound saying, "Hm, Sheila's been painting again, huh?"

Yup, yup! And I was helping. She sneezed.

"Dachshundeidt," I offered and was rewarded with one of those stares of dachshund disdain. "No, matter, dirty dachshunds are why we have an ocean. Let's go. It's bath time."

Nope, nope, nope! It'll wear off. No ocean needed at this time.

I leaned down to grab the hound thinking I'd won the round until I noticed the paint was still wet and transferring to me. Most days during the rehab of the Redstripe's Inn went pretty much that way. We did some work and cleaned the hounds. We'd work some more and return to hound cleaning. I hoped we'd not eventually run short of ocean. The dachshunds surely hoped we would.

Paris had a different sort of cleaning problem. She developed an affinity for wet plaster. We'd catch her with a wet, grayish white nose while hovering near lick marks on walls. We were concerned about what the plaster mix might do to her dachshund insides. Carson prescribed beef flavored vegetable oil which pretty much took care of any problems. Still, for that solution, the ocean came in handy again.

Mrs. Carson, between advising and cooking, made another contribution to the cause. She convinced Cirtron and Sheila and Jill to drag the old boat from the back of the inn out to the front. Once it was placed upright, she filled it with dirt and sand and planted flowers. She'd painted the entire thing white and then added red letters.

REDSTRIPE'S INN
ROOMS BY WEEK OR DAY
INQUIRE WITHIN

When she was done, she called us all out to look. It really was nice and I asked her, "Carson! This is wonderful. Did you take care of this all alone?"

"Nope., I had lots of help."

I looked down at the hounds, always underfoot, and noted they were pretty well plastered with red paint. Another ocean bath was in order, but the ersatz boat sign, even with some drips of paint drifting down in red streaks from Carson's lettering, made a fitting presentation.

A lot of the work was in the detail. But the biggest problem was the roof. It leaked. It sagged. It looked like a conservancy for birds and gave shelter to unseen rustling things. It would have to come off and I worried about losing the little protection from the weather it offered while we did the work. I was discussing this with Mike and Cirtron with the accompaniment of the plaster fiends as background percussion. Thump! Crash! Giggle! Woof! It was the sound of hammer blows, the loud rustling impact of falling plaster and then the delighted laughing of Jill and Sheila followed by the approval from our dusty canine chorus.

Cirtron minimized my concerns. "A roof? Ah! How much d'trouble can dat be? We have all of us t'work, mon."

I explained, "Well, first off, I think it would fall on just us three, the work that is, hopefully not the roof, as I don't like the idea of the women up there with loose hammers over anyone's head."

Mike, had no expression on his face, "No, that might not be wise." Thump! Crash! Giggle! Woof! "Certainly not wise."

Redstripe's Inn

"No," I said. "Not wise. And this is not going to be easy. A lot of those rafters need to be replaced, we have to get roofing materials and I think we need a flashing around the top of the outside walls."

Cirtron asked, "Flashing? I have heard of dis, a sport in de United States, no? Why d'we need such?"

Cirtron's missed communication between our cultures left my eyes watering. "No, Cirtron, it's a metal strip, nailed down on top."

"To keep the water out," added Mike.

"Ah," said Cirtron.

"Oh boy," I said while I massaged my temples and thinking it was times like this which made me feel I living inside a bad comic strip.

The issues did penetrate Cirtron's rasta brain and he stood up. "Okay, den, we need d'help. We shall have such and d'roof pieces, too. Ya' mon. Do not worry. Dere is no need for dat."

Cirtron left us, made his way out back and I heard the old truck's engine hack its way to life. I couldn't help but think Cirtron was going out to borrow a construction crew like he'd borrowed most of the materials to rebuild the inn. The concept no longer seemed strange to me. That was scary.

Mike rose and stretched as if he'd just finished a big meal. "All right then. That's taken care of. I'm going to see what I can do with some of those rafters from underneath. Maybe we can replace some or just run some new ones alongside."

"You do that. I'll be along in a minute." I sat by my lonesome for a bit wondering what magic Cirtron would conjure this time. The women had not stopped. I could still hear them. Thump! Crash! Giggle! Woof! At least I knew where the dogs were but none of us saw Cirtron the rest of the day.

Redstripe, Paris and Belle selected five minutes before midnight to conduct a test of the emergency dachshund warning system. They gave the equipment a rigorous and thorough test including barks, howls, growls and snorts. I could imagine doggy saliva dripping from front teeth exposed

Dachshunds in Jamaica

by snarling lips. A semi truck in full engine breaking mode could have snuck down Norman Manley Boulevard unnoticed or at least unheard over the dog din. Dachshunds do not make the habit of rising from comfy covers for no reason. We knew something major needed attention. We found it outside the front of the inn. It was Cirtron. He was waving a beer bottle and standing next to two Monét style haystacks. The piles were thatching materials. I understood immediately but I did not know how to thatch a roof. I was used to plywood, tar paper and shingles, not a roof that might be blown down by the big bad wolf. I told Cirtron so while the hounds conducted a long nosed inspection of the two piles.

Cirtron waved his beer at me. "Did I not tell you not t'have de worries, mon? Irie! I brought d'help long also. Look, mon." He pointed out to the beach. I looked. A line of more than a dozen Jamaicans, single file, was making the down the beach towards the inn. Each carried two six foot long bundles of thatch, one on each shoulder. As I watched, they approached and dumped their loads to begin a third pile. Without speaking, they turned and left. They must have been going back and forth from somewhere up the beach all night. A small bird could have built a nest in my open mouth.

Cirtron laughed. "Wenna sun comes, day come and build d'roof for us. Gotta help, though. Respect."

My partners in the Redstripe rehab stood around us in the Negril night. All had questions.

"Who are these people?"

"How do we pay them?"

"They're going to build a new roof? What if it leaks?"

"How does this work?"

I just closed my mouth before that little bird took up residence.

Cirtron laughed again. "No problem. Day know how, even use d'flashing like Jack say to do. Day be friends, mon. No pay. Trade."

Carson piped up, "Wait a minute Cirtron, are you talking about what I think you are?"

 Redstripe's Inn

Sheila shared Caron's concern. "Cirtron, what have you promised?"

Cirtron went on and shook his head. "No, mon. Not dat trade. Day have 'nuf be it anyway. It'll be fish."

"Fish?" I blurted, "We don't have any fish! Where do we get fish?"

"De men, mon. Day get d'fish."

Jill frowned. "I don't get it."

I didn't get it either. But Cirtron had waved his magic Jamaican stick again.

He told us, "Day all be fishers. We let'em come 'cross the land for d'inn wid dere boats an day fish on de reefs. Then, we buy d'fish for d'guests and day sell others up an down d'beach. Keen?"

I understood perfectly. Not only had Cirtron gotten us a free roof, he'd managed to supply us with fresh seafood right at the ocean's edge. A magic jamaican stick indeed and a very savy business man. Mike said something for the first time. "That works."

It certainly did. By sundown of the next day, we had a new roof.

With the new roof installed, things went along without fear of leaks and weather intruding on our repair efforts. I taught Cirtron and Mike how to sweat copper pipes with flux and solder and small torches for the new water supply lines and we replaced the drains with plastic. I insisted we add some vents to help things drain from the new sinks and toilets and showers and all seemed to work. The only casualty was Redstripe's tail. She became a little too nosey while Cirtron was soldering a pipe and the hot lead dripped on her rear end appendage. She healed up just fine. But at the time, she bolted off like a little dachshund rocket and actually took an unplanned ocean swim. Any aerospace engineer would have been interested in her speed over the sand. We did run into one more problem that needed the wave of Cirtron's magic Jamaican stick.

Jill and Sheila had torn down, demolished, turned to flakes and powder, a wall between the kitchen and dining area that

Dachshunds in Jamaica

was in need of their ministrations. The wall was likely ready to fall anyway and Jill and Sheila did not take long to put the thing out of its misery. We had lumber, but were short on plaster and concrete filler for the new wall. I was examining the remaining bags of plaster and 'crete when the three dachseteers came out from somewhere to help me with my calculations. Noses pushed into the bags and came back out powdery white. Well deserved sneezes ensued.

Oh! We thought there might, SNORT, be some food in there, SNORT. Uh, no? So where is it? The food, that is.

I ignored them. Cirtron joined us. I asked him, "Hey, we're a little short here, any ideas?"

"Ya, mon. Day all tree be short. Canna make de legs longer, no."

We like our legs just fine, thank you. They reach the ground, don't they?

I held my breath just for a moment and said, "No, Cirtron, not the dogs. We need more plaster and concrete for this wall. Can your friends get us some?"

"Ahhhh. Maybe later. Soon come."

I knew what that meant. It meant like forever. In Jamaica, "soon" could mean within minutes, days or even years. Cirtron was telling me we might not get any more bags of 'crete or plaster for a while. I looked at him and said, "So, fine. Would it be such a rare concept to go into Montego Bay and buy the stuff? We have the truck. All we need is a few bags."

Cirtron scratched at his dreadlocks as if he might stimulate a thought. "I'll go inna truck. No problem, mon. Irie"

I felt relieved but I should not have. Two hours later, Cirtron returned with the back of the truck full of glass bottles. And they stunk. Beer bottles, wine bottles and rum bottles, all empty save for dregs, filled the back of the pink and coral pickup and the smell would have dropped flies or at least made them fly in woozy circles. Before I could object, Cirtron explained. "We mix d'bokkles wid de chert and den we build d'wall. Irie. Keen?

 Redstripe's Inn

An' look. Day pay me to take de stuff!" He handed me a pile of jays. Not only had Cirtron solved our problem, we could use the bottles to fill the wall and it likely would look pretty cool, he'd made some money as a Jamaican recycler. The idea was not new. The light would go through the bottles in the wall, the bulk of the glass would save on materials, and the result would be as good as any plans from an overpriced architect. It was just a matter of cleaning things. We had the ocean for that, as always.

The wall and the roof and the plumbing all functioned well. The dachshunds continued to use the outdoor plumbing, but that was their prerogative and probably a good choice. For me, I was thrilled when I managed to get my computer back on-line and connected with the rest of the world. This involved a satellite dish, installed by some folks from Mo-Bay, and also gave us phone service and television. We had to run a cable all the way out to the road and place the dish out there as the trees near the inn blocked out access to whatever those guys had in the sky. But it worked. I had to pay real money for this setup. Cirtron had no friends, cousins, acquaintances, uncles or aunts that could "borrow" radio signals. A small television found a home on the porch and the dachshunds were happy to watch the cop shows, the animal shows and the boring news each evening in the fading light. Seldom did any of the humans get a chance to pick a channel. The TV went to the dogs. Life would have been perfect if we could have found a remote that had buttons large enough for dachshund paws.

While my new connections allowed me to resume my work, there was a task that fell to me with my new connections and skills as a geek. I contacted, made arrangements and created internet links to a travel agency. Castaways Travel agreed to list Redstripe's Inn as a recommended travel destination. The company posted pictures of the inn, our rates, the "how to get there" information and began to book guests for our little place on the Negril Beach. As guests began to dribble in, stay with us

Dachshunds in Jamaica

and then return home, their comments about us as hosts were published by Castaways. Most of them were nice.

The clientele we developed was an odd lot. Some were kids on college breaks, we had a few honeymooners on a budget and quite a few were single women. They came to Negril after nasty divorces or breakups in order to find new romance. But they only found rum and middle aged wannabe Romeos. Carson made up the difference in disappointment with her lectures about life, holding court at the dinner table, and the hounds became our therapy dogs for sorry souls. It was not unusual for the dachshunds to pick a guest bed in which to snuggle for the evening and allow peaceful furry dachshund thoughts to calm the dreams of our guests. We didn't have mints on the pillows and we didn't turn the bath towels into funny fuzzy origami animals, so the dachshunds became part of our amenities offered at the inn.

My computer delivered an odd e-mail one morning while I was looking at future bookings from Castaways. It had no return address and I nearly trashed it thinking it was junk. It wasn't. The message read,

Please forward to Colonel Michael Johnston

Kindly report to La Guardia Airport ASAP. Contact Mr. Roland Greenlay of security. Travel arrangements have been made at the International Airport in Montego Bay, Jamaica.

Vss

Colonel? How did Vss find Mike here? Who was Vss?

Mike knew what it was when I showed it to him. He left an hour later and that was it. He'd come quietly, helped and left suddenly. I don't think he even said goodbye to the dogs before he climbed into a taxi bound for Mo Bay. That was a shame. It was a shame for him so far as I thought. The dogs moped for the next three days.

 Redstripe's Inn

Dachshunds in Jamaica

Kingston and England

Carson, standing over her stove top pots and oven, stopped me when I came in one evening about six o'clock. I didn't see the dogs hovering about Carson's ankles; they must have been still out in the front near the beach and harassing passers by. They were missing the chance to lick up the spills from Carson's cooking. But they were just little dogs, after all, and had the freedom to follow their own doggy brained agendas. Still, I thought it odd that they were not being dachshunds on the spot at the moment with the prospect of nosing around the food spills on the floor.

Carson said to me, "Hey, Jack. We've got two more guests today. At first I thought they were from Kingston, but I guess they're really from England; somewhere from around a place called Loughbourough." Carson pronounced it Luff burrow; I had no idea if that was correct or not. I supposed Jill, being born a Brit, would know. "I'm going to have dinner for them ready in just a bit. I'll fix you a plate, too. They seem pretty interesting and I thought you might like to meet them and talk with them, maybe get some ideas for one of your books, you know?"

Carson surprised me. She had only a grudging respect for my writing. She thought it foolish and a waste of time. In her view, I didn't have a real job. Knowing that, I had to consider her suggestion seriously. The new quests must have impressed her in some way or other and I felt she was using me, the resident writer, to have something to show off and impress the guests. If nothing else, Carson had a decent knack for business. Regardless, I thought, fair enough. I'd join the pair for dinner if they'd have me and maybe even get some writing fodder in the bargain.

"Uh, yeah. Sure Carson," I answered, "Are they already in the dining room? I'll go talk with them. When's dinner?"

Redstripe's Inn

"Five minutes. Go be polite if you can."

I nodded and headed into the next room; it was what we called the dining room. It most certainly did not live up to its name. The room was just an extra near the kitchen in which we had placed an oil cloth covered longish table and benches. The walls had accepted some white paint, had a window in one, and the room had a ceiling fan installed that whirled slowly when it was in the right mood. It must have been a good fan day, it was spinning, and the guests, a man and woman, looked relaxed and comfortable in the Jamaican heat.

"Hi there," I said. "Can I join you? Carson says she'll have dinner in just a few minutes. Maybe we could talk over dinner."

"Most certainly, yes, please," said the man. "Missus Carson has told us you are a writer, is that true?"

"Yep, that's the rumor anyway. I always enjoy meeting people and just talking. It gives me ideas for later on and I never know what might end up in my notebook. Can I ask you some questions and things? If that's all right?"

The man replied, "Yes, of course. You may ask two."

Before I said anything more, I had to think about how to respond to the offer of two answered questions. I took a moment to study the pair. They were middle aged. Both were dressed moderately, not fancy or flouncey, but well. The man sported no hair at all. It was tough to see if he was truly bald or had chosen to closely shave off the remains of thinning hair. The woman had the tightly curled black hair common to those of African descent and it was restrained by a scarf tied in the back. Neither was smiling, but the man's eyes were grinning.

I decided to take a chance and swallowed the bait. "Would that be just two questions or would it be two questions each?" I was relieved when they both laughed.

As Carson brought in the plates, baked chicken with a mild jerk sauce with boiled potatoes and some heavenly carrots, the man said, "Please sit down, please do." I slung one leg over a bench and took a seat and began to ask some questions about the couple's background, origins and how they had come to

Dachshunds in Jamaica

be there at the Redstripe's Inn. My inquiries brought forth much more than I expected and we talked long after the plates were cleared.

Les and Delores explained they had been both born in Kingston but had left Jamaica for England when in their teens, before they had married one another. At first, their accents confused me; a hard Brit softened by, not Patois, but certainly a Jamaican influence. This was not surprising, I supposed, considering their history. Les offered that they often vacationed in the Caribbean, but he'd never been to Negril in his youth as his Kingston based family had never owned a car. Delores shared that she was a teacher back in England somewhere in the Midlands, I think I heard her say, and that it was a very hard job. Les most certainly had some opinions about Jamaica and some parts of the world in general that he had chiseled in stone over time. I was fascinated by the views he offered.

Les was in a lecture mood. "As I said, I was born in Kingston, but as it happened I left nearly forty years ago. Yet, as I see, not much has changed. The economic status of these people, the Jamaican people, is controlled by forces set in motion such a long time ago." Between his blended accent and the tone of his baritone voice, I had a thought that I would not mind having this guy read me a bedtime story. His voice was musical. "Europe and the United States have somewhat shut out the Jamaican's international trade in some respects. Other countries, say in South America, are being subsidized by the Americans causing the Jamaican product to be more expensive. This has forced the people to look to tourism as an industry. There is a reason the Jamaican government does not want the Jamaican dollar to leave this country with tourists. The money must stay here. This situation has continued back from a very long time."

Les had more. "Now, think about the people on the beach, all selling one sort of thing or another. Visitors here often shun them and are fearful. People can be openly rude. But that is not needed. Tourism is what keeps parts of the island going, economically. The beach people should not be feared. They

are the simple entrepreneurs in a challenged economy. Think on this. If these people wished to commit crimes as a way of making a living, they would be elsewhere and not demeaning themselves on the beaches of Negril. These people are not to be feared, they are to be complimented."

I wanted to listen to more, but Les was interrupted by the appearance of the dachshunds. Delores looked down at the hounds and said, "Oh! Hello little people!"

Did you hear that? She called us people. Finally, we get a little respect! Yup! Is there any food left?"

Delores did not know about dachshund attitudes and that they'd arrived for treats, not a congenial visit. She reached down for Redstripe and took her into her lap. "Les, lift up one of the dogs. They're so cute."

I took Belle and Les picked up Paris with a "Yes, dear."

With three dogs settled in three laps, Les continued with his lecture.

"Now, consider the famous musician from Jamaica, Bob Marley. People from elsewhere do not know the man brought himself up out of the ghettoes of Kingston. And this is typical. Most outside the island see the people only as painted by the pictures of the travel agencies. They do not have the true vision and…"

I could have listened to Les all night. If memory serves me, I believe I did. The dachshund snores served as the punctuation for Les' lessons.

Dachshunds in Jamaica

The Dachshund's Photo Op

I had given up on shoes weeks ago. I'd found they were nothing more than collectors for beach sand, and as my soles toughened by going barefoot, I found the whole shoe thing more a nuisance than a help. It was easier to brush sand from my bare feet than to try to clean out the same from my Docksiders. I was seriously becoming at risk of going completely native. I did not think it was a bad thing. My toenails had a different opinion. They were always dirty. Shoeless, Cirtron and I and two of the hounds made our ways north up the beach to see what there was to see one early morning. Redstripe and Belle trotted along with us on our slow, and barefooted, walk up the beach and away from Redstripe's Inn. No vendors bothered us. Cirtron was obviously a native son and the sun had darkened my own skin to the point that I no long looked touristy. I probably appeared more as some fellow who had dropped out of someplace and was now a legitimate resident of Negril. There is certain honor among thieves, Cirtron and I may have appeared as we belonged and were not to be bothered. The only thing that slowed us down was a quick squat and squirt by Belle and a little of a stop and drop by Redstripe. We covered the offending offerings of the dogs to the gods of the beach by sweeping sand over their places of demarcation with our bare feet.

    Brushed Away Resort, an establishment on the north end of Negril Beach has, among other things, a signature quirk that it very special just to them. They have these really neat foam mattresses that are very pink, have their BAR logo printed on them and the things are good to use both for cushions on beach lounge chairs and for floats for folks that want to just hang in the waters of the warm Caribbean Sea just off the sand. It is an upscale sort of resort and the rumors imply most of the clientele is young and buff. Travel agencies are quick to advertise the work-out gyms available at the place and the management does not complain. It really is a nice place. But it is also for those tourists to Jamaica who would like to see the nitty gritty parts of the culture from a distance. Guests rarely leave the grounds to explore elsewhere. More suntan oil is consumed than stomach filling food. Cirtron and I and Redstripe and Belle, on our morning beach walk, came up to the guard house on the south edge of the resort. The resident and mostly sleepy custodian of the beach peace eyed us, peered at the dogs and motioned us through but with a wave to stay towards the water. 'Not to bother the guests, do you see?

Redstripe and Belle had been snuffling along, gently disturbing everyone on our walk and were both pretty much coated with sand. I was thinking a quick ocean dip might clear this sand issue up but I sensed the dogs knew what I was thinking.

Excuse us? No, we are just perfectly fine, thank you very much. Salt water is not needed at this point, if you don't mind. Although, if you would like to carry us a bit, that would be acceptable.

I figured one more day of sand coating would not hurt the hounds and just walked on, Cirtron at my side, the dachshunds continuing to act as scouts in front of us, behind and to both sides. An "event" was being staged just ahead.

In the United States, it is not uncommon to find all sorts of magazines selling women's fashions. If one would look closely at the glossy photographs in the catalogs that come unsolicited to one's mailbox, one might see many tropical backgrounds for the models, some of which are from Jamaica and other islands nearby. Women look at the pictures for the way the clothes and swimsuits fit. Men look at the models. The background, often very beautiful, is often missed. The models in these catalogs often look to be tall enough to play professional basketball. But that is a photo-trick. It is not true. Cirtron and I and the dogs were approaching a photo-shoot for some magazine. The models were there, anorexic looking young women, small, tended by older grizzled ladies and the

Dachshunds in Jamaica

photographer had seen younger days too. Black trunks with open lids containing all sorts of picture taking and lighting equipment littered the beach. Lights on stands and wires were around and a large piece of aluminized plastic lay on the sand to reflect sunlight up against the normally shadowed parts of the model's bodies. The girls were posing for a photographer who had likely no memory of his own hair and were turning this way and that while standing on the plastic. Redstripe and Belle darted forward before I could say a word.

I said it anyway. "Belle, Redstripe! NO!" Too late. This was going to be trouble.

The dachshunds were probably thinking, *Cool! New friends? Any treats around here?*

The hounds hit the plastic, the models began to scream, the cameras were still clicking and the situation had all the earmarks of turning into a major disaster. Oh boy.

When the two hounds hit the plastic, there was another problem. The claws on their little dachshund paws pierced the plastic and left holes. It was just a moment of time; the camera was still clicking while the dachshunds were busy perforating the shiny plastic. But the bald photographer dumped his camera and began to yell.

"Somebody get these blasted animals out of here! I can't work like this! Get them out! Get them away now!"

The models recovered quickly and looked down at the dogs.

"Well, aren't you two too cute?" One reached down and picked up Belle, another reached for Redstripe. Cirtron and I just stood. I was thinking maybe a tidal wave might be a good thing at the time. The models fussed with the dogs while the photographer fussed with his camera. He must have had some sort of digital preview mechanism and exclaimed,

"Oh my god! Look at this!"

I thought, *"Look at what? Don't we have enough to look at? Cirtron does, he can't take his eyes off these young girls."*

The photo guy went on, "This is fantastic. I can't believe it! All those holes and dents in the plastic made reflections that shined little stars all over the girls' bodies! I could never have done that! I never thought of it. Fantastic! Put those dogs down. I want more shots!"

The dogs were lowered onto the plastic, the models preened and turned and the camera clicked and whirred as film advanced. Some guy with a black shirt came over to speak with us and asked, "Are these your dogs?" The man's shirt was one of those tight tee's He was well muscled, wore an earring in his right ear, and was cocking his head to one side. His squeaky slurry voice was in contrast to his build. His chino pants, bulky through the thighs, clinched at the ankles above sandals, were black to match his shirt

I had to say, "Yes."

Cirtron chimed in. "Ya' mon. Day be ours."

Black shirt squeaked, "Well, fine. Very good. You see, our photographer likes the effect from the, ah, dogs. They are what breed? Actually, it is not important. We are doing another layout in Mexico, near Cancun, next week. If you would be so kind, we would like you and the dogs to join us there, at our expense of course, for another session. We will arrange your transportation out of Montego Bay. Would you need transport from here to there? We have a small plane we use for just such things and..."

I never heard the man take a breath.

I felt I needed to slow this black shirted muscle person down, just a bit. I also thought it might be a good thing to oil his voice.

"Hold on, my friend, I don't mean to be rude, but who could authorize all this, assuming we'd agree. You can't just whisk us off from here on a whim, can you? Isn't there someone we need to speak with and make arrangements? We can't just take off to Cancun all of sudden."

Black shirt cocked his head to one side, his earring dangling. He smiled with a manufactured set of whitened teeth. "No. Yes. I understand." He waved one hand as if to push some sort of smell out of the way. "I'm Allen Hershner. I own Caribbean Fashions magazine, we are doing our swimsuit shoots for our fall catalog. I'm lucky to be able to do as I see fit and would be pleased if you two and the dogs

Dachshunds in Jamaica

would agree to join us in Mexico. As I said, we can make the arrangements. Besides, the photographer likes the dogs. So do the girls." He turned away from us and towards the preening models and blew a kiss from his palm at them.

I was not convinced that this was a good idea by any means. When Allen turned back to us, I asked, "Fall? Swimsuits? That doesn't make sense. The two don't go together." I was buying time while I was thinking. The dogs sensed my doubts, stopped their antics with the models and stared at me. *Hey! Don't blow this one. Mexico! Cool! They've got Chiwawas and tagos and stuff!*

I corrected the hounds. "They're called tacos. Now stop it."

That was another mistake on my part. I should have kept my mouth shut, not open it up and give people reason to doubt my sanity. Allen looked at me, puzzled and said, "Well, yes, of course. I am certain we can find some tacos for you. Can you come? We can arrange for near anything." He batted at the air again, trying to dismiss another bothersome smell and seemed impatient. He wanted an answer.

I delayed and repeated that the idea of selling swimsuits in fall made no sense. I associated fall with L.L Bean, not beach fashion.

Allen answered, "Oh yes. We sell so many 'kinis and suits and those delightful thongs with the little jewels in back and all sorts of lacy things in fall. Everyone wants to escape the cold in the United States and plan trips to the Caribbean in the winter. They all want the latest. Can you come or not? It will be fun." He looked at Cirtron sideways.

Oblivious, Cirtron burst in and exclaimed, "Ya' mon!" before I could respond. I simply said,

"Well, I suppose so. Yes, we'd need a ride to the airport but I'd like to…"

"Good then," said Allen. "Where can we reach you? Here's my card." He plucked a business card from a pocket and thrust it at me. His picture was on it.

Redstripe's Inn

I took the man's card and told him, "You can find us at nine twenty Norman Manley Boulevard, here in Negril. Redstripe's Inn."

"Ah," said Allen, "Good, then." He sniffed. "Let's see. Today is Tuesday. Let's say we pick you up there, at, what was it? Nine twenty Mr. Manley's road, at around nine in the morning tomorrow. Would that work for you?" I could not figure how the guy could keep talking without ever inhaling, but he was doing it.

Cirtron repeated, "Ya, mon." He folded his arms across his chest, grinned, and I could tell he was going to be no help at all.

I answered, "Fine." *"What had I just done?"* Jill and Sheila were going to use both of us for buoys when I told them the plan. That was if I could even come close to explaining.

Belle and Redstripe were listening. *Mexico! Nachos would be nice. We could get a couple of those straw hats. Let's go! Yup, yup!*

Dachshunds in Jamaica

Arriving on a Jet Plane

There is probably a better description to use, but I must say the landing at Playa Del Carmen was intriguing. We came into the small airport from over the Gulf of Mexico and hit the runway hard and fast. Whatever brakes are used to slow a plane kicked in immediately and we were thrown forward against our seatbelts, barely able to hang on to the hounds. In a large commercial airliner, the runway is so big and the plane is so high, that the normal visual references that let the brain estimate speed do not come into play. In the case of the little Lear Jet, this was not true. We could see we were really smoking down the runway and could mark the pavement passing by just a bit below us in a blur of grey concrete and black asphalt patch. Being able to actually stop did not seem to be a reasonable option. But we did stop. As the pilot predicted, we stopped no more than fifteen feet from the end of the strip. Looking out and forward at the little remaining space in front of the plane, I wondered briefly if the Lear had a reverse gear. There did not appear to be enough space to turn around. Redstripe and Belle cowered in our laps, ears flat and thinking unpleasant thoughts about the entire situation. *And we went through that ride for what? Do we get cookies or anything? This is just intolerable and we really could do without this!*

I told them both to just shut up for a minute.

The pilot was able to turn the plane around and we proceeded to taxi over towards a small building where we could see a van waiting. Two men stood beside it wearing white pants and fresh blue shirts. TOMAS TRANSPORT was painted on the side of the vehicle. Jonathan and James moved levers on the door to the cabin, pushed something or other to let the stairs unfold and Cirtron and I, bags shouldered and dachshunds in arms, said our thank you's and clambered down the six steps and on to the pavement.

Redstripe's Inn

It was hot. It was melt the asphalt hot. It was little dogs could not stand on the ground without scorching dachshund paws hot.

One of the men approached us. He was swarthy and dark with short black hair and the compact, mesomorphic build of the Mayan people of the region. He was clutching a piece of paper in one thick fingered hand and examined it carefully. He looked at the two of us, the four of us, and said "Ah, and you would be Mr. Seetrone and Mr. Jahk?" It took me a moment to decipher his English and then said,

"Yes. That's right. That's us. Are you our driver for Caribbean Fashions magazine?"

"Si, yes, we will take you down towards Tulum. It is not far. What kinds of dogs are these?"

I started to answer but an incoming plane thundered above us, a small single engine prop plane making the next landing. The sound of the engine was piercing and I had to shout. "They're dachshunds!"

"Ah!" the man shouted back, "Salud!!"

"What?" I didn't understand.

The man grinned and tried again, this time without the noise of the plane which had passed. "El estornudo. The sneeze. God Bless you." He pointed to his nose. I knew the dachshunds were thinking my Spanish skills were down in the gutter somewhere and they both snorted. The man laughed and pointed at Redstripe and Bell, "Si, el estornudo!"

I looked at Cirtron for help but he just smiled and replied, "Ya, mon." All I could do was grin vacantly and climb into the van. Once the two men were settled up front and Cirtron and I were settled in the back with the hounds, I tried my hand at a little Spanish. For me, sometimes I feel even my native English is my second language when I stumble over forgotten words or usages. It is a middle age sort of problem. But I tried anyway with my limited Spanish. I waved my hand in front of my face and said, "Caliente!"

The second man in the front passenger seat turned and replied "Si, muy caliente. Very hot." I figured I was safe and had not inadvertently insulted someone and settled back.

Dachshunds in Jamaica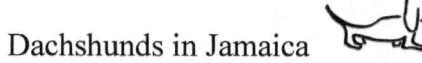

The dogs looked at me. *Yeah? So who are you trying to impress. Really!*

The first man keyed the ignition and headed the van out of the little airport and out towards Tulum.

 Redstripe's Inn

Dachshunds in Jamaica

Resort of the Lost Beach

The van pulled up to a conclave at the end of a dirt road. The tires rested on cobblestones that paved the drive in front of the entrance to the resort. A two story replica of a Spanish mission, complete with ten foot tall double wooden doors with iron pulls stood in front of the lobby, an iron bell decorated the top of the façade. Two young men in whites, pith helmets on heads, greeted us, pulled back the huge and heavy doors and motioned us through with smiles. Just inside, the dogs by our feet, we were approached by a black man in a tan suit. He wore no tie and his collar was open. "Hello and welcome! I am John. Would you follow me?"

Cirtron and I followed. The two hounds trotted along side and we entered a round building to the left. It was cool inside and John motioned us to sit on chairs in front of a glass topped desk. He took a seat behind and faced us. Welcome to the Resort of the Lost Beach. "So, you would be our guests, Mr. Jack and Mr. Cirtron." It was not a question. "May I get you a towel? And something for the dogs?" The man was not Mexican. While dark skinned, he was too tall and angular. The accent was British colonial. The facial features were African.

Cirtron answered, "Ya, mon"

I responded, "Uh, yes that would be great, thanks."

"Very good and well," said John. He turned to open a small fridge, extracted two cold damp towels and handed them over to us. He nodded, and turned back to retrieve two small bowls of chilled water, placing them down where the hounds could reach and lap. Belle and Redstripe did their slurping thing and I plied the towel on my face and neck. After the heat and dust of the trip from Playa, the cool towel was a sample of heaven.

Redstripe's Inn

I took a moment to look around, aware that the dogs were spilling water onto the white ceramic flooring. The building was not round as I'd thought. It was twelve sided and consisted of one big room. The high ceiling was of thatch. The white adobe walls were adorned with Mayan artwork and a few rugs of the same design were positioned carefully around the room. The teak desk in front of us rested on one of the carpets. A partition partially concealed half dozen computers on one side. The place wasn't just clean. It gleamed. This was not one of those high class and expensive resorts you see featured on travel television. It was one of those places only the rich know about. I looked down at the sloppy hounds and wondered if the bottom of my shoes were clean. John followed my gaze.

"Don't worry about that. We will take care of it," John said, waving a hand in dismissal. He pulled some papers from a drawer and placed them in front of us. "As you know, while we are so pleased to have you here as our guests, you are also guests of the Caribbean Fashions. The ledger has been cleared and I just would ask you sign below for our records." Cirtron and I did so with the pens John gave us and he continued as he rose from behind the desk. "Now then, may I show you the facility and take you to your rooms?" He looked down. "And you, my little dachshund friends, we have something for you also."

"Woof!"

The man smiled and replied, "Woof also to you. Welcome."

Apparently John had done his homework before we arrived. He did not have to ask about the dogs' breed. I suspected he may have known their names, too. The five of us left the building and entered the resort proper. If the front building was immaculate and quietly classy, the grounds were surreal. It was not a huge area, only a few hundred feet across bordered by buildings on the back side and the ocean in front. A serpentine sea wall constructed of coral rock and mortar separated the grounds from the beach A pool with a swim up bar, an outdoor covered dining area and a winding water

Dachshunds in Jamaica

channel were the main features. Railings along little foot bridges over a water channel were of rough hewn yet polished wood. The landscaping looked as though each and every bush, flower and blade of grass had been trimmed to millimeter exactness with a straight razor. John bent down to the pavement and retrieved a lone leaf and placed it in a pocket. "Ah," he said. "Excuse me." The two dachshunds bolted towards the grassy areas ready to explore and wreak havoc. Ears flapped. Tails stood at full alert. *Any squirrels around here? Are there? There have to be squirrels. What kind of place would this be without those furry little bushy tailed demons? They gotta be hiding here somewhere! Yup, yup!*

John was gesturing and pointing out details. He explained the little building at one end was an exercise gym, there was an air conditioned dining room ready to serve at any time and a set of stairs that led up to the entertainment area; it contained, said John, a dance floor, gaming tables and another bar.

While sometimes there are surprises, the Resort of the Lost Beach was one of those, sometimes things in life are painfully predictable. Proof of that came with a distinct sound.

SPLASH!

Redstripe had stumbled over the edge and into the wandering channel. John responded immediately and hurried over to the paddling hound while saying, "Oh, no. Oh my. We certainly cannot have this. No, not at all." He dropped to his knees at the water's edge and reached down to grab Redstripe by the back of her neck. He wet his suit to the shoulder. Rising and cradling the little dog who was disgusted and trying to shake off the water, pretty much of the rest of his tan suit was soaked too. John handed the newly bathed dog to Cirtron. "There, excuse me. My apologies, please. I will see to extra towels in your rooms."

Cirtron held the dripping Redstripe while I tried to explain this was our fault entirely and I was so sorry about the man's suit. "It will be taken care of," said John. "Let me show you to your rooms. Please do not mind my jacket."

I was getting dizzy. The dachshunds were both intrigued and annoyed.

You know what? A place like this should really have signs up. That first step off the edge over there is a real danger. A dachshund could drown that way. Yup!

John let us into a set of adjoining rooms. There was one for Cirtron, one for me. The dogs would have to choose and I already knew I would likely be the one with furry sleeping partners. While the rooms were amazing, well appointed with stocked refrigerators, wondrously tiled floors and nearly suite like in size, the part that got to me was the baskets set out on the floor tiles below glass topped tables. There were two in each room. One held dog biscuits, the small ones the dachshunds liked, and the other held rawhide strips. Bowls of water were nearby. Clay bowels of shining fresh fruit were set on the glass table tops. Flower petals were strewn around them. I was trying to take all that in when John showed us the hand held remote controls for the air conditioning and ventilation systems.

Our host left us as the dogs were burrowing into the treats. Cirtron announced, "I'm gonna go t'da pool. Going to rid m'self of the hot and dust and tirst."

"Fine by me," I answered, "But I doubt they have Red Stripe here. You'll have to rough it."

"No problem, mon. Heineken. See y'later. Ya' mon? Irie?"

The dogs were asking to be raised up onto the low bed in my room. I accommodated them and told Cirtron. "Go. Knock yourself out, huh? I'm going to take a shower and we'll catch up with you in a while. I suppose those magazine people are around somewhere or maybe they are on their way."

"Ya, mon. Be t'later den." Cirtron left and I was alone with Redstripe and Belle who were making themselves at home on the bed. Belle rolled over onto the remote for the air and ventilation systems and lights began to blink. I had a thought she might know more about how to use the darn thing than me and turned towards the fridge. The stuff in there was cold, wet

Dachshunds in Jamaica

and welcome. The dachshunds remained on the bed, on their backs, feet in the air with half closed eyes.

Not bad for a Mexican motel. We'll just rest awhile and look for squirrels later if no one minds, don't you know. Yup, yup.

I got a shower in, dressed in clean clothes and lay down with the dogs for just a bit. I drifted off and dreamed of squirrels with little sombreros.

The dachshunds and I did not stay sleeping in our luxurious room for too long. An hour later, we got up and headed out through the sliding glass doors to look for Cirtron at the pool. The three of us made our way out, over one of the little bridges and towards the pool and swim up bar. There were no splashes. But my dream of squirrels and sombreros was washed away by my vision of Cirtron. He was at the swim up, a glass in hand and surrounded by five of the models from Caribbean Fashions. He was playing the role of real rasta royalty, telling tales likely founded in little fact. Rasta men don't wear swim clothes. He was seated on a submerged stool, one elbow on the bar, in his denim shorts and I think I saw his underwater feet still were clad in sandals. As I approached, dachshunds padding behind me, I could tell the models could not get enough of him. I jumped in, waded over and caught his attention. I looked at him and silently mouthed,

"Sheila."

He winced and shrugged. I heard two splashes and the models broke off to rescue two dachshunds who had jumped into the pool. I would have thought the little water spaniel wannabes would use more common sense. Maybe they just wanted to get a share of the attention. Cirtron frowned. "Y'spoil d'fun, mon. Ah. Irie. Tirsty?"

Before I could answer, someone clapped me on the shoulder from behind. I twisted around to see Allen, owner of Caribbean Fashions, who greeted me with a huge smile. "Well hello! Are we all rested now? I am so glad you could make it over here! Mr. Cirtron and I have been waiting for you, just talking to the girls, you know. My photographer is going to have such fun with your dogs. Thank you so much for coming! The plane ride was to your liking?"

The man still talked without breathing. I told him, "Yeah, and thanks. This is great." I took a moment to glance around and take note of the bikini clad models with the dogs, my grinning Rasta companion, and the drink with a little umbrella in Allen's hand. While I was not really surprised that he was wearing speedo style swim trunks and a gold chain around his neck, I still felt clobbered by cliché. The man would not quit talking.

"We can talk about plans for the shoot at dinner. It'll be fun and the dinners here are just lovely. And everyone is just so nice. Be sure to bring the dogs, after all that's why we're here. I am certain the kitchen can come up with something for them. Didn't you say they like tacos? Or was it burritos?" He put one finger on his forehead and went on. "Oh, I can't remember. But I suppose it really doesn't matter, does it?" I had to stop him. He was making me shake.

I interrupted and asked, "So, the food here is, uh, lovely?"

"Oh, yes, just lovely. Heavenly, really."

"Heavenly?"

"Yes, absolutely heavenly. Of course, you know the girls don't eat much. They just pick. I understand, but it is such a waste. On the other hand, I always try to watch my own weight too, but being here is so hard. Of course, the resort does have a fully equipped exercise gym. Did you see it? It's all mirrors and exquisitely clean. Maybe you'd like to join me in the morning? That's when I get my best workout and I always think it is the best to pump it up and get rid of all that dinner from the night before. What do you think? Do you lift?"

I had a moment's respite from the assault on my nerves when one of the models approached. She carried a dachshund under one arm but I could not tell which one. The dog was a soaked mess and it looked as though the little hound had just gone through a car wash in a convertible with the top down. The model leaned over and kissed Allen on the cheek. "Allen.

Dachshunds in Jamaica

Shut up." She leaned back and adjusted her grip on the hound in arms. "You're boring the poor guy."

Allen held one hand to his mouth. "Oops!"

"*Oops indeed,*" I thought. Dinner promised to be an adventure. When I'd had enough of Allen, the models and wet dachshunds, I excused myself and called to the hounds. Cirtron stayed behind and resumed telling his stories to his rapt audience. Back in our room, now officially the kennel, I set out to dry the dogs with towels and the in-room hair dryer. Save for coating the clean towels with a layer of short dachshund hair, it all worked out even if the dogs turned out a little fluffy. The hounds settled back on one of the beds and I pulled up a chair, thumbing the remote control for the television for something to watch until dinner. I'd not even finished my "guy surfing" thing through the channels when the hounds came to full alert.

And you think you are going to watch what? Not that stupid news stuff, we hope. No, no, no. Animals please, find some animals. Yup!

They made sure I understood the rules by beginning to bark. We settled on a documentary about Mexican crocodiles. It was all in Spanish. The only part I could understand was that these animated reptilian suitcases portrayed on the screen would have been happy to have the dachshunds as an appetizer. I told the dogs this but they had a different view.

Nope, nope, nope! We'd bite 'em. Yup! Right on the tail, yup!

All I could do was watch crocodiles, listen to the drone of Spanish I could not comprehend, and wait for dinner. I wondered idly if the models actually had names. While watching crocs and wondering, I heard Cirtron return next door. The dinner hour was approaching so I rose to dress, leaving the dachshunds and crocodiles to their own devices. Dinner, as I suspected, was going to be of great interest.

I left the room, a dachshund under each arm, to meet Cirtron on the patio that served our adjoining rooms; the kennel was left and Cirtron's pad was right. With some minor discrepancies, we'd chosen similar outfits. I'd picked a dark

 Redstripe's Inn

blue shirt with epaulets above white slacks and Cirtron wore a navy blue tee shirt with white gauze pants tied at the waist. I handed him a hound and we walked off to the outdoor dining area. I had no idea what we would do with the dachshunds, promised tacos or not, and felt a little apprehensive. My nerves began to sing at a louder volume when we approached tables with white linens, crystal glassware, gold flatware and chairs draped completely in white cloth. It looked like a place for white ties and tails and the only tails we had were furry and sticking out from under our crooked arms to the rear.

Allen and the girls, and other folks I assumed were the photo crew, were already seated at a long rectangular table. Everyone turned their gazes towards us and I seriously thought about padding down over the beach and jumping into the waters of the Gulf of Mexico. But Allen, bless his lacey heart, saved the moment. "Jack! Mr. Cirtron! We've been waiting! So good to see you! Are your accommodations alright? Did you have a chance to relax? Yes? Oh, how could one not relax here. Now, give the dogs to Marna and Keesha." He pointed at two of the models. "They will take care of them. Please sit down, both of you."

Allen rattled on about something or other but I didn't hear. I was relieved to see the other dinner guests were dressed pretty much as Cirtron and I. And now I knew that at least two of the models had names. We handed over our burden of of hounds to Marna and Keesha and took seats. Suited waiters brought everyone leather bound menus, arranged napkins in laps and the hounds settled in with Marna and Keesha with rear paws braced on pretty thighs and front paws on the table. Our host rose and saw it necessary to trot around the table and point out selected items to each of his crew.

"Try the Beef Wellington, it's super! Look at the garlic prawns, oh my, but don't kiss anyone. This avocado stuffed chicken is something else. See the Taipei in crème sauce? You'll need a couple of extra minutes on the treadmill for that one. Did you review the wines? They have a cabernet that is pure velvet." The man could have used a baton and his running culinary commentary was making me feel stuffed just

Dachshunds in Jamaica

by listening. The dachshunds never took their eyes off of him. Marna and Keesha and the other models were fooling with the dachshunds and giggling. Their laughter and snickering was constant. It was a bad case of hypergiggleosis.

After orders were taken and dinners arrived, talk turned to the shoot in the morning. We would begin at first light. Everyone should be on time. The crew was to set up before sunrise. I did not say much through dinner. The talk was of photography, wardrobe, concerns for weather and things of which I had no understanding. I had to admit that Allen was right. The food was amazing. The dachshunds thought so too as they were fed from the models' plates with food the models would not eat anyway. Redstripe and Belle were happy to snatch morsels of steak, chicken, shrimp and fish from delicate fingers with expensive manicures.

Hey. (chomp) this stuff is pretty good! We should come here more often! Beats the dickens out of pancakes, don't you know! Yup, yup, yup!

Keesha, holding Redstripe, was seated right next to me. The girl was perfect; she was clear, hand blown glass in human form. I feared if I brushed her arm, she'd break. She made an attempt at dinner table talk. "So, I'm told you're an author?"

"Yeah. I write books and columns."

"Really? Would you put ME in one of your books?"

"Gee, I don't know. I write mostly about dogs."

The other models broke out in raucous laughter and one said, "Well, then Keesha would be PERFECT!"

The hounds had an opinion. *Hey! Where'd all these cats come from. We hate cats!*

If I had not guessed before, the exchange told me I was as much out of my element as a fish on a freeway.

 Redstripe's Inn

Dachshunds in Jamaica

Glamour Photography

Belle, Cirtron, Redstripe and I joined the crew on the sand in front of the Resort of the Lost Beach just as the sun was sneaking a peek up over the waters of the Gulf of Mexico. The sand was littered with equipment; there were lights on poles, open trunks of clothes, tarps, cameras and, of course, the models. A couple of older women were fussing with the girls' hair and outfits. The photographer saw the four of us and stepped up.

"Okay. You're here. As soon as the girls get ready, we put the dogs down and I start shooting. I'll cue you to take them off to the side while we do the outfit changes and then you bring them back. Understand?"

We understood. But I thought maybe a 'good morning' might have been nice, or maybe, 'hi, how'd you sleep?'

"I slept well, thank you, to the sound of snoozing hounds," I wanted to say, but the opportunity was not present. This was business. I must admit I've taken a look, now and then, a long time ago, at some "fashion" magazines, but I was not prepared to be standing on the other side of the camera. These folks were serious. I looked over at Cirtron. He was frowning. He was not the center of attention as he'd been the day before. All eyes were on the models.

A rhythm developed. Belle and Redstripe would parade around on shiny tarps while the models stood, preened, smiled and were directed by the photographer. "Towards me! Hands on hips, please. Look up! Smile now! That's it! Next set now."

The models would change into new outfits from the trunks while standing behind blankets held up by the older ladies. Belle and Redstripe would get a little rest and we'd start all over. The photographer would repeat his litany, "Towards

Redstripe's Inn

me! Hands on hips, please. Look down! Smile up now, that's nice. Good. That's it! Next set." His directions were punctuated by the click of his shutter. The dogs were getting tired and began to pant.

Say, is there lunch yet? Or a little of that flavored water? We're getting a little tired of all this.

Allen, who had been standing to one side called a halt. "Everyone is getting tired and hot. I can see sweat on the girls and they're going to ruin the clothes. Let's do some water shots now. I'd bet the dogs would like a little swim."

Belle and Redstripe had other opinions. *No, actually, We could do without that. The pool would be fine, but there might be crocodiles out there and we are too tired, just now, to bite tails if you don't mind.*

Amazingly, for once, the dachshunds did not get their way. Two of the models grabbed a hound each and headed for the water. I could not see from inside the photographer's camera but I did watch a shot that promised to put dachsunds in the forefront for fashion advertising. Standing sideways to the camera, one of the models leaned down to soak her long hair in the salt water. She had Belle in arms. She stood up and, holding Belle under the little dogs forelegs, tossed her head and wet hair backwards in an arc while water flew out in a spray. I don't think Belle was too thrilled, but I thought it looked like a nice picture to send home.

Allen did insist on a group shot of me, Cirtron, the dogs, himself and a couple of the models. He promised to send a print to us in Negril. I guessed I might have to crop the thing in the interest of matrimonial harmony if it were to be displayed at Redstripe's Inn. The models were way too friendly.

The shoot ended and we went back to our rooms to clean up and get ready for a little rest and relaxation. I bathed the hounds in the bath tub to rinse out sand salt water. They were not pleased. I did not use the hair dryer. I figured they would air dry in the Mexican sun. We all gathered once more at the pool and swim up bar where the models presented Cirtron and

Dachshunds in Jamaica

me each with one of the swimsuits they'd worn during the photo session.

"Don't worry. We washed them. We get this stuff all the time and we thought maybe you guys could take them back to your girls? They're neat. Maybe you could, take them back like souvenirs?"

I looked at the suit in my hands. There was not much to it. I did not think Jill would be impressed. But I tried to be respectful. "Thanks! Thanks a lot! How nice." At best, I figured Jill could use the suit to replace her shoe laces.

I leaned over to whisper to Cirtron. "I think we need to catch the next Lear Jet out of here."

"Ya' mon. D'dogs be tired. Time for home, mon."

I felt relieved by Cirtron's comment. Even he sometimes used common sense that is not so common.

 Redstripe's Inn

Nothing Ever Stays the Same

It was not a dark and stormy night. It was a bright and humid morning. The sun was up over the top of the eastern hills and the ocean was quiet, contemplating the coming events of another day. Sleep slipped away from me and my senses woke, one by one, hearing first, then eyesight greeted by the amber backs of my eyelids. My nose came alive.

I could smell my own bad breath, the oily odor of the hound still sleeping in the bed and the less than romantic body fragrance, left in place by sleep, of my wife under the sheets next to me. But something was missing. All was silent and I did not smell coffee and breakfast. I willed my eyelids to rise and saw the sunlight radiating its way in as a squarish stream through the bedroom window. Belle woomfed in her sleep and Jill rolled over. I pushed back my covering sheet and hoisted myself out of the bed. My skin was cool and sticky with dried sweat after my pores had opened in sleep. I really needed a bath, a mouthwash, a toothbrush or, at the least, a dip in the ocean. I padded barefoot down the hall and into the kitchen where Cirtron was looking around, seemingly disappointed that Carson was not up to make breakfast.

"Hey Cirtron. Where's Sheila?"

"Ya' mon, Sheila still be lazy and sleepin'. No Carson dis morning? We must den make some t'eat on our own, hey? Gonna turn on d'stove an cook some."

I agreed. "Yeah, we can do that. There's flour and some milk and eggs. I can stir up some pancakes and 'tell you what, you can brew up some blue mountain. We'll get stuff together and let everyone sleep, okay? And, I think we have some oranges around here somewhere, too. If we don't burn anything too badly, we'll be heroes."

Redstripe's Inn

"Ya'mon. Miss Carson, she can still keep de sleep too. May be it is dat she be more den tired after she met de boyfriend on de beach last night. Hah! May d'story t'tell! Maybe you putta in your book."

While I knew Cirtron was the ultimate optimist, I said, "I don't think so, Cirtron, just make the coffee and cut up some fruit."

The clinking of the mixing bowl and banging of the frying pan summoned the hounds. Redstripe and Belle wandered into the kitchen in anticipation of food. Paris did not show. I'd mixed the pancake batter in a bowl, set the frying pan to heat and turned to Cirtron. "I'm going to go and rinse off in the ocean, okay? I'll just dip in and come right back while the pan heats. You want to get the water for the dog bowls?"

"Ya, mon."

I headed out the front, over the sand, dropped my clothes near the ocean's edge, high stepped into small waves and dove into the warm Caribbean waters. Most of the night smells rinsed off and I washed out my mouth with the salt water, taking a mouth full, swishing and spitting the brine back out and into the sea. Once back on the sand, I used the edges of my palms to scrape off as much wetness I could and dressed. I was damp. But it was humid anyway and the moisture left on my body that was being absorbed by my clothes was cooling in the morning breeze. I turned towards the inn. I could smell pancakes and coffee.

Cirtron was flipping pancakes and the two dachshunds were milling around his ankles, ears perked and ready to make demands. There was still no sign of Paris nor the girls and Carson. I did not think much about the women sleeping in, but I was surprised Paris had still not shown. "Cirtron? Where's Paris? I'd thought she'd be in here by now with the smells and all that. Odd, hey?"

"Ya' mon. Little odd for de little dog. Check 'pon her, maybe. She eat way too much for such a little ting and maybe get sick, mon."

Dachshunds in Jamaica

"Yeah, maybe so. I'll go and find her. Keep an eye on breakfast, would you? Don't let stuff burn. Carson would give us trouble on that. I don't want to hear about it, okay?"

"Ya' mon. Irie." Cirtron continued his flipping.

I padded down to Carson's door, Paris usually slept with the woman, and I hesitated. Intruding on a female senior citizen's privacy was not my idea of a party. But my need to make sure Paris was alright overcame my reluctance. I opened the door, just inches, and looked in. Carson's left arm embraced Paris' long body and the dog's head rested on the woman's chest. The dachshund, without moving, aimed her eyes in my direction. Okay. Paris was fine. After all, she was getting older and maybe just wanted to sleep and let the other hounds get the pancakes.

This was not so for Carson.

She lay there on the bed with Paris, covered by a light sheet. Her jaw was slack and her stilled eyes were half open. She was not moving and I knew that the date Cirtron suggested she'd had last night had been with a much higher authority than some flashy charmer from the beach. Paris knew this too. She'd stayed and ignored the smell of pancakes.

I really did not know what to do. I tried what I'd seen in the movies. I approached the side of Carson's bed and tried to use my fingers to close her eyes. It didn't work. But I could tell, when I touched her, that her skin was cool and not flexible. The numbness that started in my hands and feet had not yet worked its way up to my legs and arms when I heard Cirtron enter the room behind me. He saw the state of things right away.

"Ah. D'time, she come. 'Ya, mon. Not so hard t'see she now be wid Ga."

Cirtron walked over to the bed, extricated Paris, and held her to his chest. "D'little dog, be proud, mon. She has been waiting wid d'lady 'till we come. A good dog." Jill and Sheila must have heard something or other, maybe just smelled breakfast, and came into Carson's room to join us. Thankfully, they were silent. They could see and tears began to spill with darkening comprehension. Cirtron continued to cradle Paris, the ladies muffled sobs, and I could smell burning pancakes.

We turned around and silently padded as a group to the kitchen. Cirtron, Paris still in arms, shut off the burner and put the pan with the burned pancakes aside while the rest of us took seats. Coffee was brewed. Nobody expressed an interest. Cirtron, with Paris, joined us, seating himself on another chair at the table.

Sheila said, "Oh my god."

Jill asked, "What do we do?"

I replied that I did not know and Cirtron just sat in silence while scratching Paris' ears.

With my elbows braced and my forehead resting in my palms, I spoke down to the wooden table. "I guess we need to call somebody, a doctor or someone. There must be some way to handle this and arrangements here, even in Negril." I thought a little more and said, "But, boy, I don't even know where to start. What are the rules here? Carson, like the rest of us is from the states, sorry Cirtron, and I wonder if we have to deal with some embassy stuff in Kingston or something." I looked up to see Jill and Sheila just staring at me. There was no help there. They were way too upset and looked it. Cirtron spoke. "Best be it I call Basi," and he produced a cell phone from some pocket, keyed it with one hand and held it to an ear. I could hear a voice buzzing through on the other end. Cirtron said, "Chobble nuh nice anna we inna big chobble. De lady Carson, she gwey wid Ga," and then fell silent a moment. Then, "Irie, so 'tis. An, ya' mon, she be family. Mo'time. We get d'whites, eh?"

My patois was getting better and I understood the single side of the conversation. Cirtron had said there was trouble and that Carson had died and gone on to God. He had affirmed this, said she was family and said he would see Basi later. He added that they would be getting some overproof rum. That last part did not make sense. At least I hoped it didn't. My mind was gibbering over the concept of using rum as an embalmer. I assured myself this could not be. I pushed

Dachshunds in Jamaica

that thought aside and said, "Cirtron? What was that all about?

"Not t'have de worry, mon. Basi, he will explain 'pon he gets here. I'm gonna take d'truck and get soma ice, irie?

"Ice?"

Cirtron looked at me, wide eyed. "Ya' mon. Be it she be hot t'day as always."

I got it and shivered. "Oh. Right."

Cirtron stood, smiled, handed Paris to Sheila and left the room. Having nothing to do that I wanted to do, I grabbed the burned pancake pan, scraped out the worst of the black stuff and placed it with the remains on the floor for the three hounds. Jill and Sheila were still just sitting and staring out from wet faces. The dachshunds seemed to be oblivious and attacked the pan. *That's it? Burned pancakes? Sheesh! Carson will hear about this, yup, yup, yup*

But Carson would not be listening.

I poured coffee into mugs for the three of us still at the table. The coffee cooled, untouched, while we talked. Jill was first to say anything. "There must be laws about this sort of thing. What can Basi do? At home, we'd already have called an ambulance and then, I suppose, we'd have to call a funeral home and make arrangements and take care of all of this. I mean Carson is…" Jill stopped. She just could not say the word.

Sheila interjected with little help. "Oh my god. I think I'm going to be sick. We can't just leave her back there! This is Carson! What are we going to do, just sit here 'till Cirtron's uncle shows up and says god knows what? Jill's right. What is he going to do? And, Jack, I don't like this ice thing. It's sick." The tears started up fresh. As usual, the problem was homing in, guided to landing by Jill and Sheila, to perch on my shoulders. I was having a hard time finding a place for my emotions to roost while I contemplated the mess. I tried to reassure the two girls.

"Sheila? Jill? Listen a second. Just hang on a moment. I have something to tell you about Cirtron." I told the story about me and Cirtron on the beach when he told me, with the cigarette butt as a teaching tool, that Jamaicans did not waste anything.

Jill looked at me, frowning. "What does that have to do with this?"

Sheila said, "Yeah, that sounds like Cirtron, always the optimist. Huh!"

I went on, "You two know about all the building supplies we got to fix this place, right?"

It was Sheila's turn to frown. "Tell me about it. And tell me where the bills are. I haven't seen a one."

I rubbed my chin to relieve some of the tension I was feeling about what I would have to say next. "There won't be any bills. Cirtron and I just, sort of, got the stuff from friends of his."

"You stole it all!" This came from Jill.

"What!?" That was Sheila's contribution.

"No, no. We didn't steal it. The supplies were extras. We just did everyone a favor by taking them." I knew I was beginning to sound like Cirtron.

Sheila's and Jill's jaws tightened. Before they could lash out I rushed to explain. "See, Cirtron always finds a way. It must be a Jamaican thing. I don't know, but he always does find an angle, right? That's what I'm telling you. Jill, remember when Uncle Basi rescued us when our van broke down on the highway? That was really Cirtron's doing. Sheila? Do remember telling us the story about that bar you and Cirtron were at in Wisconsin and the locals were giving you trouble? You told me Cirtron played his flute and calmed everyone down. The man has a knack. And if he says Basi can help, I believe him. You should, too." I ran out of arguments and took note that the three hounds had left the room; the frying pan had been scoured clean.

Before the girls could answer, I rose from the table. "Where are you going?" Jill asked.

"To light some candles in Carson's room until Basi gets here and Cirtron gets back."

I left the kitchen with silence behind me, stopped to reach into a closet for candles and matches, and re-entered Carson's

Dachshunds in Jamaica

room. I found the three dogs on the floor, all seated like furry sphinxes and keeping watch. Their eyes were bright and their ears were perked forward at right angles to their heads. No prince, princess, king or queen could have expected more honor than the three dachshund guard. Paris must have told the other two and somehow they understood. It was good enough for me. My hands shook while I lit and placed the candles and I finally cried. But, standing there in maudlin misery, I thought that if I believed in one person communicating with another, from one plane of existence to the next, which I did not, I would have heard Carson say, "Oh for cripe's sake, Jack.. Get a grip! All I'm doing here is to go and find a new place to trade! Besides, it's your turn to cook."

 Redstripe's Inn

Dachshunds in Jamaica

A Jamaican Celebration

I spent a good part of the rest of the morning on the porch in a chair. I only hoped Basi would have advice about what to do and the nasty and practical issues of a deceased person lying on a bed in the inn were making me think thoughts I did not want. I never noticed the passage of two hours but I did finally hear a car engine in the back of the inn. I got up and raced around the side of the Redstripe's Inn to see Basi pulling in with a trailer in tow. It was not much of a trailer and it held a long crate like wooden box, the purpose of which was obvious. Cirtron, in the pink pickup, pulled in at the same time. Basi levered himself out of his old tan Chevy and Cirtron popped out of the truck. The two men conferred and I could not quite hear their words. I just stood.

Basi broke off with Cirtron and came to me. He hugged me. "So, de likkle chobble, ya? We ha d'tings to do now. No problem, mon, d'lady be part of the family. You too."

"Basi, Cirtron told us you would help with, uh, this. I don't know who to call or what to do here. I want to do it right, there are all sorts of things to think about, but I don't know the rules. What do we do?"

Basi took a step back from me. He said simply, "Ah, de nine day. Dats what we do."

"Nine days?"

"Ya mon. Lemme tell you and be peaceful. Irie?"

I was not hopeful just then, but said. "I'm listening."

Basi explained, using his best English. "In Jamaica, the way d'people most are buried is not so much different as from where you come. We have d'cemetaries and d'funeral men and the government licenses and all dat. Day even say how deep d'hole must be and where. But, in my grandfather's time on d'island, tings were a bit different, keen? And soma dat still rule out and away from the towns. You see, much of the old ways come from the Maroons and the Ashanti and even the Carribs. All have come to d'island an left d'mark and d'blood. Nowdays, more than not of dis is forgotten. But, not all. We can now take Ms. Carson to the family place and give her the nine days to help make her way. We gonna have d'party and such. All will come."

I began to understand Basi was offering an old fashioned Jamaican burial. I also wondered if he should not be lecturing in some posh American college about Jamaican culture to students of sociology. But I had to ask, "Are we going to be doing something illegal? And I know nothing about what beliefs Carson held and this sounds, geez, a little tribal or something." I had visions of a moonless night with torch brandishing dancers surrounding a funeral pyre, but Basi laughed. "No, all with respect, mon. Private. No man. An you should know what is said wisely, 'Belief kill and belief cure."

That last I would have to think on but I still had questions. "What's this about nine days?" "Ah," said Basi. "In d'past, and in soma da places in d'country, when someone would die, nine days would be let by for two tings. First, d'time for waiting gives d'spirit to go round and take care of business. Den, it gave time for all d'people t'come and join for the journey and pay respect. Now, most have ways t'get round and about so the nine day is just a word for the last day. It is no longer important to be waiting so long. We'll take d'lady up to the family place and give her the nine day. But now, we have a likkle work. Basi clapped me on one shoulder and turned to shout at Cirtron. "Cirtron! Ja get d'ice, mon? And we need a sand bag, mon."

Cirtron answered Basi, "Ya, mon, ice in the back of the truck. Gonna go for a bag and filla wid sand."

"Irie," said Basi.

Of course I had to ask. "Ah, Basi? What's the sand bag for? Some kind of ritual?"

"No mon, see, d'belly wanna swell in d'dead an d'bag keeps it down. We n'want dat, not so pretty and can be stopped wid de bag, mon."

Dachshunds in Jamaica

I did not know what to say but I was very, very glad that the dachshunds had eaten the last of the pancakes and not me. Basi looked at me and said, "Ah, irie, it will be okay. Cirtron and me, we will take d'lady out to the box and arrange. Yes? You n'worry. Let d'family help you now. You take d'job to get the Sheila and your lady ready to go. Also d'Redstripe and the other two. Redstripe has been in the mountains before. The girls gonna be happy t'see her and her small friends. A fun time, no sadness" Basi left me and went into the inn.

I did not watch what Basi and Cirtron did with Carson. I did see them leaving out back with a bed sheet wrapped bundle with the three dachshunds following. The realization that I'd not heard a single bark from a single hound all morning left me a little dizzy. I felt I was dreaming but did my part and called for Jill and Sheila. "Jill! Sheila! We're going up into the mountains! Basi has Carson in his trailer and I guess we're going to bury her up in the family plot or something. There is going to be party!"

Jill was first to come to me and stand to speak. Hands on hips, feet planted for battle, she said, "What? We can't just do this. We have to call somebody!"

Sheila was next, "Are you nuts? Are you trying to get us all arrested?" All I could do was to tell the girls to out back and get into the car with Basi. I told them the dachshunds were already out there and we needed to get going. They looked at each other and looked back at me and Sheila said, "Are you sure?"

"No, I'm not. Do you have any better idea right now? I'm all ears."

Basi was already in the car behind the wheel and Cirtron was in the seat beside him and waiting. Jill and Sheila and I and the three hounds squeezed into the back. It was tight. Each of us held a hound and Basi started the engine, engaged the transmission and we were off to the mountains. It was not a pleasant journey and the trailer behind us, bumping along with Carson on her bed of ice and her sandbag on her stomach, did not paint pictures of peacefulness in our minds. But we did make it over the dirt roads, the somewhat cleared

Redstripe's Inn

lanes and harrowing switch backs to where Cirtron and Basi claimed home in the hills of Jamaica. The usual goats that blocked all the roads must have been on vacation. We were greeted by a crowd when we arrived. Their high pitched voices and grins reminded me of a carnival atmosphere. Everyone seemed way to happy for the occasion. I was all odd.

The people seemed not to notice the trailer. Several women and children approached the car. "Ah! Cirtron! Ya' bring back d'Redstripe!" Two little girls, one leaning in through each of the two back windows screamed as a duet. "Three! Three! Dere are three Redstripes!" I had to smile. Jill and Sheila just sat with the dogs in laps. I lifted my own lap passenger, Belle, out through the window and pointed to the two ladies to do the same. "They'll be fine. Let them go with the little girls," I advised. I knew neither Jill nor Sheila was nuts about the idea, but they handed the dogs out through the windows. The little girls took the hounds and ran off squealing. I could still hear them shouting, "Three Redstripes! Three now!" I figured I could correct them later and clambered out of the car, and took a look around. There were people all over the place. Two more cars pulled up behind the trailer and six or eight more climbed out of the vehicles. I was standing on packed sandy dirt. Cabins, huts really, occupied the outside of a one hundred foot circle, each standing above the soil by a little less than a foot and roofed over with rusted corrugated metal sheets. Chickens and snoozing goats rested below the structures on the cooler soil. A small structure to one side drew my attention.

Not more than ten foot square, it was just four wooden poles supporting a newly thatched and sagging top of palm leaves. The top drooped in the middle. A small table, chest high, sat crookedly underneath and was draped with a white cloth. A basket with some sort of bread occupied the middle and two bottles of rum stood guard, one to each side of the basket. I could read the labels; Appleton was a local brand.

Jill and Sheila left the car to stand and stare around. Basi was bent down fiddling with the trailer hitch and saw me looking at the little four pole structure. "Ya' mon. The bread there, d'journey cakes, day for the lady t'eat on her way to d'next. D'rum, she be for later wid d'rest and the nine day." I thought it odd that I understood. Basi straightened up and yelled to a pocket of men lounging near one of the cabins. The stood and stretched and came to the trailer. They picked up the Carson crate and carried it over to the little structure with the rum and bread and placed it on the ground.

Sheila and Jill were having some major adjustment problems. Sheila shouted, "I can't believe this!"

I could only repeat what Basi had told me. "Belief kill and belief cure."

Jill was upset too. "What in the world does that mean?"

I answered. "Actually, I don't really know."

I could see by looking at the faces of Jill and Sheila they were not pleased. Apprehension blasted out from their frowning features. I tried a diversion. "Look, over there, see the little girls playing with the dogs?" The three hounds and a group of girls were on the ground near one of the huts and collecting as much dirt into fur and clothes as was possible. "Why don't you two go over there and make friends. I'm told we're family. Go be polite. I'll figure all this out, okay?"

"You sure?" asked Jill.

"Yeah."

"I thought you just said you didn't know," Sheila challenged.

I sighed. "Just go and play, would you? Be nice. I'll take care of it."

I braced for another onslaught of questions and doubt, but the two of them pivoted and stomped off towards the girls and hounds. I'd lied to Jill. I wasn't sure about anything. I needed to talk to Cirtron and Basi who were suddenly absent from view. The crate and the four pole mini-gazebo were burning their images into my mind like an over-exposed photograph. I could hear the dachshunds barking and woofing; most of the noise was contributed by Belle and Redstripe. I could tell after much practice of listening, that Paris was making only a desultory contribution to the din. I looked around for Cirtron and Basi.

After wandering about the enclave, smiling at people who addressed me with words I did not understand, I found the two men behind one of the huts. They were speaking and gesturing to three Jamaicans who were filthy and holding rusted shovels. Sometimes I am dumb and sometimes I am not. In this case, I concluded the three dirty men had been digging and I knew what for. "Cirtron, Basi! I'm glad I found you. What do we do next?"

Cirtron remained silent. The diggers looked on and Basi said, "We carry d'lady's box to the place, mon. Wanna help?"

"Yes, I can do that. You mean like right now?"

"Ya'mon. D'ice only last for so long, keen?"

I keened all right and understood, in the Jamaican climate, that time was important.

I answered simply. "Okay, let's go."

In silence, I followed the men, Cirtron and Basi, to the crate resting on the ground beside the last minute shrine of rum and bread. We all bent down, grasped the wooden bottom and lifted. It was heavy and leaking water from melting ice. I did not want to think about what was going on inside the box. Men, women and children began to gather around us as we stood holding the crate. Three of the little girls, each with a hound and with two of the women leading Jill and Shiela, all approached us as we stood. "Now d'lift, tree." directed Basi.

I was confused. I followed suit to lift and lower as the other men placed the crate back on the ground. Then we all lifted it up once more, but this time at nearly the level of our heads. My arms were complaining. The men grunted as we lowered the ersatz coffin once more to the ground. We did this three times. It was up down, up down, up down. No one spoke or made any sound during this elevator exhibition powered by muscle. "Now we go," said Basi. We did. So did everyone else. It was a parade, a procession without cars. My guess is we carried that Carson crate better than two hundred yards to an open area, filled with jungle overgrowth and some sticks with faded letters that rose slightly above the greenery.

Dachshunds in Jamaica

The crate had no fancy brass handles. We simply shouldered it and I could feel blood trickling down my back from where the wood was digging into my skin. There was a hole fit for the crate; it was freshly dug out of the floor of the Jamaican landscape. Broken tendrils of roots decorated the top and it looked damp. The dachshunds in the arms of various people were still and peered at the hole and then twisted their heads to look about. *Where's the squirrels that dug that thing? They must grow bigger here than the ones back home.*

We lowered the crate to the ground right next to the hole. Two of the men jumped in and raised their arms to receive the burden as the rest of us levered it up once more and handed it down. I felt my arms were going to leave me and fly off somewhere. With some juggling, Carson, in her crate, finally rested at the bottom of the excavation. The women of the parade group began to wail, Jill and Sheila began to cry and the hounds began to bark and howl and the two men climbed out of the grave. Two men that had helped carry the crate began to scoop dirt into the hole with their feet and two others produced the rusty shovels to help. It only took a couple of minutes and it was all over. Basi came over to me and stared into my eyes. He smiled and nodded.

I returned his gaze. "Is that it?"

"Ah. Be peaceful, now. Do you not know that all of us come from d'earth and den return? 'Tis natural and n'ting to worry 'pon. Let d'women wail and cry, dis not be far d'men, y'see. Hmm?"

The entire thing was a little too Zen for me at the time. "Thanks, Basi, you've done too much. I'm just having a little moment here, if you don't mind." The entire affair got worse when I heard what I thought was Carson. My mind must have been rented to pirates or something.

"Jack?"

It couldn't be. I looked down at the grave. "Huh?" The hackles on the dachshunds rose up; there were three long reddish brown stripes along the dogs' backs. The hounds went still.

Redstripe's Inn

"Look up, you fool, not down! Where did you think I was going? You know, you could give me a little more credit here if you don't mind doing so!"

I looked up and about to see tree limbs waving lightly in the hot breeze. "I'm fine, Jack. Let the others know so if you wouldn't mind and remember, you need to work on your cooking. You need to use a lot less oil."

"Oil?" I felt frozen, even in the heat. A shiver took residence along my spine that did want to leave.

Carson continued to sound in my head. "Yes, oil. You don't want all that cooking to be so greasy like your Sicilian relatives like so much. Now remember, tell 'em I'm fine."

"Okay."

"Just between you and me though, I do have one regret.

"You do?"

"Yeah, I never got a chance to visit that clothing optional joint up on the north end of Negril. I was meaning too. I really also meant to get around to reading your books. Sorry about that. I'd like to get hold of them now, but shipping might be a little complicated."

The image of Mrs. Carson on a nude beach left me unsettled but I just thought back, "Don't worry about it, Carson."

While it was becoming obvious to me that I must have missed a payment due on my last bill for my reality credit card, I was grateful that no one else seemed to have sensed the interchange.

Basi picked up where he had left off and said, "No mind. Now we go back down an drink and eat and rattle de trees on de ninth day for lady Carson. Ha! You like rum?"

"I'll manage. Let's go." I looked over at Sheila and Jill and pointed with one hand back down the way we'd come. I was not going to have an easy time explaining what had just happened. Maybe only the dogs would really ever know. Maybe we'd keep it to ourselves. As the sun set, hot food was brought out from somewhere or other in metal buckets. There was pork and chicken and, I think, goat meat, all cooked up separately in spicy sauces. The buckets were placed on plank

Dachshunds in Jamaica

tables supported by logs laid sideways on the ground. The dishes for the food for guests and friends and relatives were little Styrofoam picnic bowls. Plastic spoons were used. It was odd but it worked. Reggae music blared from a boom box and the crowd of people began to dance. I didn't know what to expect. I was thinking of ladies with fruit on their heads stomping to some local cultural ritual of passage. Maybe there should be rattles or tambourines or something. That was not happening. The scene, when I filtered out the dirt jungle floor and somewhat ratty garb of the crowd, reminded me more than not of some late night club in a big city in the states. And the rum flowed. I found a tree to sit against and rest for a while. I had no idea where Jill and Sheila had gone. Cirtron came over to me, squatted down, and I noticed he carried two bottles of rum; they were the high proof stuff. He handed one to me. It was already open. Unseen tendrils of air bearing the smells of ganja swirled around my head and found their way to my nose. The party and dancing and music brought to my mind an image of an Italian wedding or maybe Greek. The rum replaced the red wine, Chianti or Ouzo but the atmosphere seemed the same. A couple of minor and good hearted skirmishes between the men broke out on the edges of things. Cirtron interrupted my thoughts.

"Drink, mon. For Carson. It is d'ninth day." I rubbed the back of one thumb against my forehead.

"Yeah. For Carson. The ninth day." I took a swig from one bottle and was rewarded with the most painful sensation I'd ever had. I was imagining all of the tissues in my throat burning off in grease smattering smoke as the liquid made its way down to my stomach where it plopped like molten steel. I gasped and curled forward, grasping my chest with both hands. I held my breath, afraid to exhale, with the worry that I would breathe fire out like some dragon and crack my front teeth from the heat. The bottle, grasped by the neck in my right hand, dipped over and spilled some of its contents onto my knee.

Cirtron sat down next to me and laughed. "Ya not drink d'rum much? Slow now. Not so much." I caught my breath,

 Redstripe's Inn

filled my lungs with air and said, "I suppose I need to get used to it, huh?"

"Ya' mon." Cirtron took another swig from his own bottle and laughed again. I was not amused. Jill and Sheila staggered up to us and it was obvious they had taken the opportunity to feel the same discomfort from the rum as I had just experienced.

"Hi, guys! Do you mind? We need to just sit a while. Can we share your tree?" It was Sheila who spoke, but Jill nodded and the two of them plopped down next to me. Paris, Belle and Redstripe appeared out of the dark. *Hey, the food here is pretty* good. Yup. But we were wondering if we could find a warm place here, gotta rest up a while.

Sheila and Jill's request to just sit turned into an issue of somnolence. Each had cradled her own head in an arm and they were soon reposed on the ground. Paris and Redstripe nosed their way between the two women and made them selves comfortable while Belle climbed into my lap. Cirtron held his finger to his lips, smiled and wandered off. I just sat and looked out over the dancing crowd which was beginning to thin. I must have drifted off for a bit. When I came alert, just for a moment, I noticed someone had covered the three of us and the dogs with a couple of blankets. In the dim light I could see a label that read:

SEARS HOME FURNISHINGS—100 PERCENT VIRGIN MAN MADE MATERIALS

I drifted off again after checking by feel for the hounds, Sheila and Jill, and then dreamed of Carson and cornfields. Deeper in my sleep, she came to me and said she really would get around to reading my books. I said that would be okay and very nice, no hurry.

Dachshunds in Jamaica

Home Again

The sun woke me up. Jill and Sheila were still snoring from under one of the SEARS blankets and the dachshunds were in no mood to move; Belle was the only one exposed to the morning daylight and I could see that her belly was still distended from the treats of the night before. I looked to one side and saw that the bottle of rum Cirtron had given me was stuck into a depression in the ground and appeared nearly half empty. Had I drunk that? No way. I stood up, casting my own blanket aside and my central nervous system told me that, yes, it was possible, probable, that much of the contents of that bottle was sloshing around inside of me. My teeth felt as though they were coated with caramel candy. I winced at the sound of Basi's voice as he approached.

"Time to leave. Wake d'ladies and I'll find Cirtron." Basi's task was not difficult. Cirtron was under his own blanket on the other side of our tree. I did my part and reached down to shake, in turn, each of the women.

"Hey guys! Rise and shine! It's time to go!" I was greeted by comments not fit for mixed company. Personally, I did not feel I was ready for mixed company either so I let the curses aimed at my general character hang in the air without comment. With little complication, we all made it to Basi's car and tolerated the trip back to the inn. I am pretty confident nobody remembered much of the perils of the return. That was a blessing. We did not speak about the fact we'd left Carson in the ground in the hills of Jamaica.

Later that afternoon, we gathered in the kitchen. The dogs could not seem to settle. Scampering feet carried long bodies from room to room and back. Long noses investigated one corner after another and then repeated the inquiries. The dachshunds were searching for something missing and I knew what it was, who it was. Redstripe, Paris and Belle would have to come to their own canine conclusions. We all knew what the hounds sought, but we all knew we could not explain. *Something's not right here. No, no, no.*

"Well," started Sheila, "now what?"

Jill offered practicality. "We deal with our guests and finish the repairs and just keep at it, that's what."

"Ya' mon," added Cirtron. "An now we have d'extra room t'rent." We all knew Cirtron was trying to be positive, but we all frowned at him anyway. Cirtron turned and found something to study on a nearby wall.

"Okay," said Sheila, "but who is going to cook? Not me. And the nearest McDonald's is in Mo-bay."

Jill chimed in, "Jack will cook. He's good."

"I am?" I was about to do a desperate wriggle out.

"You are. You know it. You're the reason I never cook at home. Actually, I think you're better with the kitchen than with your writing, if you must know," my wife told me but then softened a little. "Um, I mean as good as."

I mentally forgave her and said, "Actually, Carson said it was my turn to do the cooking, now that you mention it."

"When did she say that?" asked Sheila.

"Yesterday." The word hung in the air a moment then dropped and landed on the table with a thud. I'd been thinking of the little time I'd spent alone in Carson's room while I was lighting candles and the words just slipped out of my mouth. I also thought of the graveside chat I'd had.

Jill looked at me very carefully. "You must be wrong about that. Yesterday was the day Carson…"

"I know."

"You're too weird," stated Sheila.

"I know that, too. She also mentioned that you should all know she's fine."

Sheila brushed away the uncomfortable moment. "Never mind. Cirtron and I have something we need to tell you two. We were going to wait, but with what happened, we want to explain it now."

While I was grateful Sheila had turned the conversation, I was a little apprehensive. Surprises are not high on my list of

Dachshunds in Jamaica

fun things. I'd place them pretty far down along with roller coasters and dentists. "What is it?"

Sheila produced a file folder. "Cirtron and I decided we want to give you and Jill half of the inn. My god, you took care of building most of it and we are getting to be as close to you as anyone now. In a way, especially now, we're trying to hand back some of the things Carson gave to us here and in Wisconsin. Take a look in the folder. All the papers are in there and now we'll have four owners for Redstripe's Inn, me, Cirtron and the two of you. It's all in there and all official.

Jill and I were stunned. "Sheila, Cirtron, I don't know what to say here, this is wonderful, but you must know we can't sign this. We just can't."

Sheila began to laugh and Cirtron grinned. "No problem, mon." Sheila added, "Don't worry about it, you already signed. So did Jill. We're all partners. Everything is filed at the bank."

"What?! I didn't sign anything. What are you talking about?"

"Jack, look at the last page, it's already signed."

I flipped through the document to the end while Jill looked on. I could not believe it. At the very end was my signature, Jill's below it, with two official looking seals stamped into the paper. "I didn't sign this!"

Sheila explained, "Well, no, not technically. Carson did it for us. She copied your sigs because we all figured you would fuss about this. For what it's worth, I think she is, was, a pretty good calligrapher."

Sheila was right. I couldn't tell the signatures from our own but said, "You mean forgerer."

"Don't be unkind. Carson was trying to help and she did. We wanted this. We tried to get Carson's name there too, but she wouldn't budge. Maybe she knew something."

Thinking on the work done and the work to do, I felt I'd been handed the consolation prize at the company party. Everyone else had received matching luggage and I got an ugly lamp. Before I could craft an intelligent response, Jill broke in. "Sheila, this means so much. I can't tell you. But, you know we can't stay. We have a house and a family back home and eventually we have to go back,. at least for now. Maybe some day we could work something out, but now? It just won't work. Jack tried to tell me this before but I guess I wasn't listening."

Cirtron spoke, "Ya have d'family here, now. Dis can be home. Did you learn no ting in the mountains? One people one blood. An all your blood be welcome here. Y'know dis be true, mon."

Sheila said quietly. "You have to stay. We need you to stay. There's one more thing."

Here it comes, I thought. I figured I'd just been had again. "Oh? What's broke now?"

Sheila smiled and reached over to pat Cirtron's arm. "Nothing is broken. In fact everything has been working just like it's supposed to work." Her eyes stayed focused on Cirtron and she said, "I'm pregnant."

Jill gave a little yelp which summoned the dogs. All three dog alarms went off and I don't think anyone heard me say that I could really use a Red Stripe.

Dachshunds in Jamaica

Epilogue

Carrie Rose Armstead was born the usual nine months later in Carson's bed. At birth, she had a mix of features blended from her northern European mom and her Caribbean father; her skin was the color of light chocolate and her lighter hair was tightly curled. Cirtron and Sheila could not quite bring themselves to name her Carson. The Carrie Rose name was close enough. Her last name was Sheila's as Cirtron did not have one. Even a few days after her birth, I could tell she had an attitude that would take her a long ways. The dachshunds knew it too.

C. Rose would do the normal cry and scream thing when ever she was not comfortable, was hungry or just in the mood for mayhem. Redstripe and Belle and Paris would come running, full barks at full volume, only to be silenced by the next wail from C. Rose. Ears would perk and dachshund paws would back pedal in perfect discretion. There was no question who was in charge. For a change, it was not the dachshunds.

Jill and I had stayed in Jamaica way longer than we'd planned. We'd not spoken of this for quite a while, but I brought it up while the two of us sat on the porch one evening. My pipe was sending smoke tendrils up into the Negril evening air. I'd just cooked us all dinner, going easy on the oil as instructed. It seemed a little tough to keep things from burning with a minimum of oil in the pans, but who was I to argue with a ghost?

"Jill? I think it's time to go home."

"What's the hurry?" Jill asked.

"It's just time. We need to go back and deal with the house, get Belle back to the states, and just end all this. The inn is done and running. The web site is set; I've shown Sheila how to handle that. The baby is born and healthy. It really is time."

Redstripe's Inn

Jill can be stubborn. One of her best skills is wearing me down. "The house can wait. The kids are around. Besides, you've got your computer connections now and you've been working. Why leave? We're fine." Jill may have been breathing too much ocean air.

She went on. "Jack, let's stay at least for while. Come on. Mike and Kim can handle the house sale, dispose of everything and wire us a check. Simple."

Mike was our attorney who loved Chivas Regal and Kim was our accountant who drank nothing stronger than iced tea. But Jill was right. They could handle our affairs with probably no more fees than the cost of a round trip back to the Midwest via air and our sons Jonathan, and Jeremy could help expedite as needed.

I was not convinced. Not yet. Snap decisions have never been my favorite way of doing business. "I need to think about it. Okay?"

"Sure. Think all you want. But I know you want to stay."

My answer was to summon the dachshunds. "Belle! Redstripe! Paris! C'mon! Let's go down to the beach, ladies. Wanna swim?"

The dachshunds did come scampering out from somewhere, but I knew they did not want to swim. Oh, no.

I told them, "Hey you three, come along with me while I walk my pipe. I have some thinking to do."

The 4 of us, fourteen feet between us all, settled down out on the sand and studied the sun. Belle decided to offer a couple of coyote-like howls at the setting star but the other two just dropped down and lay with noses on paws to look at the last waves of the day sneak up over the sand. I was thinking.

I said to myself, *"Maybe it might not be a bad idea to hang around and watch Carrie Rose grow up for a bit. But this is silly, we need to go home."* Out loud, I addressed the hounds.

"What d'you three think? Should we stay?"

I was answered by a canine chorus of exuberant approval. I'd been outvoted by dachshunds.

www.ingramcontent.com/pod-product-compliance
Lightning Source LLC
Chambersburg PA
CBHW020634230426
43665CB00008B/164